D0930448

# Ecstasy and holiness

# ECSTASY AND HOLINESS

counter culture
and the open
society

Frank Musgrove

Indiana University Press
BLOOMINGTON & LONDON

150423

301.449
M 987

Copyright © 1974 by Frank Musgrove
First published in the United States in 1974
by Indiana University Press
All rights reserved

No part of this book may be reproduced or utilized in any form
or by any means, electronic or mechanical, including
photocopying and recording, or by any information storage
and retrieval system, without permission in writing from the
publisher. The Association of American University Presses
Resolution on Permissions constitutes the only exception to this
prohibition. Not for sale outside the United States, its
dependencies and the Philippine Islands.

Library of Congress catalog card number: 74–6081
ISBN: 0–253–31906–4

Printed in Great Britain

# Contents

# Tables

# Acknowledgements

Chapter seven is based on field-work carried out in the urban north-west. The author is indebted to the Social Science Research Council for financing this inquiry and to Mr Roger Middleton for carrying out the interviews.

The author is also deeply indebted to the individuals and groups who, when approached by research workers who explained the nature and purpose of the inquiry, willingly cooperated either by talking about their outlook and beliefs or by writing answers to questions and making written statements about their experiences, hopes and fears. The names of persons, organizations and places have been changed in reporting the outcome of these inquiries.

# 1

## Introduction

### Youth and society 1963–73

Ten years ago the author published a book entitled *Youth and the Social Order* which examined the position of youth in England in the early nineteen-sixties.[1] The present book was first conceived as a reappraisal of the position of youth after an interval of a decade. The research for the first book was carried out between 1961 and 1963, for the present book between 1971 and 1973. It soon became apparent that a crucial change had occurred: between the first period of research and the second, the 'counter culture' had intervened. This intervention was wholly unforeseen in the early 'sixties. But it has transformed the position and prospects of youth – indeed, it has largely deprived the concept of youth (as 'teenagers') of its utility. The focus of the new book therefore became the counter culture itself.

*Youth and the Social Order* examined the problem of youth in terms of their status and power. There was, indeed, a conflict between the young and the mature, but the conflict arose not from significant differences in outlook and values, but from the deteriorating power-base of the young. In the past decade a radical change seems to have occurred: the conflict today is rooted less in problems of power than in differences in values. It is true that today the young probably talk more about power and authority than they did, but the problems of hierarchy and legitimacy which they discuss are not specifically related to age. They are concerned with questions of dignity and deference which arise wherever there are subordinate and superordinate positions. Thus the National Union of School Students makes common cause with assistant teachers in general and members of the teachers' movement, Rank-and-File, in particular; the French university students who went to the barricades in May 1968 made common cause with adult workmen. Ten years ago it was possible to examine the position of youth without reference to peculiarly youthful values (except to show that they did not exist); today an examination of differences in values must be central to any analysis of inter-generational strife.

In the nineteen-forties Margaret Mead argued that the values of the young must be radically different from those of their elders, because of the 'rapidity of social change'.[2] In the nineteen-fifties numerous investigations were carried out to see if she was right. She was not. At the same time David Riesman told us about the omnipotence of the adolescent peer group.[3] He was wrong too. Careful and competent research conducted in both America and Britain in the 'fifties and early 'sixties showed only the sheer efficiency with which adults transmitted the cultural standards to the young. This daunting Anglo-American efficiency was probably surpassed only in France.[4]

In the early nineteen-sixties Abrams and Little could find no evidence that the young in England were in any sense a new political generation: 'There has been no breakthrough and there is little prospect of one.'[5] The author's studies of inter-generational relationships in 1962 showed young people highly critical of their supposedly omnipotent peer groups and deeply respectful of their elders' views.[6] These English studies were broadly congruent with many carried out in North America at that time, for instance Riley and Moore's inquiry into teenage 'other-directedness'[7] and Kahl's investigations of the attitudes and aspirations of 'Common Man' boys.[8] Of course there was deviant behaviour in the form of juvenile delinquency, but the young were not propounding a new value-system with its own claim to legitimacy. Westley and Elkin's dispiriting research in suburban Montreal led them to conclude that 'adolescents, by the age of 14 or 15, have already internalized the ideals of the surrounding adult society . . . they do not reject adult values or participate in an anti-adult youth culture.'[9] Even James Coleman (in *The Adolescent Society*) only succeeded us showing that sociable, non-intellectual, athletic middle-class youth were precisely like their suburban parents.

There was no student revolt. In American universities students were complacent, in English universities suicidal. The Jacob Report of 1957, which reviewed postwar American research into the characteristics of college students, described them as quiescent, even gloriously contented, offering no radical questioning or re-appraisal of their society.[10] In England the picture was much more sombre but no more challenging to the established social order. The student was not a long-haired rebel but a potential suicide or case for psychiatric care. A study of five hundred psychiatric cases at Oxford between 1950 and 1961 showed that referral rates were three times the national rates for the same age, sex and social class.[11] This was at a time before psychiatric treatment in universities had become fashionable. Ferdynand Zweig's deeply depressing study of English university students in 1962 showed them anxious and joyless, harassed and guilt-ridden, unadventurous and conformist. 'They are not angry young men', 'there is little doubt that the young are becoming old before their time.' 'The students I interviewed did not strike me as young and carefree, on the contrary, they struck me as old, laden with responsibility, care and worry, with nightmares and horror dreams.'[12]

Ten years ago the young were fighting to get in; today they are often fighting to get out. They have now seen that there may be viable alternatives to 'straight' insider positions and styles of life. Ten years ago protest was about status and power; and it took one principal form – massive movement towards earlier marriage. In 1921 some 5 per cent of new husbands were under twenty-one, 15 per cent in 1965. For new wives the corresponding percentages were 15 and 41. This was the major adolescent rebellion of ten to twenty years ago, the most significant invasion of the adult world, the most determined assault to secure status in a society which increasingly denied it. This in itself was a major social change, brought about principally by the increasingly unequal distribution of power and status between the age groups. And it typifies the conflict – a rebellion not to beat their seniors, but to join them.

In *Youth and the Social Order* and elsewhere,[13] the author conceptualized 'the problem of youth' ten years ago in terms of the weakening power base of the young, and de-emphasized the commonly alleged conflict of values. The weakening of the power-base of the young was interpreted partly as the outcome of demographic change, and partly as the outcome of the stratagems of the mature, not least their structuring of formal education. As improved life-expectancies had converted the pre-industrial age-pyramid into a post-industrial column, the young appeared to be trapped beneath a pillar of apparently immortal middle-aged men.[14] (Only the replacement of family by bureaucratic employment, which made possible the artificial death of retirement, gave some ease to the situation.) The Census data for 1961 showed that young people in their early twenties, though better educated than their elders, in terms of the status of the jobs they were able to get actually constituted an inferior social class.[15] Age groups did not differ in values; they differed profoundly in status and power.

The author interpreted the invention of the adolescent in the late-eighteenth century (by Rousseau) and his further elaboration more than a century later by Stanley Hall, as an ideology which legitimized the denial of status to the young.[16] The adolescent's supposed inadequacies – his alleged instability, lack of realism, proneness to fantasy and his celebrated 'crisis of identity' – justified his protracted exclusion from responsible statuses and extended disengagement from the central institutions of society. Legislation ostensibly intended to protect him in fact segregated, belittled and enfeebled him. Schooling created what it was intended to cure. Ten years' ago the author advocated a massive exercise in deschooling and the reduction of the school-leaving age to twelve.[17]

It now seems quite inadequate to conceive the changes in values and behaviour among young people in the early nineteen-seventies in terms of these simple notions of conflict and power which appeared appropriate ten years ago. It is true that there are some indications that student activism in England and Europe may have been most common among those least likely to get good jobs. Some interpretations of the French revolution of May-June 1968 suggest that the rebels were not trying to destroy 'the system', but to urge reforms which would ensure that they found a place in it.[18] Richard Startup's research into student activism in a British university in 1969 similarly suggests a link between a desire to reform university government and a sense that the university is unlikely to lead to the fulfilment of one's occupational expectations. 'This relationship is particularly strong in the Arts faculty.'[19]

The author attempted to test this alleged relationship in the research he carried out in 1972 with various groups of university students (reported in full below in chapters five and six). He could find no connection whatsoever between support for 'counter-cultural' values in general, or for activist values in particular, and expected occupational disappointment. University students of music did not, in the main, expect to get the jobs they really wanted: only a third of them expected to do so. But their support for counter-cultural and activist values was very weak. It is true that polytechnic students of painting and sculpture were even more despairing of getting their ideal job: only a tenth expected to do so. And their support for counter-cultural values was very strong. But when we compare the optimists with the pessimists in each area of academic specialization, there is no difference between the strength of their counter-cultural attitudes. When we compare the frustrated students of painting and sculpture with the frustrated students of music, the difference between their levels of support for counter-cultural values is high and significant.[20] The university student of music who has set his heart on playing the cello in the Hallé but expects, in fact, to become a teacher in a secondary modern school, shows no sign of developing activist attitudes.

Most of the students of painting and sculpture want to be self-employed artists (most of the music students want to work for organizations, whether an orchestra or the BBC). But most of the art students, like most of the music students, expect to become school teachers. It is in the nature of their ideal work, rather than in their expected job frustrations, that we find the clue to their counter-cultural values.

Rebellious art students at Hornsea College of Art in 1968 were not seriously worried about actually getting a job, even a well-paid job. They were bothered about the very success of their college in placing its graduates in lucrative commercial careers. Staff and students wrote an account of their rebellion as it progressed.[21] The students' protest was against their very occupational success:

> The art student, still considered a crackpot locally, is wooed by a bourgeois culture, by the business, fashion and advertising world, and, for the few, by the Bond Street market . . . Disinherited, and disentangling ourselves from any place in the local community in which we lived, we were being harnessed in a new and large-scale way in the bourgeois cultural machine . . . Never before had artists been in such demand.[22]

The chairman of the college's governing body, in a letter to the *Guardian*, considered the successful placement of students in industry

as an attested truth, and the 'relevance' of the college courses as a
self-evident good:

> I accept wholeheartedly the place of Hornsey College of Art as a
> practical training ground, and its past strong and proved associa-
> tion with industry which successfully fits people for jobs. This is
> surely highly commendable and right . . .[23]

This is precisely what the students of art found regrettable and
wrong: not their failure to find a place in the established economic
order, but their inability to engage in work as they conceived it:

> We protest against the protestant, clean, decent, self-denying,
> miserable glorification of work. I believe that this hope to work
> for one's living by living in one's work is a reason why many of
> us choose to come to art school. This is why we really kick when
> our hopes are frustrated and we find the same alienation forced
> upon us as upon our parents: the alienation from which we are
> trying to escape.[24]

The most compelling research evidence, in both England and
America, is that student activists in the late 'sixties were precisely
those who were unconcerned about jobs. This is one broad conclusion from inquiries conducted by Stephen Hatch in three British
universities in 1969. 'The protesters clearly put greater value upon
education and ideas as ends in themselves, whereas the opponents
of protest were much more likely to see a university education as
a means towards certain extrinsic ends.'[25] It was the non-protesters
who had an 'instrumental involvement' in higher education. For the
protesters, its job-getting function was in any case largely irrelevant.
The roots of student activism are elsewhere than in job-frustration.

## The extension of youth

Over the past ten years the link between age and behaviour appears
to have weakened. In 1960 behaviour was finely age-graded and
youthful behaviour was efficiently phased out between sixteen
and twenty. There is now an increasing number of youths aged
forty.

In 1905 Stanley Hall deeply regretted that American adolescents
failed to act their age. They were all premature men. But in the
author's research of a decade ago, the concept of 'acting your age'
was a powerful means of regulating the conduct of 15-year-old boys

and girls. Today even women's tights are not age-graded, jeans are not age-specific, and skirt length is a poor guide to age.

In the nineteen-thirties Arensberg and Kimball made their classic study of the Irish peasantry. They found a remarkably high proportion of boys in their forties.[26] But industrial-bureaucratic societies were requiring an inexorable step-wise progression towards maturity and death. The steps were marked out with precision by developmental psychologists and reinforced by institutional arrangements. 'Streaming' was invented in schools so that children of the same chronological age could be locked forever together as they made their inexorable step-wise progression through their years of schooling. Adult organizations (social, economic and political) established youth departments in which the young could be kept appropriately youthful. The Albemarle Report on the Youth Service in England and Wales was published in 1960. It made its own uniquely disastrous contribution to the rigid age-grading of English society and to the segregation of the young. In retrospect it can be seen as the culmination of a century-long programme of building barricades against the young. In the 'sixties some of the barricades began to fall. The Latey Report on the age of majority, which appeared in 1967, was a public signal and acceptance of change.

But youth now exceeds its proper term in part because more 'youthful' occupational roles are now available to the mature, especially perhaps in some of the personal-service professions, in a vastly enlarged academic profession, and in the expanding world of entertainment. And in the widening marginal world of leisure, familiar behavioural linkages rapidly dissolve : age, sex and social class are only loosely linked with conduct. It is virtually impossible to tell at a glance, or even closer scrutiny, the age, sex and social class of anyone on a horse or skis. Only bingo has found a firm location in age, sex and social class.

Ten years ago there was a 'problem of youth'. Now we are problems for life. Formerly, the problem of youth meant juvenile delinquency. It was a problem found among 13- and 14-year-olds of lowly social origin, poor academic attainment and bleak prospects in life. Ten years later the problem of youth which has come sharply into focus has a radically different location : it means rebellious young men (and women) in their twenties, of good social background, high academic attainments, and apparently unbounded prospects. Formerly the problem of youth was associated with privation; now it is associated with privilege. The new problem is far more subversive of the social order than petty theft and mindless vandalism. It is a principled attack on traditional social institutions, an adversary culture with well-heeled allies in high places. In the later 'sixties it could count among its allies the Director-General of the BBC and the Provost of King's (both youthful far beyond their proper term).

When the author began his explorations of the emergent values of the contemporary world, he expected to find distinctive values among late-teenagers which would mark them off sharply from anyone older. (After all, they themselves had advised: 'Trust no-one over thirty.') He found, in fact, that the world divides at age thirty-six.

The construction of a scale of counter-cultural attitudes (relating to issues which included communes, pollution, power, ambition, technology and a simple life) was the first step in the research (see Chapter five). A forty-eight item scale was found to be reliable, and its apparently rather heterogeneous items highly intercorrelated, when it was tried out on 150 university students drawn from all areas of academic study. If the scale had not 'worked', the research would have been abandoned at that point. There would have been no good reason to suppose that the counter-culture as a reasonably coherent constellation of values existed. But the scale effectively sorted people out in a predictable way. If students of computer science had proved to be very high scorers, and students of painting and sculpture low, it would have been abandoned as obviously invalid. There were, indeed, some surprises in the scores of some groups; but the general pattern of scores made sense. The scale seemed to be a useful instrument for exploring the strength of counter-cultural attitudes in various age and occupational groups.

Further groups of college, university, polytechnic and grammar school students completed the scale. The age-range of these initial subjects was sixteen to twenty-two. There were wide variations in scale scores, but variations were related to field of study rather than age. (There was, indeed, some indication that counter-cultural attitudes might be stronger at twenty-two than sixteen : the fifty grammar school sixth-form boys were remarkably 'straight'.) But when 18-year-old arts specialists were compared with 21-year-old arts specialists (and similar comparisons made among science specialists), their scale scores were virtually identical.

Older groups were matched, as far as possible, with the more counter-cultural (artistic) younger groups. Thus the older subjects were drawn from professional actors (and American social planners), but principally from university extra-mural courses in fine art and drama. It is true that their dramatic and artistic interests found only part-time expression, but it was felt that if older adults in the 'normal' population were likely to have counter-cultural sympathies, they would be found in such groups. In the event, if they were older than the late thirties, however strong their artistic proclivities, their scores on the counter-cultural scale were almost invariably low. Some 600 individuals completed the scales. It was only among those over thirty-five years of age that a significant decline occurred. The willingness of people to indicate support for counter-cultural sentiments, though never strong in more than a minority, dwindled to insignificance in later middle age. But the counter culture was clearly not solely, or perhaps even primarily, a teenage phenomenon.

*An intellectual journey*

The preliminary work with the scale of counter-cultural attitudes was carried out in 1972. It suggested that a counter culture did, indeed, exist, at least as a complex of sentiments, attitudes and beliefs. An American sociologist has recently made the obvious point, that there are 'fundamentally two ways of defining what a counter culture is':

> On the ideological level, a counter culture is a set of beliefs and values which radically reject the dominant culture of a society, and prescribe a sectarian alternative. On the behavioral level, a counter culture is a group of people who, because they accept such beliefs and values, behave in such radically nonconformist ways that they tend to drop out of society . . . It is important, however, to distinguish between counter cultures as 'groups of ideas' and counter cultures as 'groups of people', because these ideas . . . are such that it is impossible to behave completely according to their mandate.[27]

Along with further studies of the counter culture as a group of ideas, the author planned studies of the counter culture as groups of people. These field studies were carried out in the urban north-west in 1973. The counter culture as groups of people also existed. (An account of this work is given in Chapter seven.) When beliefs were translated into action, at least to the point of 'dropping out' and living on social security, the practicalities of an exiguous existence tended to overshadow more abstract theorizing. But the counter culture as people matched in a remarkable way the preceding study of the counter culture as ideas: there was a striking symmetry between them. The study of beliefs in action brought a dynamic aspect to the static mapping of attitudes. Conversations with groups and individuals in squalid 'pads' gave insight into the transformation of the counter culture over the past seven or eight years: the loss of innocence and naiveté, the growth of intellectual and organizational sophistication. The fieldwork also confirmed the age distribution of counter-cultural support – there were no teenagers in sight.

After establishing the counter culture's existence, the problem was to account for it. The author's earlier conceptualization of 'the problem of youth' in terms of a simple conflict model seemed increasingly inadequate. This inadequacy was first apparent to the author when he went to California as a visiting professor of sociology in 1969. The counter culture was luxuriant and highly visible on the university campus. The Beatles had been deified, and in Monday morning lectures one witnessed a languid process of resurfacing after the weekend freak-out. (One also noticed all the pet dogs, often secreted in lecture theatres, wandering out into the aisles at the lecture's climacteric; and one wondered at the probable loneliness and desolation behind the apparent togetherness.)

The author's research seminar for doctoral students comprised twenty people ranging in age from their mid-twenties to late-thirties. Twelve were executive dropouts. They were men who had already obtained high academic qualifications and had enjoyed secure and important positions and generous salaries with Boeing, IBM and similar organizations. They had no intention of returning. When they decided to leave their employment, their only uncertainty was whether they should join a university as doctoral students in sociology or a commune in Oregon. Universities and communes appeared to have a striking equivalence: they were places where dropouts dropped in. (In fact a number of doctoral students left the university for communes during the course of the semester.) They had not returned to the university to further their careers, they had returned because they rejected careers. They interspersed their sociological studies with painting in water colours and oils and denouncement of Governor Reagan. Their livelihood seemed precarious. But there was no simple or obvious sense in which they had been deprived or oppressed.

California, the home of the counter culture in the nineteen-sixties, is the richest society on earth. (It is also remarkable for its high rates of immigration from elsewhere in America and for its spectacular urbanization and population growth.) The counter culture in California appeared to be associated in some way with wealth and opportunity. And yet it was marked by frugality, a determined effort to reduce personal consumption. It is true that in the rhetoric of the counter culture, 'alienation' was a key word, and the power structure of the 'military-industrial complex' was a major target. It is true, also, that a major war was being fought in Vietnam – but by poor rural whites and negroes in the main. The counter culture did not recruit from the populations actually at risk.

The author decided that in his study of counter-cultural attitudes in England, he must try to get behind the rhetoric of 'alienation' and discover how those who scored high on the scale evaluated their lot and their world when they made pertinent comparisons. The pertinent comparison seemed to be with the world in which their parents grew up, as they perceived it, and perhaps with the world in which they thought their own children would grow up. When the subjects who took part in this inquiry made these comparisons, if they were high scorers on the counter-cultural scale, their perceptions of the present were very positive. In particular they singled out the absence of restriction and constraint, the existence of unparalleled opportunity. Their protest was against a future as yet unborn but perhaps conceived. The present was uniquely beneficent.

The dogs on the American campus led the author to suspect that the counter culture was connected not with alienation but with anomie – with loneliness, a sense of social dislocation and uprootedness. In order to investigate the possibility he invited the subjects of his inquiry to complete a short 'anomie scale', and to say who they were (see Chapter six). Scores on the anomie scale were in fact highly correlated with counter-cultural scores; and the self concepts of high scorers were devastatingly negative and harrowingly lonely. (The sense of uprootedness and social isolation also came out strongly in interviews with persons actively 'into counter culture'.) Ecstatic counter cultures in the past have also been marked by this same paradoxically pervasive pessimism and melancholy.

An attempt to interpret the contemporary counter culture was made through historical-comparative studies (see Chapter three). Economic expansion and opportunity, as in California of the nineteen-sixties, appear, on the face of it, to be associated with subversive counter cultures in the contemporary world; comparable historical periods of economic change might be expected to have similar counter-cultural accompaniments. The analysis of the attitude scale scores suggested a very close parallel with the Romantic counter culture, in all its complexity, which accompanied the classical industrial revolution of the nineteenth century. There was an obvious case for scrutinizing periods of great economic change in history for their possible counter-cultural connections. The results of this comparative study, which was made after the empirical inquiries had been completed, and was in some measure prompted by them, were the most surprising in this programme of research.

Others who have made comparative studies of counter cultures have started from the very opposite position : they have selected historical phenomena which appeared *prima facie* 'counter-cultural', and have proceeded from there. In selecting his periods of economic change, the author was by no means certain at the outset that counter cultures would be associated with them. Indeed, economic historians have not usually been looking for counter cultures and have ignored them as irrelevant if they encountered them. Except, then, for more modern times, this historical excursion was a genuine voyage of discovery.

Pre-selected counter cultures examined by sociologists usually include medieval monasticism, and Robert Owen's New Harmony venture in Indiana. 'Monasticism provides an almost prototypical example of the successful counter culture', maintains Westhues.[28] The kibbutzim of Israel and Noyes' Perfectionists at Oneida are other frequently cited examples. Karl Mannheim examines similar phenomena as 'utopias' and takes medieval chiliastic movements as a prime example. He claims, indeed, that this was 'The decisive turning point in modern history . . .'[29] The difficulty with selecting counter cultures on *a priori* grounds is that their characteristic features are taken as self-evident and non-problematical. By contrast the author set out to test his hunch that discrepant, discordant, 'unhelpful' and even subversive beliefs and social movements were associated with periods of major economic change and, if this proved to be the case, to examine what they had in common. There is an obvious danger of reading into the past what one has found in the present. All intellectual inquiry is dangerous.

Two sub-scales which emerged from statistical analysis of the attitude scale immediately suggested on the one hand the values and attitudes of Godwin and Shelley, and on the other the more conservative, but nonetheless deeply critical attitudes of Southey and Ruskin. The classical industrial revolution of the late-eighteenth and early nineteenth centuries was in any case an obvious period for comparative study; the complexities and differences of emphasis within Romanticism-as-counter-culture appeared to characterize the counter culture of the nineteen-seventies. The author turned to a re-reading of Romantic literature. The anarchism, attacks on authority and the family, the rejection of the work ethic and deep interest in communes (and drugs) which are to be found in the writings of Godwin and Shelley were clearly represented in one aspect of contemporary counter-cultural belief. Southey and Ruskin were far from being anarchists, but their interest in the environment, their distaste for technology, their concern that work should be 'expressive' and human corresponded closely with the second sub-scale. The circumstances in which the Romantics grew up and spent their lives seemed worth comparing with the life-styles of those who support the counter culture today (see Chapter four). Similarities might provide clues to the shaping of counter-cultural beliefs.

Other obvious candidates for inclusion in a comparative study were (starting with the earliest in time): the neolithic revolution, the industrial revolution of the high middle ages, the Italian Renaissance, and the commercial revolution ('the birth of capitalism') of the late sixteenth century. Historical scholarship has not commonly stressed, and often has not even alluded to, 'dysfunctional' counter cultures in any of these periods of great economic change.

For the author the great surprise was the Italian Renaissance (see Chapter three). The romantic interpretation of the Renaissance by Jacob Burckhardt and his followers suggested that successful banking and commercial enterprise were somehow linked with exuberant and untrammelled artistic creation. The orderly, systematic and successful pursuit of wealth co-existed with, and in some sense provided the conditions for, the ecstasy of artistic excess. Historical scholarship of the past twenty years questions both the artist's exuberance and the banker's success.

Nevertheless, the spectacular wealth – if not the sustained economic growth – of Italy during the Renaissance is scarcely in doubt. The new problem was more interesting, and finally illuminating, than the old: not why was a period of great wealth accompanied by a subversive counter culture of frenzied artistic creation, but why was it not? The historical research of R. S. Lopez over the past twenty years was of particular value in the author's attempt to understand the connections between artistic activity and economic life during the Italian Renaissance. Lopez elucidates the relationship between art, economic life and a stationary or even falling population. It is precisely with regard to its stagnant population that Renaissance Italy differed from the other (at first blush roughly comparable) epochs under review.

The Italian Renaissance, then, did not fit in, as expected, with the author's comparative historical material. But its lack of fit helped to explain the rest. The sobriety, solemnity, restraint and prudential calculation of the Renaissance artist in the service of his masters suggested that a nation's great wealth is insufficient in itself to account for counter-cultural actions and beliefs. The counter culture is not simply a symptom of surfeit, as some have maintained. The answer appeared to lie in the circumstances which underlie great economic growth – notably the upsurge and movement of population which promote social dislocation, bring into question traditional statuses and call for new rules of conduct in an uncertain and changing world.

The other periods of economic change under review were notable, like our own postwar world, not only for their unprecedented wealth and new ways of organizing economic production but for their bursting population and the intensity of migration. And in all cases dysfunctional beliefs flourished, and threatened the very progress that brought them forth. In the earlier periods irrationality and ecstasy were less self-conscious; but they were the essence of the Dionysian mystery cults of Neolithic times. They characterized the chiliastic movements which accompanied the economic transformation of the high middle ages; and the new capitalism of the later sixteenth century grew with a crescendo of witchcraft accusations and trials. The core characteristic of all counter cultures appeared to be irrationality and its invariable accompaniment was technological advance, economic development, but above all population growth.

Comparative studies which start with a collection of apparently similar counter cultures seek to 'explain' them by the features they have in common.[30] There is no reason why the social contexts which gave them birth should not also be contrasted and compared. But explanation starts from common features of counter cultures and works outwards; and having defined counter culture as retreat from the world, the banal conclusion is that the world was experienced as noxious and retreat was sensible.[31] This has the virtue of simpli-

city and the vice of tautology. Counter cultures are locked in the
dynamics of economic change.

## The dialectics of utopia

Karl Mannheim equated utopia with ecstasy and considered it essential to life. He wrote before the term 'counter culture' had been
coined; but the reality he described and tried to explain was the
same. (Utopia was not the impossible: it 'seems unrealizable only
from the point of view of a given social order which is already in
existence.'[32]) Utopia and ecstasy, said Mannheim, were essential for
being a man, not a thing. In the final chapter of this book we shall
return to Mannheim's remarkable prescience, forty years ago, of the
contemporary counter culture and the problems raised by its existential base. Here his insight into the dialectical relationship between
utopia and society is our concern.

American sociologists have usually examined the counter culture
and mainstream society as polar extremes, mutually exclusive value
systems and social realms. Their favourite metaphor is 'social island'.
They may make some passing reference to 'centripetal forces' which
somehow keep the counter culture tenuously in touch, but their
analysis is in terms of irreconcilable opposites. The political aspects
of the counter culture are an embarrasment to this thesis. They are
either de-emphasized or denied.

Westhues has no conception of dialectical process in the formation
of counter cultures :

> Counter cultural beliefs lead to their adherents cutting themselves
> off from mainstream society and severing the ties that bind them
> to the dominant order. A counter culture that would be satisfied
> with some modification of the wider culture is no counter culture
> at all.[33]

The political aspects of the counter culture are summarily dismissed :
'The counter culture is only marginally political, if at all.'[34] It has
withdrawn from social and political involvement : 'It is an entirely
new and different reality that members of a counter culture bear in
their minds and seek to embody in social islands that exist in the
midst of the rationality of the dominant order.'[35] The two worlds
divide over rationality, and transcendental experiences dissolve
social bonds : 'The importance of the transcendental experience for
sociological purposes is that it ruptures the bonds that integrate the

individual into his rational society . . .'[36] Others have similarly interpreted the experience of drugs as a process of 'desocialization', a necessary preliminary to 'resocialization' into a new social order.[37]

This had been the central puzzle running through the inquiries reported in this book : the nature of the social bond. Men are bound to society by work, by marriage and family, by property (the main test, before the twentieth century, that one was actually 'in'), and by the division of labour itself. The counter culture can be defined in terms of its rejection of all these bonds. And yet the author's empirical studies of the present and comparative studies of the past indicated a more complicated and involved reality. The great difficulty has been, while pointing up crucial differences, to sort out the nature of this involvement. A simplistic interpretation of the counter culture as revulsion, surfeit or reaction, leads to an account of polar extremes, mutually exclusive positions. In fact there is a more complex relationship of interaction, interpenetration, exchange and influence, in the realm of ideas, of institutions, and of interpersonal relationships. The politics of the counter culture ties it to mainstream society. The relationship is dialectical.

Mannheim likewise concluded that the relationship between utopia and the existing order is a dialectical one :

> By this is meant that every age allows to arise (in differently located social groups) those ideas and values in which are contained in condensed form the unrealized and the unfulfilled tendencies which represent the needs of each age. These intellectual elements then become the explosive material for bursting the limits of the existing order. The existing order gives birth to utopias which in turn break the bonds of the existing order, leaving it free to develop in the direction of the next order of existence.[38]

There are, indeed, problems of definition in this passage: what, exactly, is an 'age', and how, exactly, does one know its 'needs'? But the essential process described seems to do justice to the emergence of counter cultures and the transmutations of both counter culture and mainstream society.

There are many possible ways of looking at dialectical processes of confrontation, interaction, exchange and transformation. The concept of 'marginality' seemed especially useful : it presupposes contiguous rather than mutually exclusive social realms and suggests a penumbra of experimental values and actions around a more stable, inner core. Margins embrace, enfold and confine, but they may in some circumstances melt and lose their clarity of definition. Transactions take place across the boundary, and there is movement back and forth. This image seemed far more apposite than one of irreconcilable opposites.

Any study of the counter culture must be, in equal measure, a study of the straight culture, at least at the points where they most vigorously interact. In his empirical studies of the present, and in his comparative studies of the past, the author has tried to catch the ambiguities of the counter culture's relationship with the dominant society. The chapter on the Romantics, for which there is abundant biographical material, especially attempts to capture this relationship at the level of personal relationships with 'Establishment' figures. At the ideological level the book deals throughout with the opposition and interaction of counter-cultural 'Dionysian' and straight 'Apollonian' sentiments, perceptions and beliefs.

The areas in which the opposition and interaction of the counter culture and mainstream society are most vigorous relate to issues of power and authority on the one hand, and work on the other. One chapter (eight) is therefore devoted to issues of power and authority in contemporary society and to the counter culture's position; another chapter (nine) is similarly devoted to work. Mannheim maintained that '. . . the sociologist can really understand utopias only as parts of a constantly shifting total constellation.' To catch total, shifting social constellations is a difficult task. This book represents an effort to do so.

*The last paradox*

There is a final paradox which haunts this book : that rich societies have produced a counter culture marked by frugality and low consumption. It is a product of plenty which has opted for poverty. But it would do violence to the facts to characterize it as ascetic in the manner of a Trappist order. In many respects it indulges the senses and glories not in restraint but in abandon and exuberance.

The argument that the counter culture arises from surfeit and revulsion finds no support in our analysis. The social scars produced by high and rising rates of economic production are, indeed, deplored by members of the counter culture : and there is a deep awareness of the social costs of high technology. But low consumption is a tactic for attenuating social bonds and reducing dependence on the economic system (both Godwin and Rousseau advocated frugality on these grounds, as a means of enhancing personal freedom and autonomy). It may also be seen as a political weapon, a means of subverting an economic system which is an instrument of social injustice.

But in the counter culture no-one wants to be *too* poor. It is quite obvious even here that poverty has ever been a fickle ally of freedom. The aim is a sort of genteel poverty, with the concept of gentility radically revised. (The revised version has, in fact, strong aristocratic overtones.) But when we maintain – as we do throughout this book – that the counter culture is proleptic of cybernetic abundance, this is not to argue that the counter culture prepares its members for gargantuan consumption. Very wealthy postindustrial societies are well able to support a new, enlarged and conceivably more civilized, and perhaps more venturesome, version of the genteel poor. They may, indeed, find it acutely embarrassing not to do so. Their safety-nets can be strong but more generously and humanely conceived than social security. The contemporary counter culture may seem a far cry from Cranford, but in an important sense it may be very close to Barchester Towers. When counter culture and mainstream culture have transformed each other through dialectical opposition (and straight society has learned in the process the folly of producing all that it is capable of doing), this may indeed be the final synthesis.

# 2

# Aspects of the counter culture

*The counter culture in transition*

The counter culture is a revolt of the unoppressed. It is a response not to constraint, but to openness. It is a search for new interactional norms in the widening, more diffuse margins of postindustrial societies. It is most satisfactorily conceptualized not as a revolutionary ideology, but as an exploratory curriculum, a range of experiences and exposures through which the postmodern generation seeks a sense of significance. It flowers in the shadow of futurity: a form of anticipatory socialization (often re-socialization) for long life in the loose social networks of a highly plural, non-mass society. It is not a 'youth culture'. It is a rebirth of Dionysian culture which has striking historical parallels. It insists that we are men, not things: that existence precedes essence. It defines the proper (human) categories which make us holy. It is unique in its promise that humanity can finally be human.

Hippies and student activists made the modern counter culture between 1964 and 1968. For a comparative study of 1,496 student riots and demonstrations 1964–9, see E. L. Blackman and D. J. Finlay, 'Student Protest: A Cross–National Study', *Youth and Society* (1973). They are now an irrelevance. Hippies are quaintly archaic; student activists are experts in the legal niceties of university committee procedure. But the counter culture was born in Sproul Hall, Berkeley in the fall of 1964. The police who encircled Sproul Hall were almost as numerous as the students who occupied it. Eventually more than six hundred police moved in to arrest eight hundred students. Culture and counter culture defined their respective positions through long autumn days and nights on the Berkeley plaza.

It is as easy to highlight the absurdities as the drama of those days. Lewis Feuer has done so.[1] Joan Baez sang 'We Shall Overcome', courses were started on the nature of God and the logarithmic spiral, and Mario Savio, the sophomore student leader, bit a policeman in the left thigh. Later, sexual intercourse was performed before large audiences. In one of its many aspects, the disturbance at Berkeley in the fall of 1964 was an orgiastic rebellion. But in spite or possibly because of this, the year 1964 is in a real and importance sense the hinge of modern history. The birth of the counter culture marks a major discontinuity in the history of our times.

By 1967 there were probably a quarter of a million full-time hippies in America; it is estimated that approximately three-quarters of them came from middle-class or upper-class homes.[2] Both active participants and sympathizers were of superior scholastic attainment. When the Muscatine Committee reconstructed the events of 1964, they found that 'The students arrested in Sproul Hall included an unusual percentage of scholastically able young people.' When they sounded opinion in the student body at large, they found that '. . . three quarters believed the leaders of the movement to be idealistic and motivated by moral values. On the whole, support was stronger among those students with high scholastic records than among those with low records.'[3] The counter culture remained tightly tied to university students in the mid-sixties. The 'situationist' students who disrupted the University of Strasbourg in 1966 were as highly moral as the Berkeley students. Their attack was against the degrading and meaningless 'spectacle' of a consumer society (but the judge before whom they appeared singled out their 'rejection of all morality and restraint'). It was French University students in May 1968 who attempted deliberately to extend the new morality into the world of adult workmen. They sought to disolve the boundaries between students and society. Stark antithesis began to yield to interpenetration and diffusion.[4]

Charles Reich is correct in relating the origins of the counter culture to student generations: 'One chronology is based on the college class of 1969, which entered as freshmen in the fall of 1965. Another important date is the summer of 1967, when the full force of the cultural revolution was first visible.'[5] But already, in the late 'sixties, the location of the counter culture was shifting. Marcuse saw the wider significance of events in France in 1968 when he wrote of 'the rebellion for the total transvaluation of values, for qualitatively different ways of life . . .'[6] The age-range of counter-cultural support was widening: 'Despite ample evidence that most hippies are young (under thirty) and that most of their critics are old (over thirty), support for the movement ranges far beyond age lines: many of the hippies' most ardent admirers, if not participants, are over thirty; and many of their detractors, under thirty.'[7]

Today in England the counter culture is synonymous neither with student activism nor hippiedom. It has broken from its base. At its core, it is true, there is a relatively small number of people who have rejected work as it is conventionally conceived and leisure which they see as its mirror-image. They are mystics, aesthetes, anarchists, music-makers, community actors, political and social activists, sculptors, painters, potters, wood-carvers, metal-workers, social philosophers, writers and poets, gardeners, poster designers and unpaid social workers. (Many of the 'social workers' are, in effect, unpaid and defiantly untrained *psychiatric* social workers.) They are typically in their late twenties; they are not university students, though many have been to universities.

They lead a shifting, disorderly, dangerous, and often very courageous life of improvization and experimentation on the meagre and uncertain benefits of social security. Many work long and arduous hours in their chosen activities. They will sometimes define themselves as 'freaks', invariably as 'alternative', but never – in 1973 – as 'underground'. The 'alternative' smokes pot, but it is highly visible and open (and receptive, even hospitable, to visiting sociologists).

The counter culture radiates from this full-time, central core in a series of concentric circles representing diminishing degrees of attachment and involvement. These widening circles interpenetrate and overlap extensively with 'straight' society; they embrace intermittent members who, for short periods, join communes and quasi-communes. (The latter may even take the form of officially affiliated adult education centres which are concerned with the quality of personal relationships, sceptical of the value of 'intellectualizing' interpersonal problems, committed to promoting 'awareness' and the openness of communication.)

Ironically, the counter culture overlaps and interpenetrates in an incongruous way current styles and ideologies of management training.[8] The post-experience course for industrial managers is a weekend freak-out.

On the far outer fringes are relatively inactive sympathizers who join encounter groups and read the underground press, Tolkien's *The Lord of the Rings*, R. D. Laing, *Gandalf's Garden*, and books about the open family. They may be vegetarian, eat health-foods, and practice yoga. But there is also a bogus accretion which takes two main forms: derelict, conventionally delinquent and mainly ill-educated lower-class inadequates, on the one hand; and, on the other, well-heeled with-it middle-class and aristocratic week-enders who wear the gear, learn the language, and smoke a joint. The former are spurious, disqualified, essentially because they are simply destructive; the latter because they follow and aspire to success in orderly, structured conventional careers. Among the latter are many with-it students who are held in deep contempt by committed members of the counter culture because they have sold out to the system. The counter culture is neither hippiedom nor a student subculture.

The circles of authentic sympathizers probably extend much deeper into middle-class than working-class society. The counter culture is selectively pervasive. While it adopts many of the values of the heroic working class – its spontaneity, sexual virility, 'ethic of reciprocity', disregard for the future, irreverance, community-rather than family-centredness, lack of career ambition, the exuberant devilry of a poacher-culture – 'uptightness' spreads more deeply into the working class as it acquires property, high wages, a taste for French wines, privacy, credit-cards, continental package tours, a university education for its children, and respectability. Beaujolais and gas-fired central heating have triumphed where nonconformist chapels, the Band of Hope and Boy Scouts failed.

The counter culture has affinities with more robust working-class values which probably found their fullest expression in mining communities – especially, perhaps, isolated gold-mining communities. Time was erratic, punctuated irregularly by exploits; and life was dangerous. The counter culture would identify with Lawrence's virile gamekeeper (contemporary working-class Eastwood finds him acutely embarrassing) and share Lawrence's contempt for the effete and impotent Sir Clifford. Among its heroes are hirsute bandits who come down from the forests to fight for justice. The pilgrimage to the East is no package tour.

Hippiedom, it was recently cogently argued in *Oz*, is now socially and politically reactionary: the values of the counter culture are safe with the middle classes. In his brilliantly perceptive short history of the counter culture, 'The Long March Through the Bingo Halls', John Hoyland sees the hippies of the nineteen-seventies as 'a pretty reactionary bunch, and the ideology they adhere to is quite dangerous':

And where does this leave the hippies? For the most part still wittering on about grooving and getting it together, but now in the most vacuous, sentimental and depoliticizing way. Hippy ideology has become the escape valve for thousands of young people who want some kind of justification for sitting on their arses doing nothing, while convincing themselves that their very inactivity makes them the purest revolutionaries of all.[9]

The middle class – notably through such movements as Women's Lib – has now made the hippies redundant:

In fact, those who are relatively well educated, those whose very freedom from toil and whose future role in society gives them the opportunity to worry about the quality of life under capitalism, are often those who experience these ideological contradictions in a particularly acute way.[10]

(In a very similar vein, members of the very middle-class National Union of School Students, whose interviews are reported in Chapter seven, looked despairingly on working-class pupils, whose awareness they sought to extend.)

The counter culture has evolved in the past six or seven years, but it is difficult to know whether its class basis has changed (or even what it was in the first place). Looking back to the 'sixties Hoyland claims that the counter culture was 'only possible because large numbers of middle-class youth were able to enjoy a leisured existence that was parasitical . . .' The American evidence is unequivocal on this score: what Reich calls rather pretentiously 'Consciousness III' – roughly the counter culture of this book – originated in the educated middle class and has retained its solid middle-class base:

The great change took place when Consciousness III began to appear among young people who had endured no special emotional conditions, but were simply bright, sensitive children of the affluent middle class . . . But even in the fall of 1967 the numbers involved were still very small. The new group drew heavily from those who 'had been exposed to the very best of liberal arts education – poetry, art, theater, literature, philosophy, good conversation. Later, the group began to include 'ordinary' middle-class students. In time there were college athletes as well as college intellectuals, and lovers of motor cycles and skiing as well as lovers of art and literature. But the core group was always white, well educated and middle class.[11]

There is certainly evidence that the American counter culture has become less élitist in its recruitment: university students of relatively inferior social background and academic attainments were joining by the 'seventies.[12] And, indeed, Reich looks forward with confidence to the day when it will generally prevail, become all-inclusive, and embrace differences of class and age: 'It is both necessary and inevitable, and in time it will include not only youth, but all people in America.'[13]

It is because of its highly educated, middle-class base that Americans have seen a parallel for their own counter culture in London's Bloomsbury circle of the nineteen-twenties and thirties.[14] Certainly, the Bloomsbury circle were distinctly alternative, and Lytton Strachey, Clive Bell and Virginia Woolf would be generally qualified for inclusion in the counter culture. They would be disqualified principally by their rationality. But E. M. Forster would not be disqualified even on these grounds, and his hostility to the arrogance and inhumanity of science and scientists, and his central concern for personal relationships,[15] quite apart from his sexual proclivities, would bring him well inside one of the innermost concentric circles of our model.

Studies of student activists in England have found no social-class bias in recruitment,[16] our studies of counter-cultural attitudes among a cross-section of university students (see Chapter five), likewise show no variation with social-class origin. (The crucial circumstances is field of study.) This may be because the English university is still highly selective and working-class students are unlikely to 'represent' in any precise way their class of origin. In England as in America the counter culture is probably closely associated with a liberal, middle-class education; rather less demonstrably with a middle-class background.

Whatever their social-class origins, people in England, as in America, who are 'into counter culture' appear to become 'classless'.

They are united by rituals of marihuana smoking, musical happenings, the search for intense experiences, breaking from family attachments, and not earning a wage or salary. We have some very fragmentary evidence within the full-time hard-core counter culture of class-based statements about fellow-members (see Chapter seven); but social-class background does not appear to be importantly linked with behaviour and beliefs.

This is the apparent conclusion of a comparative study of two hippie groups or networks in London. In 1970 Mills selected one group of hippies who were intellectual, highly educated, and generally of superior social background; his second group were less well educated, more working class and conventionally delinquent in background, and more 'into' hard drugs. But these distinctions proved, in the event, to be of no analytical value: 'I started with a concern for them (i.e. social and demographic variables) but soon came to reject them as of little explanatory power.'[17] The two socially contrasted groups proved not to be markedly contrasted in behaviour and values: both emphasized physical euphoria and sexual enjoyment, a belief in spontaneity and 'doing your own thing' rather than becoming enmeshed in bureaucratic procedures and organizations. This comparative study failed to uncover any pertinent comparisons. The clearest (though admittedly impressionistic) evidence of middle-class connotations in the fieldwork reported below in this book relates to the three rebel movements studied: the National Union of School Students, the teachers' movement, Rank-and-File, and Free School Teachers (see Chapter seven). They are only on the fringe of the counter culture, and their middle-classness shows through in a continuing addiction to the work ethic.

The counter culture has changed and is changing, but it remains (in Yinger's sense) a contraculture rather than a subculture. It is not a subculture like the subculture of doctors or Wesleyans; more radically, it is 'the creation of a series of inverse or counter values (opposed to those of the surrounding society) . . .'[18] It remains counter to urban bourgeois culture which has degenerated even from its earlier state by requiring conformity in place of daring and risk-taking, duplicity in place of honest dealing. 'Since the new values are formed so largely in reaction to middle-class values, a whole set of priorities is the reverse of traditional values. Work will be to express self rather than to make a living; enjoyment will be in the body rather than in the accumulation of objects; one will seek creative activity, not gainful activity; sex, not violence; love, not war. Love will be open to the communal, non-exclusive pattern.'[19] This is still a fair statement of the counter-cultural position; but significant changes of emphasis are now apparent.

The counter culture has been an important and often traumatic learning experience over the past seven or eight years, both for those who were in it and for many who were not. Some of its inherent contradictions (for instance, between individualism and collectivism, and between aestheticism and political activism) have become more apparent; and the counter culture has certainly become more widely diffused, and possibly more fragmented. Diffusion means less distinction between being 'in' and 'out'. In 1970 Mills found that London hippies had a very keen sense of 'a kind of line' between themselves and straight society.[20] Our own fieldwork in the urban north-west in 1973 did not suggest such a sharp sense of separation or deliberation in assuming a counter-cultural life. The picture was nearer to Matza's view of deviant activity : '. .. considerable though variable interpenetration of deviant and conventional culture.'[21] The counter culture is no longer so insulated : it illustrates Durkheim's notion of the 'unbroken connection' between social realms.

The counter culture is no less the inverse of the bourgeois society it increasingly pervades : but in seven years it has learned three sharp lessons – that hard drugs are not ecstatic but soporific and finally lethal : they do not enhance personal relationships, but destroy them; that communes are more difficult to establish and maintain than was initially supposed : instead of promoting 'meaningful' relationships, they can often survive only by keeping relationships shallow; and there are limits to a social system's being purely 'expressive': 'instrumentality' creeps in and may be a condition of survival. It is in a shift towards more deliberate organization that the counter culture has probably changed most.

The counter culture is intelligent. It is certainly capable of learning from experience. The effects of drug-use are quite apparent to a London hippie :

> Drugs make you fucking lazy, I will tell you that. If you keep getting stoned and using speed you stay out late at night and you don't get any sleep. Then during the day-time you just lay there all day. But now I want to get some energy so that I can do things.[22]

The counter culture has learned that hard-drug use makes people not only lazy but unreliable and selfish. Increasingly it has recognized the limits of expressiveness and the need for some organization in achieving effective social and political action. This is Hoyland's plea; and it is also his dilemma. It has been stated by Mary Douglas: 'After attacking definition as such, ritual as such, it is very difficult to turn about and seek the new definitions, differentiations, and rituals which will remedy the case.'[23] This is the difficult turnabout that is taking place: the counter culture no longer shows quite the contempt for competence and the ability to fix things, which Roszak and Reich discerned and approved. Political activists in particular are increasingly concerned with organizational skills, but recognize that such concern is a threat to deeply cherished values.[24] Hoyland recognizes the danger of humourless dedication to far-distant goals, the possibility that, 'as we dedicate ourselves to politics and make our revolution, the beauties and wonders of life will slip unnoticed through our fingers.'[25] The new pragmatism threatens to widen the always latent rift between the expressive-aesthetic and the political-activist aspects of the counter culture.

There is certainly a widespread feeling that the counter culture is now fragmented compared with the 'sixties. The ideal of inclusiveness cherished by the 'postmodern' generation was stated by Keniston: '. . . an attempt to include both within their personalities and within their movements every opposite, every possibility, and every person, no matter how apparently alien.'[26] Hoyland thinks the attempt has failed: 'The collective ideology, the ideas and assumptions that held the different components of this movement together in the 60s have now become so dispersed and diluted that it makes very little sense to talk about the Underground as a specific entity any more.'

This may be a nostalgic backward look to an imaginary Golden Age; and our research into counter-cultural attitudes (reported in Chapter five) suggests caution in claiming the unrelatedness of the diverse aspects of counter-cultural belief. But seven years of learning have produced greater realism, and diffusion if not fragmentation. Indeed, the realism has promoted diffusion:

> It already appears that the hippies' purely expressive solution is considered too radical as a viable solution for the society as a whole. Very few people completely drop out (which the totally expressive solution necessitates). But there is evidence (in America) that fewer and fewer people are taking the straight life in its extreme sense as their style of life either. Rather, some sort

of balance is apparently being worked out on both sides of the fence.[27]

The difficulty with the 'purely expressive solution' is that it becomes boring. Ecstasy is difficult to sustain. A protest against banality ends limply wondering what to do next. Mills has interpreted pop festivals as 'sacraments of renewal' which revive flagging zeal and fading commitment and enthusiasm. 'It was this process (of attrition) that the performers halted and swung into reverse. In the process they became the renewers of transformation and occasionally its initiators.'[28] Activist students, according to Jeremy Seabrook, have the same problem after they have graduated and left the university. The problem is how to get through Saturday night. (The heroic working class in Sillitoe's Nottingham never had this problem.) 'Many of them maintain a fragmented life, travelling across country for a few days with friends who have started a commune in a condemned house in Liverpool . . .' A brief return to their university town is not an effective sacrament of renewal. 'Very soon the career structure becomes the most important social preoccupation . . .'[29] and marriage is the final betrayal.

The full-time counter culture is peopled by a small minority and is anxious about 'wastage', recruitment and continuity. Peter and Brigette Berger point out that in America the percentage who have totally embraced the 'green revolution' is statistically insignificant.[30] But it is socially significant. Adam Curle is unwilling to prophesy whether the counter culture will erode the straight culture, be crushed by it, or co-exist with it. He concludes, nevertheless, that '. . . the genuine hippies are sufficiently numerous to constitute, I believe, a significant phenomenon'.[31]

We estimate from explorations of the counter culture in the urban north-west of England that there are probably between 500 and a thousand full-time 'members' in a population of half a million. They are predominantly male, and represent some 2 per cent of the forty thousand or so males in their twenties. This is a very rough estimate; but a similar percentage is obtained from the estimated 150,000 who attended the Isle of Wight pop festival in 1970 – some 2 per cent of the eight million or so people in England in the relevant age range.

Our inquiries into support for counter-cultural values among a cross-section of young people mainly in higher education suggests that very strong sympathy is to be found among roughly one-third of the males and one-sixth of the females (age-range sixteen to twenty-five). These proportions give strong support to the whole complex of counter-cultural values. Some 40 per cent of the males and 25 per cent of the females give very strong support to the values associated with aestheticism; but only 16 per cent of the males and 8 per cent of the females to political activist-anarchist values. (See Chapter five.) These proportions probably give a rough indication of the extent of the concentric circles of counter-cultural support around the full-time inner core.

The counter culture is thought by some to have a fragility because it is a movement based not on a social class (like social and political reform movements of the past), but on a generation. And generations grow older. But even class-based movements have commonly prospered through external allies, and the counter-cultural 'generation' appears to extend into the late-thirties and to have powerful allies who are considerably older. 'Recruits' are not typically solving the alleged identity-crisis of adolescence; they are solving the identity-crisis of early middle age.

'The age group is intrinsically transitional, unless its span is artificially extended by the refusal to move on to a way of life appropriate to the next stage.'[32] People may refuse to move on to the next stage through under-acculturation (as Keniston suggests[33]), or from over-acculturation, as indicated in the work of Kohlberg.[34] In the latter case, people have moved through and beyond the developmental stages described by Piaget, to a 'post-conventional' stage marked by devotion to personal principles that may transcend not only conventional morality but even the social contract. It is with these transcendalists that the future of the counter culture lies.

Continuity depends not only on an increase in Dionysian personalities, but on an increase in Dionysian social roles. These, as Bennett Berger has argued, are available in 'bohemian businesses', in show business, and to some extent in working-class occupations. Proprietors and managers of small art galleries, pottery and leatherwork shops, discotheques and health-food shops may have much more in common with their customers than with other small businessmen. Berger concedes that '. . . show business careers and similar occupations are in fact subject to much the same economic circumstances and bureacratic controls as are other occupations'.[35] (Our material on a theatre company, reported in chapters five and six, supports this observation.) Nevertheless, 'the image of show business careers exists in a milieu in which Dionysian excess has a long tradition and an honoured place'. A residue of heroic working-class occupations also provides opportunities for an episodic and colourful way of life, and university places for mature students (and perhaps for staff) may be similarly conceived.

## Communes

Terry lives in a squatters' community in Kentish Town and trans-lates ancient languages. He says of the community: 'The most attractive thing I find is that here people will tend to co-operate, not compete. It is one of the few places I know outside Oxford or Cambridge where it is possible to knock on almost any door and know you will be welcome. There is an alternative way of life here, although it may appear fragmented.'[36] Ex-public schoolboy Rollo Maughling, and his wife Solange, a former beautician, live in the Glastonbury Community. Rollo makes decisions by casting the I Ching and reading Tarot cards, tries to see the inner, spiritual purpose behind every action of his day, and earns a weekly wage as a van driver because it is very important to be self-sufficient and have personal dignity.[37] Neither Terry nor Rollo would describe themselves as hippies or their communities as communes. 'The alternative' has its own shifting margins, but an ideal-type commune is its central reference point.

The counter culture also expresses an extreme individualism which appears to consort ill with the commune ideal. But the indi-vidualists who remain outside the commune movement often do so with regret, recognizing their inability to cope with its demands, but paying tribute to its purposes. Mills found among the London hippies that 'The commune was the guiding image of a large part of hippie life, the nearest vision of the good society that was reached.'[38]

It is also Adam Curle's view that the commune ideal embodies the high morality of the counter culture: 'They live together in communes, earning their living, or in some senses literally making it, with the minimum of compromise with the world of the market. They run their community affairs as well as their interpersonal relationships on principles that are most seriously intended to pre-serve and increase individual autonomy and promote the fullest realization of the human spirit.'[39]

An English *Directory of Communes* (1972)[40] lists thirty-three communes which are looking for additional members. They are typically quite small (four or five members) and the age-range wide. Thus one commune of three consists of Betty, fifty-four, Pat, twenty-nine and Tony, thirty-seven. The age spread is probably similar to that in America, where a survey conducted in 1970 showed that 67 per cent of commune members were twenty-three years of age or more, and 42 per cent were over twenty-five.[41] The aims and organization of the English communes vary considerably. A number, like those run by the Philadelphia Association and the Richmond Fellowship, are alternatives to mental hospitals. The eleven members of the Sarum House Buddhist Community recognize a range of traditions ranging from Soto Zen to Tibetan Vajrayana. But typically the communes are at a formative stage, feeling their way towards a philosophy and appropriate form of organization.

They also appear to be predominantly middle class. The Stoney-marsh Commune in Hampshire has five members and describes itself as follows:

> Sons and daughters of the middle classes and mostly in our twenties, two of us are qualified teachers, and the rest rejects of our academic system, having dropped out at various stages. Three of us work on local farms, picking up basic skills. In the future we want to work our farm organically and produce most of our own food . . . We are a pretty close knit group, and have got to know each other very well during the last few months; breaking down barriers in relationships with honesty and sharing; working out fears and hangups by confronting them. We all feel that we have grown tremendously from this, and if we have a common direction, it is to keep travelling on this path towards the unknown and thereby realize a greater spiritual harmony with each other and our environment. Through self-discovery and awareness we can put ourselves in a stronger position to catalyse a change of consciousness in others. We have no desire to escape from society's problems but feel that any real change for the better must start at an individual level.

The same tentative, exploratory views are expressed by the nine members of Parsonage Farm commune. They value spontaneity but recognize that 'In living communally . . . individual spontaneity cannot be entirely free . . .'. They know they have a long way to go before they can claim to be a commune.

Fundamentally we are work oriented; this is our main common denominator at present. We do know that we are not into religion, mysticism, occult things, 'hippy' philosophies, or drugs. We are concerned about the exploitation of man and resources and we would like in our own way to develop ways of keeping exploitation to a minimum while still maintaining a pleasant standard of living. Whether this is possible or whether we are kidding ourselves we are not sure.

The commune movement reflects the misgivings about the modern 'nuclear family' which have recently been expressed by some psychiatrists and anthropologists. In a celebrated lecture, Edmund Leach claimed that, 'Far from being the basis of the good society, the family, with its narrow privacy and tawdry secrets, is the source of all our discontents.'[42] The attack on the family is made in the name of mental health and personal freedom: in spite of its evolution into the 'companionship family' and the emergence of 'joint-conjugal roles', its authority structure is seen as archaic. These views echo through the notices in the *Directory of Communes*.

The Birchwood Community was set up in 1971 'by people who didn't want the traditional consumer cell of mum and dad in suburbia, but were not altogether certain what they did want. No clear cut ideology. Nine adults and three children living in a large house with eight acres of land. Hope to expand to around twenty-five. Most of us earn bread outside the community. Not dropouts but anti-rat-race; not free love yet but aiming to loosen the possessive stranglehold which characterizes many couples and child-parent relationships. Still at a very early stage, but some ideas are beginning to emerge. Income-sharing, encounter groups. Madness. Now reached the stage of moving from a community (basically a house sharing structure) to a commune (basically a relationship sharing structure). Fairly idle, fairly anarchic, not very trendy, a bit timid.'

The Selene Community is more certain about its ideology. It is a commune, standing 'between the coldness of the nation and the rigidness of the family.' It is based on love which means sharing and a commitment 'which is intended to last forever'.

We are also deeply in love with the Earth Mother and her old pagan religion, with the moon and with the trees and with all of wild nature, and we worship when the moon is full and sometimes on the old festivals of the sun, too. We want more people to join us permanently, people who are sensitive and rational, interested in plants and people and mental and emotional creativity . . . We are not interested in the traffic of ephemeral relationships. Our commune is our home and our tribe and the home of the Earth Mother. Without love, encounter is worthless; with love you would not go away.

The commune explosion of the late 'sixties produced an estimated four thousand communes across North America. Three carefully conducted, independent studies showed that by 1969–70 they had typically evolved a high degree of organization, however informal and orgiastic their origins. Berger investigated some twenty communes engaged in subsistence farming in northern California. Sex roles were sharpy differentiated: cooking and milking goats were undertaken by the women; only men with no special skills were relegated to the kitchen. And 'exclusive sexual access is a norm that runs deep . . .'[43]

Speck made a three-year (1966–9) study of American communes and found a fluid line of demarcation between them and the wider society. Many members had paid employment, but in jobs well below their training and abilities. Many left for the 'straight' world, and some returned. Sexual relationships were much as Berger found them: 'Though the opportunity for sexual freedom and experimentation was there, the sexual activity and pairing was most conservative.'[44] Speck (a psychiatrist) has higher hopes of the 14-year-olds who show signs that they are 'beginning to break through the sexual inhibitions of older youths and adults.'[45]

Westhues emphasizes the separateness of American communes, their existence as 'intentional islands'. He also stresses the formality, and even the rigidity, of their organization. He investigated twelve directly, and a further sixty by questionnaire. The values their members strongly support are: close interpersonal relationships, total honesty with other people, doing things with other people, a sense of community, greater sensitivity to other people, and the opportunity to be creative. 'Intellectual concerns, politics, drugs, and sexual permissiveness received much less support.'[46] The communes rarely last for more than two years, but 'at least a third of their members show a stable commitment to some kind of communal way of life.'

The more explicitly political communes are less visible, often with good reason. They do not advertise in the *Directory of Communes*.

They are usually urban and are associated with political action – Women's Lib, international anarchism, 'situationism'. The Amherst Road commune which housed John Barker, Hilary Creek, Anna Mendelson and James Greenfield, was dedicated to revolution, and its members were condemned, in December 1972, to ten years' imprisonment. But it was closely linked with loners like the anarchist, Stuart Christie.[47] Underlying the communes, whether superficially 'retreatist' or more obviously 'activist', is a concern with, and rejection of, power as it manifests itself in families, formal organizations, the nation-state, or international relations. In opposing power some have learned to embrace it. For a detailed study of the extent, recruitment and aims of English communes, see A. Rigby, *Alternative Realities* (1974, Routledge & Kegan Paul: London), published after the above was written.

## Micro and macro levels

This book examines counter cultures at the micro level of individual belief and action, and at the macro level of structural social change. At the micro level values appear to be prior, at the macro level demographic and economic change appears to be the 'independent variable'. Our conversations with people 'into counter culture' in an urban area typically revealed a long personal history of predisposing attitudes and values; a comparative study of historical periods characterized by notable Dionysian movements suggests that counter-cultural values emerge in a context of rapid population growth, economic expansion, and consequent social dislocation. At this level values are not 'prior': they do not precede and promote social and economic transformations, but follow in their wake. The problem is why economic reorganizations which require above all system and order and handsomely reward them promote values which are penalized and undermine them. In his study of seventeenth-century science Merton stresses the importance of distinguishing the personal attitudes of men of science from the social role played by their research. Likewise it is important not to confuse the personal values and motivations of contemporary hippies with the counter culture's long term social role. This is the distinction between micro- and macro-level analysis.

The counter culture is a form of deviant behaviour (though not necessarily in the limited technical sense of 'rule-breaking'). Recent studies of deviant behaviour have tended to de-emphasize personal values which push people into action. The work of Becker,

Lemert and Matza plays down 'causes' and concentrates on the nature of the social phenomenon. Appropriate values arise after the deviant has become deviant, and not before. Motivation is post, not prior.

Matza employs a concept of 'drift', which is the temporary, episodic release from the bind of convention. This is not compulsion or commitment: 'It is, instead, almost the opposite. During release (from the bind of convention) the delinquent is not constrained to commit offense; rather, he is free to drift into delinquency.'[48] Suitable motivation may arise after he has drifted in, and prevent him from drifting out, as Becker argues in his study of marihuana users: '. . . instead of the deviant motives leading to deviant behaviour, it is the other way around; the deviant behaviour in time produces the deviant motivation.'[49]

Becoming a deviant is seen as a social process: deviants have 'deviant careers' shaped by 'career contingencies' which push the actor from one point to another: 'Career contingencies include both objective facts of social structure and changes in the perceptions, motivations, and desires of individuals.'[50] These rather simple notions – including labelling theory, which defines a deviant as one to whom the label has been successfully applied – have been considerably refined;[51] but the structure of events in some sense outside the individual, in which he becomes almost unwittingly enmeshed, remains an important explanatory concept.

Mills gives great weight to the impact of the transfiguring experience. (He also uses labelling theory to explain the hippie's sense of outsider identity: The label once attached, the box is sealed almost irrevocably.'[52]) The events are decisive turning points in the passage from not being a hippie to being one. 'Becoming a hippie was experienced as a kind of total transformation, which the young person half-knowingly brought upon himself.'[53] The transforming experience might have been the impact of Beatlemania, a visit to North Africa, the first drug injection. Prior values are not entirely discounted, but 'In becoming a hippie the experience of transformation was critical . . . The crucial element was always some intensified experience . . .'[54] Mills might be writing about Saul on the road to Damascus. There was a marked discontinuity with the past. The event marked a new self, a new beginning.

The only comparable transfiguring event we have found in our field work was the first experience of school teaching – usually described as 'shattering' by members of Rank-and-File and by teachers in Free Schools (see Chapter eight). But the full-time members of the counter culture did not recall decisive turning points or single, critical events. They explain their present position by giving full-scale life-histories which illustrated the essential continuity of their values. This was also true of the three educational protest movements: the National Union of School Students, Rank-and-File and the Free School teachers. The teachers also mentioned the trauma of class teaching; but, like all our other subjects, emphasized prior values and attitudes. The other common factor was the experience, while growing up, of social isolation. Our subjects had been moved around a good deal as children and had often felt an extreme sense of social dislocation.

This appears to be one important link with our macro-level analysis: the transformation which is subsumed under the general heading of 'post-industrialism' can be understood only with reference to 'the extraordinary importance which movements of population assume as both a catalyst and ingredient of social change.'[55] Put very simply: post-industrialism creates a lot of lonely people. (The first student protest movements at Berkeley in the mid-sixties were closely connected with loneliness in the sense that they attracted disproportionate support from students away from home for the first time[56] or living in apartments rather than fraternities.[57])

It is true that an historical 'stable state' is a romantic myth, an imaginary rural utopia in terms of which anyone who moves from his place of birth is a deviant and a threat to established order; it is equally true that modern plural societies make possible the relatively unstressful assimilation of migrants, through 'pluralistic integration'.[58] Nor does recent research confirm Eisenstadt's simplistic proposition that 'every migratory movement is motivated by the migrant's feeling of some kind of insecurity – and inadequacy in the original social setting.'[59] Nevertheless, post-industrial societies are characterized by rapid population movement and growth and the the rise of 'transilient man' involved in world-wide communication networks. Transilient man is not necessarily rootless and marginal in a pejorative sense; but a shifting life in extensive social networks calls for a new social ethic which the counter culture provisionally and experimentally provides.

Loose social networks constitute an 'open' society. But modern technology and bureaucracy, it is often said, spell greater restriction and constraint. This claim calls for critical re-appraisal.

Technological change has not only advanced exponentially, claims Schon: it has become increasingly pervasive. All new technology is disruptive, but the vein of technology mined in the past half-century is uniquely disruptive.[60] In fact, as Leach has argued, technology may merely produce substitutes (like nylon for red flannel) and the consequent social change is minimal; when it produces new additions (like television and electronic computers), the consequences may be more far-reaching.[61] But even additions may be by-passed: they do not pervade; they over-ride. Technological additions, maintains Leach, have been mainly in the field of communications, in the form of supra-cultural communication networks. New motorway systems leave ancient villages to turn in upon themselves and pursue their traditional life. In traditional societies communication systems are bounded, hemmed within the perimeter of groups which can sustain face-to-face relationships. With the rise of supra-cultural systems, 'the communication network has developed an autonomy of its own which is potentially not bounded at all.' Such networks co-exist with local systems without destroying them. Leach recognizes that the interfaces between technology and society are multi-faceted, but maintains that 'it is the communications facet rather than the bulk production facet which matters most.' In its most characteristic modern form, technology is easily evaded; and it is unlikely to reduce cultural variety since it usually provides alternatives among an array of equally viable possibilities. The real danger to human variety is not technology but science, which offers the one and inescapable truth.[62]

Bureaucratic constraints are as illusory as the harness of technology. Merton, rather than Weber, gave us a picture of bureaucratic rigidity and overconformity. In a classic essay, he claimed that, since bureaucrats 'minimize personal relations and resort to categorization, the pecularities of individual cases are often ignored.' Rule-observation is obsessive. 'If the bureaucracy is to operate successfully, it must attain a high degree of reliability of behaviour, an unusual degree of conformity with prescribed patterns of action.'[63] In fact, even bureaucracies are today in a state of flux.

Peter Blau wrote about the dynamics, not the rigidities, of modern bureaucracy, and illustrated rule-adaptation and revision to meet changing circumstances.[64] More recent investigations have shown modern bureaucracies obsessed not with rule-observation but with flexibility, even to the extent of creating chaos, confusion and uncertainty about rule application, to the dismay of bemused clients who wish to know where they stand. Meticulous and unbending rule-observation is a serious disqualification in a modern bureaucrat.[65]

So, too, are reliability and loyalty. Crozier has described the secular trend for bureacracies to become less bureaucratic in this sense. Personnel are more interchangeable, and organizations can be content with a more temporary loyalty. 'The modern organization can tolerate more deviance, restrict its requirements to a more specialized field, and demand only temporary commitments.'[66] The loyal servant is an encumbrance because he expects excessive protection in return.

And bureaucracies are increasingly decentralized. The centre cannot handle and process the rising flow of information, and decision-making is perforce displaced to the perimeter. Schon even sees the counter culture itself, a shifting network of relationships without firm centres, as the model of modern bureaucracy. Far from being the negation of contemporary bureaucracy, the amorphous counter culture of loosely-connected, shifting centres is created in its image.[67]

The open society has weak grids and groups. Mary Douglas sees grids and groups as two (independent) sources of social constraint. The grid is 'classification, the symbolic system'; the group is 'pressure, the experience of having no option but to consent to the overwhelming demands of other people'. A 'closed' society, in these terms, will have strong groups and grids, and 'Strong grid and strong group will tend to a routinized piety towards authority symbols; beliefs in a punishing, moral universe, and a category of rejects.'[68]

Mary Douglas interprets Dionysian counter cultures as a reaction against oppressive groups, and especially against constricting grids; but she also interprets them as an expression and consequence of relaxed groups and grids. She cannot have it both ways. Countercultural students, she claims, are reacting against an overstructured grid, 'the experience of which has always driven people to value unstructured personal experiences . . .'[69] Certain Londoners who are deeply implicated in the impersonal constraints of our urban-industrial society may think and even behave likewise.[70]

But her Durkheimian 'principle of symbolic replication of the social state' leads to a contrary conclusion. The beliefs and conduct of the Ancient Israelites were the outcome of their experience of strong groups and grids, and these in turn reflected their state of siege. Their adherence to rule, the legalism of their priests, and their rejection of the Dionysian mystery cults, simply reflected their social state. To expect them to stop preaching a stern sexual morality, vigilant control of bodily boundaries, and a corresponding religious cult would be asking them to give up the political struggle.'[71] The Dionysian Dinka of the Sudan, with little sense of sin, pollution and taboo, for whom trance is a central cult and incest defined in the most generous categories, live in a more expansive and benign environment and experience lighter social constraints. It is not over-structered but relaxed grids which lead to Dionysian effervescence and luxuriant marginality. 'In all cases, it is the lack of strong social articulation, the slackening of group and grid which lead people to seek, in the slackening of bodily control, appropriate forms of expression. This is how the fringes of society express their marginality.'[72] This is the interpretation which accords with the thesis of this book.

# 3

## Ecstasy and economic order

### Technology and ecstasy

The contemporary counter culture is often damned as 'parasitical'. It impedes rather than promotes orderly economic progress. It is lacking in 'relevance'; its supporters are 'irresponsible'. They are prepared, it is said, to take but not to give. Periods of great economic growth and change are sustained by quite different men: self-disciplined, pre-eminently rational, albeit capable of taking calculated risks.

Sixteenth century capitalism found such men among the puritans; the nineteenth century found them among nonconformists and utilitarians. We have them in abundance – perhaps over-abundance – today. The successful businessmen of our day – according to recent personality studies carried out by Eysenck – are above all 'stable' and introverted.[1] They are much more stable than university students (who tend to be rather high on neuroticism), and they are much more stable than the general population. But more surprising, perhaps, than this, they are not only more introverted than the general population, they are even more introverted than university students. Our successful businessmen tend to be steady, even phlegmatic, cautious, unemotional, rather inturned and not naturally convivial men, who methodically do their homework. Complex economic enterprise apparently requires no less. The problem is to account for the significant minority of able young people in advanced Western societies who, in the past decade, have rejected the economic virtues of thrift, sobriety and steady application in the pursuit of long term goals. Perhaps this is a unique phenomenon of our times? One method of approaching the problem seemed to be through a comparative study of periods of great economic change.

Economic historians have not paid much attention to apparently incongruous beliefs and values in periods of economic growth. But on close examination, five great economic revolutions appeared to have co-existed with strikingly discordant, even subversive, values and beliefs: the neolithic revolution, the eleventh-century industrial revolution, the commercial revolution of the sixteenth century, the classical industrial revolution of the nineteenth century, and the cybernetic revolution of today. All appeared to have 'counter cultures' which were at least superficially discordant and 'unhelpful', especially in their support for non-rational, 'disorderly' and highly emotional modes of conduct. But a sixth period of spectacular economic enterprise and achievement appeared to have no such accompaniment: the Italian Renaissance was, apparently, the great exception. It offered an opportunity for 'deviant case analysis'.

These highly complex – and controversial – periods of economic change are sketched very briefly below with reference to the values which appear to have supported and perhaps to have hindered them. Clearly this brief sketch can do no more than suggest possibly crucial relationships. But in the light of these comparisons, neither technology nor bureaucracy appeared to be the crucial circumstance which precipitated non-rational adversary cultures. The critical factor appeared to be population growth.

The relationship between order and ecstasy has been variously interpreted by philosophers and sociologists since Nietzsche explored the opposition of Apollonian and Dionysian characteristics and their triumphant synthesis in Greek tragedy. Spengler thought that ecstasy, an unbounded intellect and soaring imagination, could not survive 'civilization' in the sense of a highly mechanized and science-based society; Ellul laments that ecstasy can only be emasculated, incorporated, contained; most American writers on the counter culture conclude that it is ineffectually reactive. Only

Nietzsche had unwavering confidence that ecstasy would finally prevail.

The counter culture embraces madness and disorder. Its committed members describe themselves as 'freaks' and those who are not 'alternative' as 'straights'. Edumund Leach embraced disorder, too, in his counter-cultural manifesto of the late 'sixties. He was scornful of our 'all-pervasive reverence for law and order' and berated us because we take for granted 'that there is something intrinsically virtuous and natural about law and order . . .'. 'If we were logical,' he claims, 'it would be order, not chaos, which would fill us with alarm.'[2]

This is the authentic voice of the counter culture. Characteristic behaviour in the 'alternative scene' is irregular, disordered, deranged. Members of the counter culture deliberately induce abnormal mental states. Familiar perceptual-experiential boundaries dissolve. Experience is discontinuous, ruptured, dissolved, restructured. Marcuse describes the rejection of sanity as the basis of liberation, '. . . sanity defined as the regular, socially coordinated functioning of mind and body – especially at work . . .'. The alternative has rejected sanity:

> Today's rebels want to see, hear, feel new things in a new way:
> they link liberation with the dissolution of ordinary and orderly
> perception. The 'trip' involves the dissolution of the ego shaped
> by the established society – an artificial and short-lived dissolu-
> tion anticipates, in a distorted manner, an exigency of the social
> liberation: the revolution must be at the same time a revolution
> in perception which will accompany the material and intellectual
> reconstruction of society, creating a new aesthetic environment.[3]

Ellul talks of madness and machines. Madness is the only escape. Art and ecstasy are insufficient. 'Only madness is inaccessible to the machine.'[4] 'Every other "art" form can be reduced to technique . . .'

Ellul thinks our civilization is unique in suppressing and constraining ecstasy. Before the rise of modern 'technicized' societies 'the form society took expressed the psychology of the individual. This is no longer true.' In the fatalistic tradition of Durkheimian sociology, he sees modern social forms as external to man but coercive. Modern men are trapped by a society they did not even will or invent; their frenzied reactions only support and strengthen it. 'There is no doubt that the norms of our society have changed for reasons which are not "human" . . .' The technicized society makes and transforms itself. 'This new sociological mass structure and its new criteria of civilization seem both inevitable and undeniable. They are inevitable because they are imposed by technical forces and economic considerations beyond the reach of man.'

Ellul offers no hope. He is passionate for nature, art and ecstasy, but technique is all-pervasive and '. . . the invasion of technique desacralizes the world in which man is called upon to live. For technique nothing is sacred, there is no mystery, no taboo.'[5] Modern man is divorced from nature, and 'Nothing belongs any longer to the realm of the gods or the supernatural. The individual who lives in the technical milieu knows very well that there is nothing spiritual anywhere.'

The counter culture is merely 'functional', serviceable to the technological society, finally providing it with support and confirmation. It is 'integrated'. 'Ecstasy occurs . . . not as a cause but as a result of the technical society.' But ecstasy, apparently, is not ecstatic, but soporific. Surrealism, anarchism and youth hostels have '. . . performed the sociological function of integration'.[6] Movements such as today's existentialism, or eroticism in the form of a renovated Marquis de Sade or of the little pornographic reviews, are a sociological necessity to a technical milieu . . . thanks to 'movements' which integrate and control them, they are powerless to harm the technical society, of which henceforth they form an integral part.[7] Stripped down to essentials, this seems to be little more than a new version of 'the opiate of the people' with pornography in place of religion. Ellul is trapped in the characteristic circularity of functional analysis.

Oswald Spengler, like Ellul, denied the possibility of ecstasy in the advanced stages of a technological civilization. His vast organic metaphor of social development allowed no other conclusion. There would be no more poetry, Wagner or valkyries. But Spengler accepted the inevitable more cheerfully than Ellul. We could all find a sober dignity as engineers.

Spengler's 'quiet engineer', 'the priest of the machine',[8] is quiet, hard-working, self-controlled; a sad decline from the Faustian scientist who had formed Western culture for a thousand years. Modern historical scholarship shows scientists, even in the scientific upsurge of the seventeenth century, no less rigorously methodical and self-controlled than engineers.[9] But for Spengler Faustian science was intellectual intoxication, and for the Faustian soul '. . . the prime symbol is pure and limitless space'. Ellul and Spengler are agreed in this: that technology supports life but robs it of humanity; ecstasy offers no serious threat to a technological order; and modern technological society leaves no room for what is essentially human in man: his capacity to consider the infinite, to find truths hidden from reason, and to experience awe in the presence of unfathomable mystery.

Numerous contemporary social analysts likewise see modern technology as dehumanizing. But they do not all share Spengler's fatalism and pessimism ('Of great painting or great music there can no longer be, for Western people, any question. Their architectural possibilities have been exhausted these hundred years'.[10]) Technology and the regulated social organization that it entailed, do not exclude ecstasy, but provoke it. For Roszak the counter culture is an authentic quest for human significance in a devitalized world, 'an emerging balance to the gross distortions of our technological society . . .'.[11]

Technology is singled out as the prime cause of both madness and ecstasy. The connection is fairly simple and direct. Explanation is in terms of reaction against the scale and pervasiveness of modern mechanization. Toffler, like Ellul, focuses on the rate of technological change rather than its level: it is rapid change (especially an exponential growth rate), that carries a 'psychological price-tag' and leads to hippie communes. bucolic retreats, and 'future shock'.[12] Roszak is less concerned with the debilitating or disruptive effects of machines and the social dislocation caused by the diffusion of new techniques, than the limitations of scientific modes of thought. He attacks 'the myth of objective consciousness'. Hampden-Turner similarly attacks 'technological thinking' and the 'borrowed tool-box of technology' which social scientists have used to study man. He defines true man as free, autonomous and integrated, not the victim of the socio-technical system he has created: '. . . technology may legitimately be regarded as a force and value separate from man. It seems destined to grow . . . There is something almost God-like about technology . . .'[13] Slater voices similar fears: 'The old-culture American needs to reconsider his commitment to technological "progress". If he fails to kick the habit he may retain his culture and lose his life.'[14] And Charles Reich holds 'Consciousness II' in profound contempt largely because it '. . . believes in the central ideology of technology, the domination of man and environment by technique.'[15]

In fact, the disjunction between culture and the dominant social structure is probably unconnected with the level of technology or the rate of technological change. Technology is irrelevant to both frenzy and ecstasy. Successful economic revolutions are associated with population movement and growth. It is the consequent social dislocation and uncertainty and threat to established identities that most satisfactorily explain the conjunction of economic order and spectacular poetic excess. Social dislocation calls for experiments in new interactional norms. Ecstasy is demographic.

Nietzsche no less than Spengler saw in the wild exuberance of Wagnerian music the high point of German culture and the triumphant affirmation of life over death. But, unlike Spengler, he expected no decline: nineteenth-century civilization was leading to the splendours of unlimited Dionysian excess. In *The Birth of Tragedy* Nietzsche celebrated intoxication and exulted in excess. His study of classical tragedy is in fact a passionate hymn to Dionysus and his reincarnation in German music from Bach through Beethoven to Wagner. Dionysian music expresses fear, terror, mystery. But above all Dionysian excess finds its sublime expression in sexual orgies and abandonment, feverish sexual excitement bursting all bounds and ignoring all laws. Nietzsche's bitter opposition to Christianity was based on its denial of sexuality, its suppression of the deepest instinct of life.

Apollo and Dionysus represent opposite principles of personal life and social organization. Nietzsche has provided a typology which has proved useful to philosophers, anthropologists, sociologists and psychoanalysts. (Among those who have made notable use of Nietzsche's conceptualization are Spengler, Ruth Benedict and Norman O. Brown.[16]) For Nietzsche the Apollonian and the Dionysian co-exist, interact and, in the ancient world, achieve a triumphant synthesis in Greek drama: '. . . at last, by a metaphysical miracle of the Hellenic will, they appear paired with each other, and through this pairing generate the equally Dionysian and Apollonian art-work of Attic tragedy.'[17]

Apollo is judicious (and judicial), calm, rational, circumspect, guarded and restrained. He makes laws and obeys them. He is an individualist, with a strong sense of boundaries and separateness – he is never 'beside himself', he never loses himself. Even in anger decorum never deserts him: he is the perfect ambassador, the supreme bureaucrat. (And he is always meticulously and appropriately dressed for the part. He is a man to whom externals are important.) He expresses himself in the plastic arts; he moulds and shapes materials; he is a sculptor, potter, painter. He is thus an 'author' and has authority. He is optimistic, self-confident, competent: life is orderly, predictable, under control. Apollo is a law-maker-engineer. He has been fashioned most perfectly in modern times in the Grandes Écoles.

Dionysus has no sense of boundaries. He bursts any that surround him, including the boundaries of self that mark him off from others and the world. Dionysus is open, Apollo is closed. 'The individual, with all his boundaries and due proportions, went under in the self-oblivion of the Dionysian states and forgot the Apollonian precepts.'[18] Dionysus is a lyric poet and musician. He is drunk. He does not shape and subjugate nature, but is in harmony with it. 'The chariot of Dionysus is bedecked with flowers and garlands: panthers and tigers pass beneath its yoke'.[19]

The festivals of Dionysus know no bounds. 'In nearly every instance the centre of these festivals lay in extravagant sexual licentiousness, the waves of which overwhelmed all family life and its venerable traditions.'[20] In spite of this wild exuberance, or perhaps because of it, Dionysus is rather sleepy, lethargic, slightly drugged: 'It is either under the influence of the narcotic draught, of which the hymns of all primitive men and peoples tell us, or by the powerful approach of spring penetrating all nature with joy, that those Dionysian emotions awake, in the augmentation of which the subjective vanishes to complete self-forgetfulness.'[21] But for all his joy, Dionysus is a pessimist: he rejects science and its implicit self-confidence and optimism. Openness is anomic.

Writing in the late nineteenth century, Nietzsche concludes with an invitation to the counter culture. 'Let no one attempt to weaken our faith in an impending re-birth of Hellenic antiquity . . .' The spirit will be purified through the fire-magic of music. 'Yes, my friends, believe with me in Dionysian life and in the re-birth of tragedy. The time of the Socratic man is past: crown yourselves with ivy, take in your hands the thyrsus, and do not marvel if tigers and panthers lie down fawning at your feet.'

Spengler's hero is not Dionysus but Faust. But the victory will go to Apollo. Spengler's Faust has many of the qualities of Nietzsche's Dionysus, but he is more aggressive, dominative, subjugating nature rather than finding harmony with it. Faust thirsts for mastery. But he is as unbounded as Dionysus: 'The painting that defines the individual body by contours is Apollonian, that which forms space

by means of light and shade is Faustian . . .'[22] Faustian technology
is passionate, Gothic, and Faustian science is sheer intoxication:
'The intoxicated soul wills to fly above space and time. An ineffable
longing tempts him to indefinable horizons. Man would free himself from the earth, rise into the infinite, leave the bounds of the
body, and circle the universe of space against the stars.'[23]
Apollo is the characteristic man of our advanced technological
society. Curiously, Ruth Benedict draws the parallel between the
Dionysian Kwakiutl and the Americans of 'Middletown'. The South-
West Peublo Indians, characterized as Apollonians, are too little
self-assertive, too shy of exercising authority and holding office, to
stand comparison with America's organization men. But the
Kwakiutl are reckless, competitive, acquisitive: rivalry is their key
institution.[24] Nietzsche would have been astonished and dismayed
at this application of his typology. Apollo is industrial-scientific
man. He might have been invented by Max Weber. He is rational-
bureaucratic man. Dionysus is the child of tomorrow.[25]

*Ecstasy and order: a comparative sketch*

The connection between Apollonian values and behaviour and the
maintenance of complex economic systems is scarcely problematical. Different facets of the Apollonian character may have
prominence at different stages of economic growth. Calculated risk-
taking and self-assertion may be particularly valuable, and so rewarded and encouraged, at the take-off point of economic development; more restrained and devious virtues of circumspection,
reliability, regularity, and insinuation may be emphasized in periods
of economic consolidation. But whatever the precise emphasis
within the complex of Apollonian characteristics, it is never self-
indulgent, sleepy, lazy or erratic; it is invariably rational, deliberate,
and 'future-oriented'. Its drunkenness is social and its sexuality
diplomatic.

The argument about 'which comes first', changes in values or
changes in technology and economic life, raises complex issues.
Interaction and mutual reinforcement between values and economy
take place over time in a way which is too intimate, intricate and
involved to settle firmly any claim to primacy. A great deal of
evidence seems to point to the probable primacy of technology. But
the problem is not to explain values and behaviour which clearly
support the economic order and are well rewarded by it: what is

problematical are the rise, diffusion and persistence of discordant Dionysian values which impede the system and invite economic penalties rather than rewards. It is frenzy, not impulse-control, that is problematical in successful economic systems. But it cannot be dismissed as an unfortunate by-product. It is at the heart of the matter.

Gordon Childe concluded from his studies of neolithic culture and ancient barbarism that '. . . in the long run an ideology can survive only if it facilitates the smooth and efficient functioning of the economy'. But he conceded that 'An obsolete ideology can hamper an economy and impede its change for longer than Marxists admit.'[26] But apparently incongruent or dysfunctional value-systems may facilitate an economy in more circuitous and devious ways than Gordon Childe recognized. Involved functionalist arguments like Ellul's amount to little more than a simplistic 'safety-valve' thesis. This argument can be tested through comparative studies. In fact, orderly and complicated economies do not invariably provoke a Dionysian reaction; and, when they do, Dionysus is not inevitably doomed, even in the long run, to extinction or 'integration'. Dionysus often seems to flourish in lockstep fashion with economic growth and abundance. Italy in the fourteenth and fifteenth centuries is the illuminating, deviant case. At the most, Dionysian behaviour in this rich civilization of banker-poets, was muted, in a minor key. Ruskin found in the Italian Renaissance only geometry. There was no solace for a Dionysian soul amidst the stones of Venice.

Modern anthropologists have taught us not to be surprised at the peaceful co-existence of rationality and magic. They are not so mutually exclusive and starkly anthetical as Frazer imagined when he wrote The Golden Bough. Frazer saw an orderly procession of discrete stages whereby magic was replaced by religion and religion by science. It is true that magic and science are in some sense competitors: Both offer logical and convincing explanatory worldviews. Magic may be ruthlessly rational in offering a consistent explanation of the world. It is compatible with empirical experience (and when it 'fails' it is simply bad magic). Magic, it has been argued, 'combines very smoothly with even sophisticated technology because it explains its success.'[27] The coexistence of magic and rationality no longer surprises us; but their relationship and interaction remain obscure.

The neolithic revolution was a triumph for order, reason, foresight and planning. And at its centre was a frenzied corn-god, worshipped in wild dances, wilder music and drunkenness. (Pop festivals of the late nineteen-sixties are comparable but relatively restrained.) Man imposed himself systematically and effectively on nature: he domesticated animals, made pots, wove cloth, and regulated his food supplies through settled agriculture. And a demented corn-king was equated with the disciplined farmer: 'He is spoken of as himself doing the work of a husbandman: he is reported to have been the first to yoke oxen to the plough, which before had been dragged by hand alone . . .'[28] He is an inventive technician, and '. . . among the emblems of Dionysus was the winnowing-fan, that is the large open shovel-shaped basket, which down to modern times has been used by farmers to separate the grain from the chaff by tossing the corn in the air. This simple agricultural instrument figures in the mystic rites of Dionysus; indeed the god is traditionally said to have been placed at birth in a winnowing-fan as in a cradle . . .'[29] But as a corn-king he was sacrificed (perhaps in the form of a bull, as in Crete) and buried; and frenzied rites enacted his sufferings, death and resurrection.

Gouldner and Peterson have rediscovered Apollonian man in neolithic cultures through the statistical technique of factor-analysis. There is no doubt that Apollonian man fashions, promotes and guides major changes in technology and economic organization. Gouldner and Peterson examined the characteristics of seventy-one early 'industrial' societies taken from the Yale Cross-Cultural Index. Fifty-nine traits or variables of these societies were intercorrelated. Three major 'factors' were extracted: kinship, technology and ethos. The distinguishing features of ethos were precisely those that characterized Nietzsche's Apollo.

The essence of Gouldner's Apollonianism is 'norm-sending'. It is centred on authority, restraint and impulse-control; it is found pre-eminently in socially stratified, hierarchical, deferential societies with hereditary castes and classes. The social mechanisms for controlling behaviour and restraining emotion are powerful. They are ceremonial societies, notable for their elaboration of ritual; their laws are codified and authority is vested in judges; great power is accorded to chiefs and government is usually by restricted council; there is a highly organized and powerful priesthood, legendary heroes are venerated, and the after-life is seen as attractive. There is every inducement to be decorous, disciplined, restrained.

The Apollonian ethos correlates highly with technology. After cautiously considering the 'variance' of the different factors in the factor-analysis, Gouldner and Peterson suggest that technology takes precedence. It makes the largest contribution to the total system, and is more likely to influence ethos than be influenced by it: '. . . T (Technology) and A (Apollonianism) are not likely to influence each other equally, and T is less likely to be influenced by changes in A than A is likely to be influenced by changes in T.'[30] Factor-analysis vindicates both Malinowski and Marx.

The technology that Gouldner and Peterson are examining is the rudimentary technology of neolithic cultures. It embraces pottery, the cultivation of grain, the domestication of animals, weaving, basketry, herding, and the mining and smelting of metals. The connection with Apollonianism is strong: 'Insofar as Apollonianism involves a stress on cognitive modes of experience and a hopeful, melioristic view of the world . . . we should expect it to correlate positively with T. This expectation is strengthened if we recall the stress that T entails upon a plastic art, pottery, and if we note that it is in this respect similar to Nietzsche's notion of Apollonianism . . .'[31] The correlation coefficient is gratifyingly large: 'To sum up: Our evidence suggests that the higher the level of technology, the higher the degree of demanded impulse-control or Apollonianism.' There is an interesting and pertinent reference to Freud; curiously, none to Max Weber.

Gouldner and Peterson are very careful not to generalize their conclusions to all stages of economic development. Apollonianism may be important principally as a starting mechanism, at the take-off point of major technological and economic change and re-organization. It is then that restraint, frugality and discipline may be particularly necessary. A successful and prosperous economic system provides other rewards for business enterprise than spiritual satisfaction. Max Weber conceded that 'successful capitalism' in his own day no longer required the support of religious asceticism: mechanized production had its own momentum, business activity, at least in America, had taken on the character of a sport, and '. . . the idea of duty in one's calling prowls about in our lives like the ghost of dead religious beliefs.'[32] But the decline of Apollonian conduct is not the same thing as the rise of Dionysian behaviour. Neither Gouldner nor Weber recognizes, far less explains, the close association of dysfunctional Dionysian values with great economic transformations. Dionysus is there at the take-off point, too.

He was present at the birth of the great economic upsurge that occurred in Europe between the eleventh and the thirteenth centuries. Economic historians have highlighted its significance: The startling surge of economic life in Europe in the "high" Middle Ages is probably the greatest turning point in our civilization.'[33] Norman Cohn, in *The Pursuit of the Millennium*, has detailed the concurrent frenzy and irrationality.

The industrial revolution of the high middle ages is not remarkable for spectacular technological advances, although these were not negligible. There were important developments in the power-base of industry through the utilization of wind and water mills. Lewis Mumford (in his book, *Technics and Civilization*) saw great symbolic significance in the making of glass, mirrors, and optical lenses, the introduction of the magnetic compass, the manufacture of paper and, above all, the invention of the mechanical clock. Human affairs were given direction and regularity: but they were depersonalized, communication was no longer necessarily face-to-face, and man turned introspectively in upon himself.

These are interesting speculations. The facts are the expansion of cloth manufacture in Artois and Flanders, the production of metal goods in Cologne and Liège, working in iron, coal, lead and tin in England, Hainault, Eastern France and Southern Germany. Carus-Wilson has focused our attention especially on developments in the woollen industry in England in the thirteenth century.[34] The spread of the mechanical fulling mill was of great significance for the woollen industry and its widespread use made this century '. . . one of striking progress industrially, though of equally striking change and upheaval. It witnessed, in fact, an industrial revolution due to scientific discoveries and changes in technique; a revolution which brought poverty, unemployment and discontent to certain old centres of the (woollen) industry, but wealth, opportunity and prosperity to the country as a whole, and which was destined to alter the face of medieval England.' The new fulling mill needed water-power to drive it and so brought about a massive relocation of the woollen industry with consequent shifts in population. But it was a period of expanded opportunity and rapidly increasing industrial wealth. There were, indeed, unprecedented wealth and opportunity throughout Western Europe at this time. And there was dramatic and public renunciation. By the early thirteenth century the great Mendicant Orders, the Franciscans and the Dominicans, were in being.

There was opportunity, openness and social flux. Writing of

northern Europe, Postan claims that now the town was '. . . a place
of opportunity to which the villein might flee in search of freedom
and wealth.' The fact that '. . . opportunities were more or less unlimited is directly borne out by the prevailing freedom of immigration – a freedom which was not to be regulated and restricted until
much later in the Middle Ages.'[35] Openness and opportunity were
no less apparent in the south, where '. . . the greatest gift of the
Commercial Revolution was the continuous creation of new opportunities for anyone to climb from one class to another.'[36] Apprentices became masters, successful craftsmen became entrepreneurs,
new men made fortunes in commerce and money-lending, merchants
and bankers enlarged their business. The middle class waxed more
and more prosperous in a seemingly inexhaustible boom.'[37]

It was precisely in these centres of economic growth and opportunity that frenzy and irrationality were most evident. Flagellant
processions appeared in the crowded Italian cities of the thirteenth
century, prophets and wild chiliastic movements drew support
from the prosperous industrial regions between the Somme and the
Rhine. The Children's Crusade marched to the Mediterranean ex-
pecting it to dry up before them as the Red Sea had dried up before
the Israelites. The millennium was not in the ordered prosperity
of the wool towns of Flanders.

The millenarian sects of medieval Europe drew their following
from all social levels, and the well-to-do are strongly represented in
their ranks. The ascetic 'Franciscan Spirituals' who flourished in
the thirteenth century came mainly from the noble and merchant
families which were prominent in the Italian towns. Men of similar
social position, who had most to gain from the new wealth, became
adepts of the Free Spirit, along with literate and articulate clerks
and former priests in minor orders. The association between
ambiguous social position and millennial inclination is seen most
clearly in the case of the Beguines, the women – mostly unmarried
or widowed – from the upper strata of urban society, who always
played a large part in the heretical movement of the Free Spirit.
Superfluous peasant women could find work in agriculture, superfluous women in the ranks of the aristocracy could become nuns;
but medieval society had no recognized social role outside marriage
for the women of prosperous merchant families.

Cohn gives a central place, in his examination of chiliastic movements, to the heresy of the Free Spirit which flourished from the
end of the twelfth century, especially along the Upper Rhine. The

movement of the Free Spirit was anarchistic, mystical-ecstatic, and orgiastic-erotic. The adepts rejected humility and wore the robes of nobles: they acknowledged no superior authority, and claimed that no 'free man' should refrain from any act to which nature moved him. They were naturalistic, justifying their life-style and their independence as a return to the state of Adam before the Fall.

But above all – certainly in the view of contemporary chroniclers – they were given to unbridled sexual excess. Cohn's sober scholarship leads to the conclusion: 'What emerges then is an entirely convincing picture of an eroticism which . . . possessed above all a symbolic value as a sign of spiritual emancipation . . .' 'For all alike adultery possessed symbolic value as an affirmation of emancipation.'

The sexual act outside marriage was not merely of symbolic value – it was a mystical experience, 'the delight of Paradise', the ascent to mystical ecstasy. The charges of communal orgies may have been exaggerated. 'On the other hand the adepts did at times practise ritual nakedness, just as they did at times indulge in sexual promiscuity; and there is no doubt that they were asserting – as one inquisitor put it – that they were restored to the state of innocence which had existed before the Fall . . . the leader of the *Homines intelligentiae* claimed to have a special way of performing the sexual act which was practised by Adam and Eve in the Garden of Eden.' His devotees were numberless.

The rise of capitalism in the sixteenth century has attracted an army of scholars since Max Weber wrote his seminal essay and Tawney contributed historical scholarship to an over-simple sociological analysis. Few would dispute the heightened tempo of economic activity in the late sixteenth and early seventeenth centuries. The rapid rate of technological innovation and the development of complex and large-scale industrial enterprises in England after the dissolution of the monasteries have been explored by Nef.[38] The first paper and gunpowder mills and sugar refineries were introduced into England at this time. The introduction of all these manufactures into England during the last sixty years of the sixteenth century opened an entirely fresh field for the growth of industrial capitalism.' Old industries like coal mining and iron-making were organized on more complex, large-scale lines and were supported by far larger amounts of capital. It was a time of technical inventiveness, and William Lee's stocking-knitting frame is only the most celebrated of a wide range of mechanical developments. The introduction of new industries and of new machinery, tools and furnaces in old industries had brought about technical changes and methods of mining and manufacturing only less monotonous than those associated with the great inventions of the late eighteenth and early nineteenth centuries.'

Controversy centres not on the facts, but on the interpretation of these economic advances. Argument hinges on definitions and dates: the precise nature of individualism and of capitalism itself, and the period before, during or after the Reformation when individualism, capitalism, or both could be said to have arrived.

Weber centred his attention on the Lutheran revolt against the corruption of a vast ecclesiastical bureaucracy and the recovery of true Christian asceticism. Tawney saw more significance in Calvinism than in Lutheranism, and in the later, untypical features of Puritanism. In Weber's analysis values are prior, in Tawney's, economic organization. An appropriate selection of values is made by a self-confident and aggressive capitalism that has arrived.

For Tawney the triumph of capitalism is the failure of Protestantism. A successful capitalism selected from the incongruent elements of Puritan belief, the individualist creed most suited to its function. Collectivist, half-communistic beliefs were quietly dropped. The new bourgeoisie did not find the social ethic of Calvinism serviceable: 'The individualism congenial to the world of business became the distinctive characteristic of a Puritanism which had arrived, and which, in becoming a political force, was at once secularized and committed to a career of compromise . . . Its theory had been discipline; its practical result was liberty.'[39]

Weber's sociology is essentially psychological: he tied the development of capitalism to prior attitudes and values, to a new ascetic dedication to work. 'Medieval ethics not only tolerated begging but actually glorified it in the mendicant orders.' But Luther brought work out of the monastery and sanctified it for profit. One's secular 'calling' became a religious experience. It required, and handsomely rewarded, a godly discipline. But Luther's concept of a calling, it has been cogently argued, '. . . savours little of the spirit of capitalism, but only of the medieval spirit of ordered status.'[40] Protestantism was not a modernizing ethic; it was anti-ambition; it discouraged innovation, adaptation to change, the taking on of new tasks which involved breaking out of one's orderly and settled calling as ordained by God. Weber's psychology had failed to explain even the psychological profile of the new entrepreneur.

The critical issue is sequence. The debate on the connections, if any, between religious belief and economic development hinges on the correct ordering of events. All Weber's critics have pointed to highly organized capitalistic enterprise in pre-Reformation Europe. Robertson argues that it was merely displaced, by the discovery of new trade routes from the south to the north. For Robertson religion is a total irrelevance. Economic change has a strictly economic explanation.[41]

The argument from sequence led Tawney to the view that the Reformation was less the forerunner of capitalism than an attack on its consequences. Capitalism might be defined as the direction of industry by the owners of capital for their own pecuniary gain, as the temper which is prepared to sacrifice all moral scruples to the pursuit of profit, or as economic imperialism. Under all these headings it was well known in pre-Reformation Europe. Protestants dismissed the commercial development of the last two centuries as a relapse into paganism and Luther expressed 'the popular protests against a commercial civilization which were everywhere in the air . . .'[42]

The sequential span has been extended in recent explorations of early capitalism. The focus of attention is no longer the pre-Reformation or the Reformation itself, but the Counter-Reformation. Capitalism, it is held, developed in both Catholic and Protestant countries during the period of the Reformation; and those which continued to develop were those which escaped the Counter-Reformation. It was not the Reformation that promoted capitalism, but the Counter-Reformation that suppressed it.[43]

On one issue all are agreed : that early capitalism was a triumph for order and rationality. Tawney saw the Puritan movement leading to the triumph of the economic virtues : 'The Christian life, in short, must be systematic and organized, the work of an iron will and a cool intelligence.'[44] For Weber the link between Protestantism and capitalism was rationality. 'One of the fundamental elements of the spirit of modern capitalism, and not only of that but of all modern culture: rational conduct on the basis of the idea of the calling, was born . . . from the spirit of Christian asceticism.'[45] All the authorities are agreed on the central importance of rationality and order : they differ only in locating their source. For Robertson the source is double-entry book-keeping. 'An adequate book-keeping system is one of the cultural conditions necessary for the emergence of capitalism'. He sees its extension throughout Europe after the middle of the sixteenth century, following its introduction into Flanders from Italy a century before, as '. . . no doubt of great moment in the spread of economic activity and the spirit of capitalism.'[46]

Good books rather than the Good Book provide the basis of prudential calculation which is at the heart of capitalistic enterprise '. . . working on the same lines as Weber, it would be very easy to substitute systematic books for the Protestant Ethic as the origin of the capitalist spirit.'[47] Robertson realizes, of course, that this is not the whole story, but maintains : 'It is to scientific book-keeping much more than to the ethic of any religious system that we owe the rational methodizing of business life. Systematic organization is one of the most powerful agents of economic progress, and this holds good perhaps more for systematic book-keeping than of any other form.' It is not simply a matter of technical proficiency: book-keeping removes the man from the commodities he deals in, the corn or wool become shadows, reality lies in the ciphers, and '. . . the very conception of capital as "lucrative possessions" depends on the analysis of scientific accounting.'

The area of greatest agreement is in fact the most problematical. Protestantism and nascent capitalism were in fact associated with a dramatic recrudescence of irrationality.

Max Weber's examination of sixteenth-century capitalism and Protestant beliefs without reference to the rise of witchcraft was a remarkable achievement. Even Merton thought he was continuing where Weber left off when he related the Puritan ethic and temperament to the development of seventeenth-century science and technology.[48] The proper sequel to Weber is not to spell out still further the results of rationality, but to recognize and explain the concurrent rise of irrationality. Capitalism rose not only with systematic accounts, a cool intelligence and a sense of a disciplined calling, but with the spectacular recrudescence of witchcraft. Weber set out deliberately to ignore the apparently irrelevant and to make his analysis in terms of 'ideal type' religious sects. He recognized that he was presenting religious ideas in the 'artificial simplicity of ideal types', but maintained that understanding would grow only from 'an investigation of them, in their most consistent and logical forms'. Logic, if not evidence, requires the exclusion of any consideration of witchcraft and magic. It was logical that a religion defined in terms of rationality should lead not to the rise, but to the decline, of magic. This is precisely what Weber maintained.

For Catholics, said Weber, 'The priest was a magician who performed the miracle of transubstantiation.'[49] The Puritans eliminated magic as a means of salvation. It was the radical elimination of magic that the practice of worldly asceticism made not only possible but inevitable. 'The genuine Puritan even rejected all signs of religious ceremony at the grave and buried his nearest and dearest without song or ritual in order that no superstition, no trust in the effects of magical or sacramental forces on salvation, should creep in.' The Quakers exemplified the control of passions and the enthronement of reason most perfectly, waiting silently in order to overcome 'everything impulsive and irrational, the passions and subjective interests of the natural man'.

In Essex between 1560 and 1680, in a population of perhaps 100,000, some 2,500 individuals were involved in witchcraft accusations, either as witch or as victim.[50] The peak period of trials for witchcraft was 1570 95 : the period of Puritan ascendency. The relationship between Puritanism and witchcraft is doubtless complex and indirect (there was no discernible geographical relationship between witchcraft accusations and the distribution of religious beliefs in late-sixteenth-century Essex); but a relationship nonetheless exists. Surveying the whole of England throughout the whole period of the Reformation, Thomas refers to '. . . an unprecedented volume of witchcraft trials and executions (which) occurred in the century and a half following the Elizabethan religious settlement . . .' Indeed, '. . . in England witch-prosecution and the Reformation arrived together'.[51]

American scholars have also highlighted the association between Puritanism and witchcraft in England :

> . . . the history of the persecution of witches in England (also the history of the practice of witchcraft) directly parallels the career of the Puritans. The first enactments were produced by the returning Marian exiles; the persecution reached its height during the revolutionary period and in centers of Puritan sentiment : interest in and fear of witches declined after the restoration.[52]

There was a close connection between Puritanism, witchcraft and capitalism. Witchcraft was most widespread in the south-east of England '. . . where economic development was most advanced. For it may be – and this, perhaps, can be investigated – that witchcraft helped solve, in the minds of the people, some of the problems raised by that very development and by its impact upon traditional ways of doing things.'[53]

## A deviant case : The Italian renaissance

In the three economic transformations briefly reviewed above – the neolithic revolution, the eleventh-century industrial revolution, and the commercial revolution of the sixteenth century – order and frenzy are closely interlocked. There are comparable Dionysian phenomena in the industrial revolution of the eighteenth and nineteenth centuries : if Bentham and Utilitarianism are the obvious Apollonian symbols of the age, Coleridge and the Gothic Revival are firmly etched on the other side of the coin. The Romantics will be examined in the following chapter. The nineteenth-century industrial revolution has one further characteristic in common with the earlier economic transformations: it was a period of abnormal population movement and growth. The 'deviant case' to be examined below – the Italian Renaissance of the fourteenth and fifteenth centuries – was not. And Dionysian elements are strikingly absent, too.

Wilkinson has recently singled out the loss of 'ecological equilibrium' as the prime source of economic change in the high middle ages, the sixteenth century and the late eighteenth century. Ecological disequilibrium arises when population grows rapidly and outstrips resources : economic innovation restores the balance. 'In English history there can be no mistaking the intimate connection between the periodic appearance of population pressure and economic development.'[54] The neolithic revolution shows the same connection.

The build-up of population in neolithic times led eventually to the urban revolution in Mesopotamia : villages of reed huts and mud-brick hovels were the sites of later cities such as Erech, Eridu and Ur. But long before the urban revolution, a population explosion had occurred. A census of skeletons reveals its magnitude :

Small though they were, neolithic communities were substantially larger and far more numerous than palaeolithic or mesolithic groups. From Hither Asia, Egypt and Europe literally thousands of skeletons have survived from the period between the neolithic revolution and the urban revolution or the transition to a Bronze

Age economy as against the few hundred human fossils from the whole of the Old Stone Age. Yet the Old Stone Age must have lasted ten to fifty times as long as the New.[55]

The cities which developed out of further growth and economic specialization were theocracies in which priestly households managed an intricate economy and imposed a godly discipline. The high middle ages saw rapid population growth, movement, and urbanization. 'This was indeed the time when the whole of Western Europe became urbanized.'[56] Lopez sees this upsurge of population as the basis of economic growth: The increase in the population must definitely be regarded as the initial thrust which set in motion the rest.'[57]

A restless intelligentsia travelled along the trade routes from town to town. In these circumstances, Cohn suggests, social bonds were weakened and traditional relationships were undermined. But there was prosperity and there was 'openness'. 'It may be that social and economic horizons expand too rapidly . . .'[58] Dionysus is not the child of deprivation but of unnerving opportunity.

The success of early Tudor governments has been ascribed largely to the recovery of population after more than a century of stagnation. From the end of the fifteenth century England felt '. . . the quickening effect of an upward trend in its population.'[59] The sixteenth century was an age of urbanization. London grew rapidly especially between 1580 and 1625. And in these circumstances lay the source of 'anomie'.

A sociologist has explained the anomic state of sixteenth-century Europe precisely in these terms. There was, she suggests, social flux and 'rampant anomie' :

London with a population of 60,000 at the beginning of the century had nearly four times this number at the end. Rome went from 55,000 to 100,000 in the century. A German-speaking population in central Europe estimated at 12 million in 1500 grew to 20 million in 1600. Villages were transformed into cosmopolitan, multi-lingual cities, bringing together evicted peasants who had no experience of a money economy with seasoned speculators . . . An urban *nouveau riche* lived side by side with a *déclassé* nobility, the literate beside the illiterate, the rural migrant next to the indigenous artisan.[60]

The author suggests that the 'solution' was the Protestant ethic. Its consequences were more obviously deranged behaviour and irrationality. The growing town was not so much the home of decorus restrain as of bizarre sects :

> It would be wrong to presuppose undue 'rationality' on the part of seventeenth-century urban dwellers. It was in London that the sects, with their prophecies and healing miracles, were most successful; and it was there that the busiest astrologers had their practices. London was not exempt from witchcraft accusations and the city seems to have harboured every kind of popular magician.[61]

Italy in the fourteenth and fifteenth centuries was highly bureaucratic and capitalistic in its economic organization, its population was stagnant and Apollonian men conducted its affairs (and even painted its pictures and executed its sculpture) with the calm assurance which come to men of prudence, assured position, nice calculation and foresight. (It required a French invasion to give Savonarola his moment of triumph – and in many ways he too was the voice of discipline and order, sternly opposed to sexual exuberance whether in the flesh or in the arts.)

Burckhardt's interpretation of Renaissance Italy has been radically transformed by historical scholarship over the past twenty years. Burckhardt made much of the openness of Italian society during the Renaissance; contemporary scholars show convincingly that it was closed. Burckhardt emphasized unbridled 'individualism' and heightened self-consciousness, the absence of constraints, especially in sexual relationships and in affairs of honour and vengeance : 'The restraints of which men were conscious were but few.'[62] Contemporary scholarship finds closely rule-regulated conduct and circumspection where Burckhardt saw unbridled licence and licentiousness. Burckhardt saw an open society in which hierarchial distinctions were breaking down and careers were open to talents. Birth and inheritance were of little account, he thought, and '. . . the main current of the time went steadily towards the fusion of classes in the modern sense of the phrase.'[63] Modern scholarship shows rigid hierarchies, closed bureaucracies, and severely restricted opportunity. Hard-headed economic historians have substituted fact for Burckhardt's romantic fantasy.

Even Burckhardt conceded that order and system characterized the conduct of affairs, especially among the Florentines. Parents realized the keenness of competition for orderly careers in government, ecclesiastical and financial bureaucracies. 'The inborn talent

of the Florentines for the systematization of outward life is shown
by their books on agriculture, business, and domestic economy . . .'
'At all events, we have no difficulty in recognizing the city where
dying parents begged the government in their wills to fine their
sons 1,000 florins if they declined to practice a regular profession.'[64]

Ruskin had been repelled by the over-orderliness, precision and
lack of spontaneity in Renaissance art. Highly skilled technical
proficiency dehumanized art and the artist, for 'perfection is not to
be had from the general workman, but at the cost of everything –
of his whole life, thought and energy. And Renaissance Europe
thought this a small price to pay for manipulative perfection.'[65]
Renaissance art was a triumph for rationality and science at the
expense of inwardness and intuitive understanding: 'Imperatively
requiring dexterity of touch, they gradually forgot to look for
tenderness of feeling; imperatively requiring accuracy of knowledge, they gradually forgot to ask for originality of thought . . .
they were left to felicitate themselves on their small science and
neat fingering.'[66] Science was disastrously equated with art : 'But
the grand mistake of the Renaissance schools lay in supposing that
science and art were the same things, and that to advance in the
one was necessarily to perfect the other.'[67] A contemporary scholar
sees restrained and orderly art as the mirror of restrained and
orderly men : 'Composure and detachment are not merely the
passport of the well-bred man; they impress their mark on Renaissance art . . .'[68]

Alfred von Martin's Marxist interpretation of the Italian Renaissance is perhaps the most extreme characterization of its order and
rationality. It was a resounding triumph for bourgeois capitalism,
based on '. . . the systematized outlook of the bourgeousie, which
was primarily determined by economic considerations.' The behaviour of the typical Italian of the Renaissance was characterized
above all by rationality, for he had '. . . eliminated the idea of divine
power from the considerations governing his actions and indeed
from his thoughts and writings. Men had ceased to believe that
anything irrational might intentionally interfere to disturb their
own systematic designs, they thought themselves able to master
fortuna by virtu.' Savonarola and his like are dismissed in a paren-
thesis: ('The success of popular preachers of repentance was tran-
sient and sporadic'). It was an age of hard work and self help :
'Social conditions which had lacked a traditional basis had already
given way to a systematic order. Everyone had to rely upon

himself in the knowledge that neither metaphysical concepts nor supra-individual forces of the community were backing him.'[69]

Lopez re-interprets Burckhardt's concept of Renaissance individualim in similar terms. It was an age of individualism only in the sense that '. . . an individual who wanted to be outstanding had to work hard at it.'[70] It was a highly competitive age because opportunities were restricted, and good birth as well as hard work was a distinct advantage. The ideal Renaissance man '. . . came from a good, old family, improved upon his status through his own efforts, and justified status by his own intellectual accomplishments'. It was a rich society, but it was not an expanding economy in the fourteenth and fifteenth centuries, and it was less diversified than in the middle ages. 'It rewarded prudence more than initiative, experience more than innovation.'

This was a static society with a stable population and a stationary economy. There was no sense of openness and opportunity. 'Contrary to widespread popular belief, the society of the Renaissance was essentially aristocratic. It afforded economic, intellectual, and political opportunities to only a small number.'[71] Burke's recent studies of social mobility in this period confirm this judgment. There were a few striking examples of upward mobility, but fifteenth-century Italian society was becoming less rather than more open; merchant families were crystallizing into a nobility and no new families were admitted.[72]

The production of works of art, Lopez has argued, was inversely proportional to economic expansion. The value of works of art rose precisely as land values fell. Merchants invested in artistic splendour when the range of commercial investments was limited.[73] The precise meaning attached to 'investment' is not very clear; and recently Lopez has given it a new gloss in contemporary terms by referring to investment in art as 'the credit card of the élite'.[74] But the evidence for lack of business opportunity is strong: 'It is not surprising that shrewd rulers and thrifty businessmen were prepared to invest part of their capital in functional works of art and in practical culture.'

In these circumstances Italian cities during the Renaissance developed a cautious and prudential civilization. 'An essential part of the image of man at this time was the idea that he was essentially a rational, calculating, prudent animal.'[75] Men worked hard to establish safe careers in the capitalist bureaucracies. And artists also planned their careers carefully. The sculptor Gauricus claimed:

'Since I was a boy, I planned my life so that as far as it was in my power I never wasted any of it in idleness.'[76]

Italy during the Renaissance was a nation of bank clerks rather than a nation of artists and poets. Indeed, in the absence of any system of examinations or professional qualifications, poetry was written to obtain a job in a bank.[77] (Poetry was not an infallible guide to bureaucratic competence. Lorenzo the Magnificent was a poet of some accomplishment; his management of the Medici bank was calamitous.)

This orderly, rational, bureaucratic, and prudential society of limited opportunities existed during a period of population stagnation and decline. There was little movement of population; it was not an age of urban growth. Florence appears to have grown somewhat at the expense of the smaller towns of Tuscany: 'Even so, Florence in this period never topped 70,000, as far as we know, compared to its population of about 100,000 in the early fourteenth century.' The great period of urbanization had been at an earlier date: '. . . the peak period of urban growth was as far back as the years 1150–1200.'[78]

Population trends during the Renaissance have been closely studied and hotly debated; the general conclusion appears to be that there was '. . . a sharp contraction by 1350, then a seesaw on a lower level, with its bottom normally before 1450, then stabilization somewhere below the pre-1350 peak and a hint of recovery some time before the end of the Quattrocento.'[79] The city populations suffered no disturbance from incursions from the countryside. 'No longer a terminus of frontier trails or a bustling thoroughfare, the city was much like a theatre, where people shed "muddy clothes" to don, like Machiavelli, "royal and courtly ones".'[80]

With a static population went social rigidity and exclusiveness. 'In the Renaissance, opportunities were usually reserved for those who were citizens of the town. Yet citizens too had little chance to improve their lot. The guilds formerly had accepted apprentices freely and assured every apprentice of the opportunity of becoming a master. Now they became rigid hierarchies . . . Outsiders were either rejected or kept permanently in the subordinate position of journeymen.'[81]

The Italian Renaissance was non-Dionysian. Its banks and even its artistic enterprises were sustained by Apollonian men. Dionysiac exuberance and excess, in one manifestation or another, was closely associated with the other periods of social and economic achievement reviewed above. Population movement and growth appear to underlie and promote great periods of economic development and opportunity; and together they promote social dislocation and uncertainty, a sense of 'normlessness' and anomie. Traditional social rules and expectations are questioned, or lose their usefulness. The rise of witchcraft in sixteenth-century England has been interpreted as a response and 'solution' to such social uncertainties.[82] The open society is the society of opportunity and anomie. As Durkheim said: 'Those who have only empty space above them are almost inevitably lost in it, if no force restrains them.'[83] When there are no boundaries and goals are infinite – as with Nietzsche's Dionysus and Spengler's Faust – there is anomie, exhilaration and perhaps ecstasy. The certain cure for anomie and ecstasy is limited and specific goals, lack of opportunity, hierarchy and due subordination. In this book we opt for ecstasy.

# 4

## Boundaries and the romantics

### Dialectical opposition

Nineteenth-century Romanticism was strikingly like the contemporary counter culture in its explicit attack on technology, work, pollution, boundaries, authority, the unauthentic, rationality and the family. It had the same interest in altered states of mind, in drugs, in sensuousness and sensuality. Like today's counter culture it was hypochondriacal and narcissistic. Hypochondria (as well as an interest in changed states of mind and feeling) helps to account for Coleridge's drug-use and Shelley's (intermittent) vegetarianism. Like the poet in Shelley's 'Alastor' – and like Shelley himself – the markedly counter-cultural today are inclined to a 'self-centred seclusion'; yet also like Shelley and the poet in 'Alastor', they are paradoxically deeply concerned with communication and community. But perhaps the most striking and significant similarity between the Romantics and today's counter culture is this: the imagination of today's counter culture feeds on science fiction. The Romantics invented it.

We have argued that counter cultures arise in periods of rapid economic change and reorganization but find their explanation in the social dislocation and uncertainty which arise from associated population growth and expanded opportunity. Like today's counter culture Romanticism flourished not among the poor and oppressed, but among the well-to-do and highly educated. (The major public schools and the universities made a disproportionate contribution to the Romantic movement.) But the lives of the Romantic poets were not marked by great material wealth – often, indeed, by material hardship and financial uncertainty. There was a background of wealth, a context of affluence, a more or less reliable safety-net which made actual destitution unlikely though by no means inconceivable. As the nation's wealth visibly increased, the Romantics preached modest consumption. They were far from being ascetic; but they preached (and even practised) simplicity and austerity.

We have argued, following Nietzsche, that the relationship between Apollonian men and values, on the one hand, and Dionysian on the other, is 'dialectical'. The Romantics exemplify the dialectics of Apollonian-Dionysian opposition and interaction, thesis and antithesis, which seems to develop with unusual intensity at times of major economic transformation. At the personal level the Romantics lived marginal lives (often in voluntary, sometimes involuntary, exile), but maintained close links, involved patterns of interaction and interdependence, with orthodox and profoundly boring insiders, pillars of mainstream society. Their relationship to the boundaries of society were highly ambiguous. They were at the centre as well as the circumference of the new industrial society.

The opposition between Romantic counter culture and mainstream society never made dialogue impossible – continuous exchange occurred, however bitter and acrimonious, between Godwin and Malthus, Shelley and Peacock, Southey and Macaulay. Wordsworth withdrew to Grasmere, but wrote poetry deliberately intended to communicate with the 'straightest' of men in straight society, dealing with 'incidents and situations from common life . . . in a selection of language really used by men', but offering nevertheless a new perspective and a new meaning through 'a certain colouring of imagination, whereby ordinary things should be presented to the mind in an unusual way . . .'[1] English Romanticism was never so esoteric that it moved entirely outside mainstream society. It was only Gautier and his circle who assumed a position of defiant irrelevance and spoke only to a disassociated coterie: 'Il n'y a de vraiment beau que ce qui ne peut servir à rien; tout ce qui est utile, est laid . . .'[2] The English Romantics (with the possible exception of

Landor) were never so totally and contemptuously dismissive of the Apollonian Utilitarians who confidently stage-managed an economic revolution.

Peacock (like Macaulay) claimed that poets in general, and the Lake Poets in particular, had become a somewhat comic and pathetic irrelevance. Peacock examined poetry for its social function and claimed that '. . . like all other trades (it) takes its rise from the demand for the commodity, and flourishes in proportion to the extent of the market.' By such criteria, he claimed, it no longer had any serious claim to a place in society. The poet had removed himself from society: 'The march of his intellect is like that of a crab, backward.'³ (Peacock's argument from the market for poetry is especially curious at a time when Moore and Crabbe could ask 3,000 guineas for a poem, and Bryon 2,500 for a new canto of 'Don Juan'.)

Shelley's reply to Peacock in *A Defence of Poetry* is in fact an exposition of the essentially dialectical opposition and interaction of the poetical imagination and the dominant ethos of the established order. Poetry corrects an '. . . unmitigated exercise of the calculating faculty'. In his preface to *Prometheus Unbound* Shelley disclaimed any directly reformist intentions: 'Didactic poetry is my abhorence'. Nevertheless, in both his theory and practice, the poet is involved in essentially dialectical opposition to society: poets 'are not only the authors of language and of music, of the dance, and architecture, and statuary, and painting; they are the institutors of laws and founders of civil society, and the inventors of the arts of life . . .' It is in poetry that Shelley sees not a separate order of reality, but an all-embracing synthesis: 'It is at once the centre and circumference of knowledge; it is that which comprehends all science, and that to which all science must be referred.'

Malthus and Bentham most faithfully represent the dominant culture which served the industrial revolution. They were the great 'norm-senders' of an Apollonian age. They were calculators and codifiers; they set boundaries; they were interested in restraints and punishment; they were the heirs of the seventeenth-century Puritan ethic. They were preoccupied with sin, and happiness was as impossible as it was undesirable. The trouble, at least for Malthus, was sex. Compared with the corrupt institutions which Godwin hoped to reform, 'there were deeper seated causes of impurity that corrupt the springs and render turbid the whole stream of human life.'⁴

The decade 1811 to 1821 saw the biggest decennial increase in England's population (by 18 per cent); the decade 1821 to 1831 saw the largest urban growth: while the population rose by 16 per cent, the towns grew by 30 per cent.[5] Migration made its greatest contribution to urban growth in this decade, accounting for 48 per cent of the increase. The population problem was at the centre of the Romantic consciousness. The drug-induced reveries of the Romantics were haunted by the image of the sunken city.

Malthus had no more humane solution. Mankind, he conceded, had not necessarily reached 'the term of its improvement', but the lower classes could not for long be free from want. The reason was simple – sexual desire would never be abated: 'The passion between the sexes has appeared in every age to be so nearly the same that it may always be considered, in algebraic language, as a given quantity.' And in any language it was too much.

The New Poor Law of 1834, rather than the steam-engine or the cotton mill, was the supreme Apollonian triumph of the age. Bentham codified laws and preached utility and social efficiency; Malthus wanted to eradicate sex but despaired of doing so. The solution to both their problems was the segregated workhouse.

Malthus was the antithesis of Romanticism on two counts: his social arithmetic and his denial of sexuality. In his novel, *Melincourt*, Peacock portrayed the confrontation of the dominant culture and the adversary culture in Mr Fox (Malthus) and Mr Forester (Shelley). This was the opposition between the Dionysian affirmation of life, sensuality and joy, and Malthusian anti-life. Mr Forester found Mr Fox's 'arithmetic of futurity' as dehumanizing as his denial of sexuality. Indeed, Shelley found the calculations of economists, 'for want of correspondence with those first principles which belong to the imagination',[6] the most serious threat to human dignity in his time. It is on this score that he links Paley with Malthus and proclaims (in the Preface to *Prometheus Unbound*): 'For my part I had rather be damned with Plato and Lord Bacon than go to heaven with Paley and Malthus.'

## The two emphases of an adversary culture

There were two main emphases in nineteenth-century Romanticism which foreshadow in a remarkable way the split in the counter culture of the nineteen-seventies. One emphasis is represented by

Godwin and Shelley; the other by Southey and Ruskin. The first is against power and work (but accepts, even welcomes, a suitably humanized technology); the second is against mass living, pollution and machines: it is more nostalgic, backward-looking, retreatist. Both are concerned with the boundaries which limit and circumscribe man and make him less than human; but the boundaries that especially concerned Shelley and Godwin (and Coleridge) were the boundaries of apprehension and perception; the boundary that concerned Ruskin and Southey was the boundary between men and machines. Both seek to rescue human dignity: both are for the wholeness of man. But the first is at heart political, the second aesthetic. The Godwin–Shelley emphasis is activist-anarchist; the Ruskin–Southey emphasis is environmentalist-expressive.

But it would be wrong to draw the distinction too simply and sharply – just as it is impossible to mark off the different emphases clearly and unambiguously in the counter culture today. Thus there is a sense in which the interest in drugs, which distinguishes the activists of today's counter culture as well as the Romantic anarchists, is 'retreatist'. Shelley himself saw no necessary conflict between communes and drug use, on the one hand, and political activism on the other. In his prose fragment, *The Assassins*, he dreamed of a hashish-intoxicated, remote bucolic commune: effervescent, Dionysian, ecstatic. Among its members 'A new and sacred fire was kindled in their hearts and sparkled in their eyes'; 'To live, to breathe, to move was itself a sensation of immeasurable transport.' But if an Assassin entered a civilized community, 'he would wage unremitting hostility from principle'. Like the bearded bandits admired by the counter culture today, they might come down from the mountains and forests to fight for justice.

The Godwin–Shelley complex of values rejects work; the Ruskin–Southey complex rejects only its standardization, routinization and mechanization. Work is closely linked with problems of social power and authority. The trouble with work for Godwin and Shelley was not that it dehumanized the worker because it was standard, repetitive, routine; its unpardonable property was that it tied men to society.

Both Godwin and Shelley saw in technology the possibility of weakened social ties and political freedom. Shelley's regret was that industrialization had been so badly mismanaged, through lack of guidance from the poetical imagination, that it appeared to result in more work, rather than less. Godwin looked at advancing technology with fewer reservations and asked: 'Who shall say where this species of improvement must stop?' He believed that: 'The conclusion of the progress that has been sketched, is something like a final close to the necessity of manual labour.'[7] Even in his own day, Godwin thought, if all men played their part, '. . . each man's share of labour would be light, and his portion of leisure would be ample'.[8] Shelley and Godwin together are a remarkable anticipation of Herbert Marcuse.

Shelley and Godwin welcomed social fluidity and flux; they objected to 'fixed laws';[9] they de-emphasized property and the ties of family. The accumulation of private property, said Godwin, could only promote 'a servile and truckling spirit';[10] and indissoluble marriage was 'the worst of monopolies', a despotism which expressed 'the most odious selfishness'.[11]

The ecstatic anarchists of the Romantic movement, of whom Shelley may be taken as representative, vigorously explored perceptual-experiential boundaries, especially in relation to drugs and to death. In their experience of both they breached the rationality and decorum of the dominant Apollonian culture.

Drugs and dreams were the characteristically Dionysian means whereby the Romantics breached the boundaries of orderly sensibility. They explored irrationality, incoherence and disorder through opium and hashish. The supreme Dionysian expression in nineteenth-century art is, perhaps, the passionate, violent and frenzied delerium of Berlioz's opium fantasy – not itself the product of drugs – the *Symphonie Fantastique*.

Even the Romantics who did not use drugs were preoccupied with dreams. Dreams and drugs were a literary technique: Poe, De Quincey, Wilkie Collins, Baudelaire and Crabbe deliberately sought inspiration in dreams and used opium as an aid. De Quincey was convinced that opium dreams could be a creative process analogous to literary creation; they crystallized emotions and sensory impressions into symbolic patterns which could be worked into literature. Crabbe, Wilkie Collins, Poe and Baudelaire shared this conviction that the opium dream provided a literary model and a *méthode de travail*.[12]

Crabbe's dreams were scarcely liberating – they were deeply disturbing and disquieting. Coleridge's dreams were more properly nightmares, which he experienced, and which influenced his poetry, even before he began taking opium. He claimed not to take opium for poetic purposes: he was trying not to heighten sensation, but diminish it. And certainly the use of opium for sedative, medical reasons was common in his day. Both Clive of India and William Wilberforce regularly took opium for medical reasons, without any notion of literary benefit. De Quincey first obtained opium from a London apothecary to cure an attack of neuralgia. Yet De Quincey's *Confessions* published in 1821, gave a new meaning to the taking of opium. Francis Thompson appears to have begun taking it for no medical reason, but because he had read the *Confessions*. And Gautier and Baudelaire in the Club des Haschischins made no pretence that either opium or hashish had even remotely medical purposes. Their purpose was sensation, expanded consciousness. Hashish, claimed Baudelaire in his *Paradis Artificiel*, was more mind-expanding than opium, a more effective means of re-ordering consciousness and promoting sensation.

Baudelaire pursued sensation for sensation's sake with profound seriousness and without hypocrisy: The smoke of hashish rose in a blue cloud and hung over the decorative furniture of the Hotel Pimodan and the court of the fantastic prince became a sort of opium den.[13] Swinburne was a kindred spirit who rejoiced that Baudelaire had experienced 'Sin without shape and pleasure without speech'.

The painter Meissonier, who hoped for exquisite sensation and lofty inspiration when he took hashish, saw nothing but an over-ordered universe of regular, symmetrical designs.[14] Baudelaire, like De Quincey, insisted that drugs induced interesting states of mind only in minds already interesting. In fact opium seemed generally to have a soporific effect. It is in their experience of death, rather than drugs, that the Romantics often experienced frenzy, Dionysian madness, a sense of chaos and a disordered universe.

Ruth Benedict has described how the Apollonian Pueblos made as little of death as possible, while the Dionysian Kwakiutl '. . . stressed rather than avoided the despair and upheaval that is involved in death'. For the latter, death was the 'paramount affront'.[15] (Leigh Hunt used this same term more than a hundred years earlier to describe his experience of Shelley's death.)

The seventeenth-century Puritans had not merely spiritualized work: they had taken the sting out of death. Popular death-bed stories socialized children to accept death without emotion: James Janeway's *Token for Children*, Thomas White's *A Little Book for Little Children*, Henry Jessey's *A Looking Glass for Children*, and James Whitaker's *Comfort for Parents*. This popular literature made death familiar, companiable, routine in Puritan homes. Mrs Sherwood describes the ritualization of death in a late-eighteenth-century upper-class household: the funeral invitations were sent, and 'Around the centre of the paper . . . were representations of every horrible circumstances belonging to natural death – graves and skeletons, coffins and shrouds . . .' She watched the funeral's standard, controlled and formal ceremonial with detachment: '. . . when the funeral arrived with all the paraphenalia of nodding plumes, flowing scarves and cloaks, coal black sheets and mourning coaches, I stood at my playroom window which commanded the church, and gave myself up thoroughly to the contemplation of the scene.'[16]

Like Heathcliff in fiction, De Quincey in real life was wild with grief at the death of a loved one. Three-year-old Kate Wordsworth died while he was away in London:

> De Quincey returned to Grasmere, and in frenzied grief threw himself night after night upon the child's grave . . . The effect was utterly devastating to his health. The doctors sent him south to Somerset and Devon, where sunshine and healing waters slowly restored him.[17]

De Quincey's behaviour was characteristically Dionysian indulgence in uninhibited grief.[18]

Trelawney, Leigh Hunt and Byron revived strange and ancient rites to cremate Shelley in Italy. Their purpose was not to subdue emotion, but to heighten it. They were eminently successful. Byron, it is true, made something of a display of calm and asked for Shelley's skull, which Trelawney refused in case he used it as a drinking cup. But even Byron was deeply disturbed by the occasion. The wild extravagance of the rites were described by Trelawney:

> . . . more wine was poured over Shelley's dead body than he had consumed in his life. This with the oil and salt made the yellow flames glisten and quiver.[19]

Leigh Hunt also described the scene in his *Autobiography*: 'The ceremony of the burning was alike beautiful and distressing.' Wine, frankincense and Keats' poems were burned with Shelley: 'The beauty of the flame arising from the funeral pile was extraordinary.'[20] Leigh Hunt experienced death as an outrage: '. . . I had bordered upon emotions which I have never suffered myself to indulge and which, foolishly, as well as impatiently, render calamity, as someone termed it, "an affront and not a misfortune".' In death as in life Shelley had burst through the boundaries of experience.

## The man-machine antithesis

Shelley, Coleridge, De Quincey and Swinburne explored the disordered regions of society and the mind. Ruskin's concern was the shifting boundary between men and machines. This is the theme of contemporary science fiction – a theme first explored by Mary Shelley. While Shelley wrote 'Prometheus Unbound', his wife wrote *Frankenstein: A Modern Prometheus*. Modern Prometheus, she saw, was not the creative artist, but the scientist who could create a monster with electricity: not quite a robot, but an artificial man in agony because he had no place within the normal social order. In the wake of the steam engine Mary Shelley had perceived the key boundary problem of our time.

Industrial society has found the boundary between men and machines as problematical as pre-industrial societies found the boundary between men and animals. The imagination of pre-industrial man was peopled with werewolves and mermaids; fables told of toads who were handsome princes; and Titania embraced Bottom in his ass's head. The new boundary was explored by Butler in Erewhon, in the fiction of Jules Verne, H. G. Wells, today in science fiction and in the existentialist philosophy of Sartre. The problem is to find and keep one's proper (human) category; to put tools and machines in their proper (non-human) place; to recognize, in Sartrean terms, that the defining characteristic of man is 'l'être pour-soi', of things 'l'être en-soi'. Today's counter culture, like Ruskin, insists that man is unprogrammed; that he is holy; that he is not a thing.

Pre-industrial societies feared that men might be confused with animals and so lose their humanity; Ruskin feared they would be confused with machines with similar consequences. Keeping to one's own category was a question of wholeness, even holiness. In Ruskin's writing: 'His ideas on the relation between art and the social structure nearly all cluster round this man-machine anthithesis.'[21]

The boundary was shifting and uncertain, and Ruskin was concerned with pollution and contamination – the loss of integrity,

The ancient Israelites dealt with the contamination of men by animals and established categories, boundaries, classifications of meats which were clean and unclean. Dietary laws specified forbidden animals, and 'By rules of avoidance holiness was given a physical expression in every encounter with the animal kingdom and at every meal.'[22] Hybrids were abominated:

> Neither shalt thou lie with any beast and defile thyself therewith: neither shall any woman stand before a beast to lie down thereto: it is confusion. (Leviticus 18.)

(A more Dionysian pre-industrial culture faced the same boundary problem in an opposite fashion: wholeness was not simply keeping within one's proper classification but embracing and unifying diverse categories. Centaurs and Minotaurs symbolize a more inclusive solution. Leda surrendered to the sexual embrace of a swan, Pasiphae submitted to a bull.)

Ruskin abominated the man-machine hybrid and denounced it like an Old Testament prophet. It was defilement:

> Let me not be thought to speak wildly or extravagantly. It is verily this degradation of the operative into a machine, which, more than any other evil of the times, is leading the mass of the nation everywhere into vain, incoherent, destructive struggling for a freedom of which they cannot explain the nature to themselves.[23]

Ruskin used the terms 'tool' and 'machine' interchangeably. When he wrote about similar problems in the nineteen-thirties, Eric Gill sharpened up the distinction and referred to tools when the workman did things the way he intended. The machine-product was pre-determined.[24] But Ruskin's meaning is clear. Automatic, semi-automatic, or even too closely programmed tasks to be performed 'by the book' diminished human responsibility and converted the workman into an 'animated tool':

> You must either make a tool of the creature, or a man of him. Men were not intended to work with the accuracy of tools, to be precise and perfect in all their actions. If you will have that precision out of them, and make their fingers measure degrees like cog-wheels and their arms strike curves like compasses, you must unhumanize them.[25]

The Renaissance had dehumanized man in its search for a kind of perfection; mechanized industrial production in the nineteenth century was the culmination of this process. The answer lay in the recovery of the pre-Renaissance spirit and style of life and work. Humanity was Gothic. Ruskin's attack was on routinization and predictability; his plea was for imperfection: '. . . imperfection is in some sort essential to all that we know of life. It is the sign of life in a mortal body, that is to say, of a state of progress and change.' Humanity was mutability. Gothic was its purest expression, the 'restlessness of the dreaming mind'.

Ruskin spoke up for savagery. He attacked rules, regularity, punctuality and 'accurate and methodical habits'. But he was distressed because Rossetti would never keep his room tidy or go to bed at a reasonable hour; he worked diligently and systematically and his literary output was prodigious; he was reserved; he never quite understood the sense of humour and sheer buffoonery of the Pre-Raphaelites; and he failed to consummate his disastrous marriage with Effie Gray. Nevertheless, his message is clear and consistent: his argument for disorder and uninhibited exuberance was the central theme of his writing on art and society.

This was his dictum on art: 'Nothing is a great work of art, for the production of which either rules or models can be given'.[26] The characteristics of the ideal builder, the true artist, the human man, were savageness or rudeness; love of change; love of nature; a disturbed imagination; obstinacy; and generosity. And art and architecture went beyond function and utility and gloried in grotesqueness and redundance.

Southey, too, saw indignity in contemporary technology and industrialization (and also, like Ruskin, he was an environmentalist, deeply concerned with the ugliness and pollution of the new industrial landscape). In the eighteen-twenties he saw technology and population growth as dehumanizing and brutalizing. His answer was de-industrialization and population decline; his hope was that England would be saved from herself by being driven out of business by her competitors. Only industrial failure could save the nation and restore the dignity and purity of pre-Reformation society. Like Shelley (and Marx) he thought that industrialization made the rich richer and the poor poorer: 'Great capitalists become like pikes in a fishpond who devour the weaker fish; and it is but too certain, that the poverty of one part of the people seems to increase in the same ratio as the riches of another.'[27] But unlike Shelley and Marx he turned despairingly to the past rather than to the revolution of the future.

*Episodic life styles and linear men*

With the Romantics, poets and poetry moved into the margins of society, but they sustained an intense interaction at the level of ideas and of personal relationships. Peacock was obtuse in his diagnosis of 'irrelevance'; but poets were now less firmly embedded in (and constrained by) society than they were. A literary historian has described the changing world of the writer in the later eighteenth century:

> Under these new conditions it was no longer the case, as it had been up to the mid-eighteenth century, that writers were not solely men of letters. Previously they had had careers at Court, in the Church or the armed forces, but in this period there is no outstanding writer who greatly distinguished himself in any other walk of life . . . This assumption of a specialist function involved a narrowing of opportunities for social experience; none of these writers was intimately associated with those holding political power, none had moved as close to the control-room of the State as had Swift and Prior, Milton, Marvell, or Donne . . . To (this estrangement) we owe a greater grasp and penetration of the subjective, a keener analysis of sense perceptions. Deriving from it, perhaps, is an increasing tendency of poets to dwell, or to hope to dwell, in remote places. Only Byron moved for a time in the great world, by the twin rights of birth and genius . . .[28]

The life-styles of the Romantic poets and artists were episodic and their closest alliance was with linear men. They deliberately rejected commitment to a calling and orderly careers, but their intimates were lawyers and bureaucrats. This was not the artist-patron relationship of the traditional kind. Shelley neither accepted nor needed any commission from Peacock and even Francis Thompson was probably without financial obligation to the Meynells.

The early lives of the Romantics usually foreshadowed their disordered adult careers. And their youth was commonly marked by detachment as well as disorder. Landor, Trelawney, Coleridge, Shelley, De Quincey, Swinburne and Francis Thompson lived markedly episodic, non-linear lives; Wordsworth and Keats are partial exceptions; Southey stands out from them all as a rock of stability, sense and responsibility. But for his prudence, caution and final defection from their schemes, the Romantic poets might have sung their songs not by Derwent Water but in a utopian Pantiso-cracy on the banks of the Susquehanna. The linear careers of insiders with whom the Romantics maintained close connections are found to perfection in the India Office – Peacock, who thoroughly enjoyed the tidy structure of bureaucratic office, and Charles Lamb, who completed thirty-three years in his calling with greater reluctance, fretting against his slavery to 'the desk's dead wood'.

De Quincey ran away from Manchester Grammar School because he was profoundly bored. He wandered in the hills of north Wales and then spent his time at Worcester College, Oxford, as a recluse. In five years he appears to have spoken to no one. He left without completing his degree examinations because, he maintained, the examiners were contemptible. It is true that he then considered a settled career in law and even kept terms at the Middle Temple; but he never qualified, and turned instead to literature.

Swinburne wanted to be either a lighthouse keeper or a light dragoon. At Eton he was not unhappy, but was uninvolved; '. . . he was curiously detached from ordinary human activities . . . (he) quivers solitary, tremulous, aloof – as some lone seagull above the waves.'[29] He was drunk and defiant: 'His early manhood was but a constant defiance of circumstances, a hectic search for new worlds to startle or to defy.'[30] He was rusticated for a time from Balliol for being wild and drunk; he never took his degree. When his father, Admiral Swinburne, urged him to take up the profession of law, he did not take kindly to the idea. The admiral finally gave him four hundred pounds a year to do as he pleased.

Landor was expelled from Rugby and rusticated from Oxford. His father was a doctor who urged him to take up a regular career but, like Admiral Swinburne, finally capitulated and allowed him one hundred and fifty pounds a year. After a brief period as a private in the Spanish army his life was spent in extravagant escapades and eventual Italian exile supported by his brothers' benevolence. Trelawney did not go to Oxford but deserted from the navy. He wandered around Europe and the East, fought in the Greek War of Independence and married the sister of an insurgent chief. Francis Thompson's doctor father was less indulgent than Lander's or Swinburne's and refused him any support after he repeatedly failed his medical examinations at Manchester. He was briefly in the army, sold encyclopedias and later matches on the streets of London, where he was rescued from starvation by a prostitute with whom he appears to have had a steady relationship.

While Charles Lamb worked steadily at the Indian Office, his old contemporary at Christ's Hospital disappeared from Cambridge and enlisted as Silas Tomkyn Comberbacke in the 15th Light Dragoons. But Coleridge alias Silas was incapable of learning to ride a horse. The 15th Dragoons did not regret his return to Cambridge. He became a Unitarian preacher and a minister at Shrewsbury. Josiah and Thomas Wedgwood gave him an annuity. For a time he was even a quite competent administrator as secretary to Sir Alexander Ball, Governor of Malta. He deserted his proconsular office less because of opium addiction than unbearable boredom.

Orderly, structured careers were available not only in law and medicine and the Church, but in government (and quasi-government) departments at home and overseas. (Even Byron's friend and biographer, Thomas Moore, was appointed Admiralty Registrar of Bermuda at the age of twenty-four, although it is true he never actually did the job.) Episodic and disorderly careers were a deliberate choice. Lamb and Peacock followed bureaucratic careers while maintaining a lively connection with the world of poetry. Lamb was a reluctant bureaucrat, impatient to be superannuated. In 1822 he wrote wearily to Wordsworth:

> I grow ominously tired of official confinement. Thirty years have I served the Philistines, and my neck is not subdued to the yoke. You don't know how wearisome it is to breathe the air of four pent walls, without relief, day after day, all the golden hours of day between ten and four . . . these pestilential clerk-faces always in one's dish . . . I sit like Philomel (but not singing) with my heart against this thorn of a desk.[31]

Lamb would have agreed with Karl Mannheim that the bureaucrat's life produces a 'dialectical twist of the soul'.

Peacock rejoiced in his steady progression up the hierarchy of the India Office. He had no taste for solitude or exile and had no intention of yielding to Shelley's plea that he should join him in Italy. On £600 a year he could propose marriage by letter to Jane Gryffydh whom he had not seen for eight years. And £600 a year in 1819 became £1,000 in 1823, £1,200 in 1830, £1,500 in 1836, and £2,000 when he succeeded James Mill the following year. He turned his classical learning to good account by settling the problems of transport to India. He was an excellent committee man, very capable as an expert witness before official commissions of inquiry. He stayed in harness until he was seventy, when he retired with a pension of £1,333 a year.[32] Yet the link with Shelley remained strong and even survived the publication of *The Four Ages of Poetry*.

Coleridge spent the last fifteen years of his life with James Gillman, surgeon, of Highgate; Swinburne his last thirty years with Theodore Watts-Dunton, solicitor, of Putney; Francis Thompson his last twenty years under the watchful eyes of the Establishment literary pair, Wilfrid and Alice Meynell. There were good medical reasons for all these unlikely alliances; but there appears to have been no real financial dependence. In 1824 Coleridge was elected Associate of the Royal Society of Literature and received an annuity of £100; Watts-Dunton probably made a financial profit out of Swinburne;[33] and Francis Thompson appears to have made at least £100 a year from his writing in his last years of close association with the Meynells[34]. These bizarre relationships illustrate and symbolize a deeper dialectic of culture and counter culture.

The outsider position is often experienced as too open and precarious even in youth and rude health and on an independent income. Even Shelley at times found marginality disturbing. Briefly he lost his nerve and wrote enviously to Peacock from Italy, envying his tidy and orderly life, and actually asking for help in obtaining an official appointment: 'I have some thoughts, if I could get a respectable appointment, of going to India, or any place where I might be compelled to active exertion, and at the same time enter into an entirely new field of action.'[35] This was the outsider's characteristically ambiguous attitude to the boundaries of society.

Van Gogh is often considered as the epitome of the unfettered bohemian outsider who lived without regard for convention, finally establishing a commune at Arles. In fact his life and relationships parallel in a remarkable way the pattern of the English Romantics. His apparent carefree outside position is edged with melancholy; his final resting place was not a bourgeois household but a suicide's grave.

At nineteen, as an art dealer's agent in London, he bought a top hat. He travelled punctually each day from the suburbs to the gallery in Southampton Street in the city. But he became ever more lonely, and at twenty-two he spent more time reading his Bible than attending to his duties and was soon out of work. At twenty-three he was a miserably paid teacher in a private school in

Ramsgate; in his late twenties he engaged in a hopeless study of theology in Amsterdam. His shifting life was anxious and precarious to the end.

When he went to paint in the south of France it was to find warmth, colour, simplicity, new perspectives:

> . . . I came to the South and threw myself into my work for a thousand reasons. Wishing to see a different light, thinking that to look at nature under a brighter sky might give us a better idea of the Japanese way of feeling and drawing. Wishing also to see this stronger sun . . . because one feels that the colours of the prism are veiled in the mist of the North.[36]

But in his itinerant life Van Gogh maintained an unflagging correspondence with his brother Theo, a solid, dependable, bourgeois art dealer who sent him money and marketed his paintings. In the last ten years of his life, apart from a period (1886–8) when the brothers actually shared a room in Paris, Van Gogh appears to have written to Theo at least once a week, often once, and sometimes twice, a day. His first breakdown came when he heard that Theo was to marry and he feared their relationship was threatened. The Romantic outsider was astonishingly like the prostitute who turns to a protector not for material support but for a stable relationship in the uncertainties of a marginal life.

Swinburne's poem, *Atalanta*, has been described as unrestrained and passionate music, 'a latent and continuous hymn to Dionysus'.[37] Its author spent his last thirty years with a Putney lawyer remarkable for his efficient, methodical and conscientious conduct of affairs, for bland, self-satisfied, suburban decorum. And for thirty years the author of *Atalanta*:

> rose at 10.00 a.m.; at 11 he took his walk; at 1.00 he returned; at 1.30 he had luncheon; from 2.30 to 4.30 he rested in his bedroom; from 4.30 to 6.30 he worked in his study; from 6.30 to 7.50 he read Dickens to Walter (Watts-Dunton) in the drawing room; at 8.00 he dined; at 9.00 he returned to his study, where he worked till midnight.[38]

There were no more songs before sunrise, Swinburne was no longer 'a white bird perpetually winged for escape.'[39] He illustrates the fate of the counter culture that came too soon.

# 5

## The structure of contemporary counter-cultural attitudes

Investigation of the counter culture at the micro level of individual behaviour and involvement (see chapters seven and eight) suggests that values are prior to action. People adopt counter-cultural life-styles, either wholly or intermittently, because of the values they hold. Investigation of the counter culture at the macro level of economic change and population growth (as in chapters three and four) suggests that the opposite is the case: action is prior to values. Values arise from prior structural change. The link between macro- and micro-level analysis is generational consciousness.

Fifty years ago Ortega y Gasset defined the essence of a generation as 'a particular type of sensibility'. He attached great significance to it as the hinge of history: 'It is, so to speak, the pivot responsible for the movements of historical evolution.' In some instances, he thought, 'There are in fact generations which are disloyal to themselves and defraud the cosmic intention deposited in their keeping.' But generally they were true to themselves and provided the thrust of social change: 'The changes in vital sensibility which are decisive in history, appear under the form of the generation.' Each new generation attended to 'the internal promptings of spontaneity'.[1] This chapter investigates the particular sensibility of the 'new' generation, its internal promptings of spontaneity, the values which mark it off from older generations and which constitute the pivot of contemporary social change. The new generational consciousness arises from particular historical events: it mediates changes in social structure to the personal level of individual thought and action.

Empirical studies of the values and attitudes of the contemporary counter culture are comparatively few. They have been carried out mainly with student activists in America in the late 'sixties. Perhaps the most notable of these – intensive as well as extensive, sensitively perceptive as well as technically competent – were the investigations by Richard Flacks at the University of Chicago in 1965 and 1966. In the former year he conducted extensive interviews with samples of student activists, non-activists, and their parents in the Chicago area; in the following year he interviewed samples of participants, non-participants and opponents of a sit-in at the University of Chicago.[2]

Flacks was particularly interested in the relationship between activists' values and those of their parents (which was close), and the social status of activists (which was high). But the interview data indicated important value-clusters which significantly differentiated activist students from non-activists. Flacks summarizes thus:

> . . . whereas nonactivists and their parents tend to express conventional orientations towards achievement, material success, sexual morality and religion, the activists and their parents tend to place greater stress on involvement in intellectual and aesthetic pursuits, humanitarian concerns, opportunity for self-expression, and tend to de-emphasize or positively disvalue personal achievement, conventional morality and conventional religiosity. When asked to rank order a list of 'areas of life', nonactivist students and their parents typically indicate that marriage, career and religion are most important. Activists, on the other hand, typically rank these lower than the 'world of ideas, art and music' and 'work for national and international betterment' . . . When asked to indicate their vocational aspirations, nonactivist students are typically firmly decided on a career and typically mention orientations towards the professions, science and business. Activists, on the other hand, are

very frequently undecided on a career; and most typically those who have decided mention college teaching, the arts or social work as aspirations.

Four major value-patterns, which distinguished activists from non-activists, emerged impressionistically from the interview data. (Each value-pattern contained between ten and thirteen scale-items on which interviewees were scored.) The first value-pattern was 'Romanticism: aesthetic and emotional sensitivity.' This was concerned with beauty and the arts, but 'More broadly, it can be conceived of as involving explicit concern with experience as such, with feeling and passion, with immediate and inner experience; a concern with the realm of feeling rather than the rational, technological or instrumental side of life'.

The second value-pattern was labelled 'Intellectualism' ('high valuation of intellectual creativities'), the third 'Humanitarianism' ('value on compassion and sympathy – desire to alleviate suffering'), and the fourth 'Moralism and self control'. This fourth cluster related to impulse-control, acceptance of conventional authority, reliance on external and inflexible rules to govern moral conduct, emphasis on the importance of hard work and antagonism to idleness. Nonactivists scored high in this area, activists low. The reverse was the case with the first three value-patterns.

Investigations which have focused on the 'underground' aspects of the counter culture have tended to play down wider social and political interests and to stress personal 'expressiveness' and privatism. In the late 'sixties the values of seventy-eight 'students and others' living in hippie communes in the university towns of East Lansing and Ann Arbor were compared with the values of a control group consisting of students from Michigan State University. (Similar comparative studies were made with other deviant groups – homosexuals, delinquents, prisoners and drug-users.) Experimental and control groups were compared on their rank-ordering of eighteen 'instrumental values' and eighteen 'terminal values'. The hippies differed from the controls on twenty-three out of thirty-six values – more than any other group. With regard to instrumental values (relating to conduct) the hippies were less ambitious, obedient, polite, responsible and self-controlled than their controls, but more broadminded, cheerful, forgiving, imaginative, independent and loving. With regard to terminal values (relating to end-states of existence) they attached more importance to an exciting life, world peace, a world of beauty, equality and pleasure, less to comfort, accomplishment, social recognition, self-respect, national security and salvation.[3]

Content-analysis of the underground press in America (1967–8) compared with the content of *Reader's Digest* – taken as a 'straight', bourgeois, middle-brow publication – suggests that the counter-culture has little interest in instrumental, achievement values, but a central pre-occupation with expressive value. Three hundred and sixteen articles were randomly selected from *East Village Other*, *Avatar*, *Distant Drummer*, and the *Los Angeles Free Press*; 162 were elected from *Reader's Digest* in the same period.[4]

Forty-two per cent of the value-themes in *Reader's Digest* were instrumental, relating mainly to achievement; only 10 per cent of the themes in the underground press were in this category. Typically, *Reader's Digest* articles emphasized methods of occupational achievement, including business enterprises created by college students, advice concerning financial investments and taxes, the careers of well-known persons who had achieved occupational success, and so on.' Forty-six per cent of the themes in the underground press, 23 per cent of those in *Reader's Digest*, were 'expressive'. Expressive themes were mainly self-expressive, but included affiliative and religious-philosophical themes.

But 44 per cent of the themes in the underground press, 35 per cent of those in *Reader's Digest*, were 'other' Other includes political, and 19 per cent of all the themes in the underground press were in fact political (12 per cent of those in *Reader's Digest*). This high proportion of political themes consorts ill with the expressive thesis. The authors of this study attempt to explain it away (in a footnote): 'A secondary appeal of these newspapers is often to politically radical or New Left, though most of the material is designed for hippie consumption – a group known for its apolitical stance.' This is not good enough. The non-instrumental, apolitical stance is not a given – it is what the researchers set out to prove. Evidence which fails to fit neatly into the expressive thesis is given a special explanation. To explore the possible unity embracing the diversity of the counter culture is the purpose of this chapter.

## A scale of counter-cultural attitudes

In 1972 the author constructed a Likert scale of counter-cultural attitudes. This was subsequently used to explore the degree of support for counter-cultural values in various populations of students and adults. In order to establish the social and personal correlates of these values, respondents were asked for a range of classificatory information: age, sex, marital status, the part of the country in which they had grown up, the type of work in which their fathers were engaged, their subjects of study and career intentions, if they were students, and their qualifications and job, if they were adults. They were also asked to complete a short scale designed to measure 'anomie', to write ten statements in answer to the question, 'Who are you?', and to answer the following two questions which were intended to probe their 'generational experience': 'Are there any important ways in which you think the world in which you have grown up is different from the world your parents grew up in?' and 'Are there any important ways in which you think the world your children will grow up in will be different from the world you have grown up in?' Five hundred and ninety-six respondents (288 males and 308 females) ranging in age from sixteen to over sixty completed the main scale, the anomie scale, and provided personal details; 450 of these also completed the questions relating to one's self-concept and perception of generational differences.

This chapter reports work carried out with the main scale (and derived sub-scales), which shows the strength of counter-cultural attitudes by sex, area of academic specialization and age. The next chapter reports the responses to the supplementary questionnaires and indicates some probable sources and conditions of strong support for counter-cultural values.

The Likert scale of counter-cultural attitudes was constructed by asking 150 university students drawn from all academic areas to respond to seventy-two statements which appeared, prima facie, to relate to counter-cultural concern. These statements were based on a scrutiny of themes in the 'underground press' and the author's semi-structured interviews with a hundred arts and social science students on campuses of the University of California 1969–70. These preliminary explorations suggested that the counter-cultural ideology embraced some eight or nine relatively distinct value-clusters. Some of these values appeared to be not merely relatively distinct, but even opposed and incompatible. There was a central concern for purity, in various senses, coexisting with a delight in obscenity and acceptance of dirt and disorder in personal appearance and living conditions. There was contempt for bureaucratic and technical competence along with effective organization of protests, demonstrations and aid programmes. 'Alternative' social action groups attacked bureaucracy and maintained efficient filing systems. Both American students and the underground press (in America and England) might at the same time support protest movements, social programmes and radical student activism, and yet express commitment to other-worldly values of mysticism and contemplation, withdrawal and non-involvement in an urban-industrial society. There are currently signs of greater specialization both in underground publications and in counter-cultural associations.) One of the first aims of the inquiry reported below was to establish whether there was any empirical consistency or coherence among the apparently disparate elements of the counter-cultural ideology.

Among the overlapping, shifting, apparently contradictory, but deviously interconnected values of the counter culture it seemed possible to distinguish first of all an attitude to power. The gross power of government, industrial, military (and educational) bureaucracies, as well as their infrastructure of rule-regulation, are seen as exploitative and dehumanizing. Small-scale human groupings might function with less power and conceivably without fixed and formally designated positions of authority, hierarchies need be less pronounced, if they are needed at all, and in any case lower-order members should share in an organization's management. But power and authority are in any event corrupting both for those who exercise and those who submit to them: a truly human life can only be lived outside the formal power structures of society. Deference is degradation, ambition is corruption, and rule-observation and bureaucratic routine a denial of human spontaneity and autonomy.

The rejection or questioning of boundaries appeared to be a key attitude of the counter culture. The normal boundaries of sense impression and perceptual experience are as questionable as conventional social boundaries. The attack on boundaries is an attack on fixed order in favour of openness, mutability and flux. It embraces a suspicion of established social roles (into which people are 'pressurized'), as well as all systems and processes of classification. It denies the reality of distinctions of race, class, sex and creed. 'Labelling' is highly suspect, not least the labels attached to deviants, especially the allegedly insane. But there is a deep contradiction in the counter-cultural position which, by definition, establishes a boundary with 'straight' society. ('Free schools' may define themselves as alternative yet seek to remove any barrier with the local community.) But to remove or lower the boundary is to run the risk of 'selling out', of showing lack of genuine commitment and authenticity.

A third value-cluster appeared to centre on the concepts of purity and sincerity. 'Straight' society is hypocritical, bogus and corrupt. (Among American students in 1970 the most common term of abuse was 'garbage' – applied equally to pretentious scholarship, atmospheric pollution, political promises, adulterated foods and contaminated drugs.) The counter culture is a new puritanism, in spite of its dirt and disorder. It is concerned very deeply with authenticity and sincerity in personal relationships – hence the injunction, 'sleep with a stranger': the dramatization (possibly public) of non-manipulative, non-possessive uses of sex.

Naturalism is the fourth distinctive value of the counter culture. The rejection of the spurious is closely associated with naturalism, a suspicion of synthetic products and a strong preference for natural materials – including 'pure' foods. The contemporary counter culture rests on new dietary laws and a reclassification of forbidden foods. It promotes a vegetarian diet not because animals are unclean but because the kinship of man and animals is close. (This causes some uncertainty over the use of one natural product, leather.) And naturalism leads to a concern for the environment, a conservationist attitude to the countryside, opposition to unrestricted urban growth, and frequently a distaste for urban life.

Open and free communication appeared to be a fifth important value, related to the attack on boundaries, and including the exploration of new or discredited means of communication, such as touch. The counter culture is tactile: it reinstates touch as a means of communication. It is also highly visual: vivid colour in dress, personal adornment, artistic creation and domestic decor signals a less inhibited approach to personal relationships. And communication – oral, written and pictorial – makes free use of obscenities – perhaps as an expression of openness and frankness, an acceptance of disorder, and an assault on the boundaries of bourgeois propriety.

A sixth complex of values could perhaps be subsumed under the heading of aestheticism. Artistic creation is highly prized (at least in Eric Gill's sense of making things which express spontaneity and joy), and technology and the scientific method are seen as threatening to the deepest human values and purposes. A deep commitment to poetry, music, art, mysticism, astrology, Eastern philosophy, expresses the counter-culture's rejection of scientific rationality. Heightened awareness and mystical experience may be found through drugs. The counter culture seemed, fundamentally, to be seeking ecstasy. It is pre-eminently sensationalist.

The deepest values of the counter culture are concerned with the quality of human relationships: they are expressive rather than instrumental, caring rather than manipulative. Future goals are de-emphasized: present states of mind and relationships are all-important. Aestheticism is closely related to these personalistic-expressive values and yet, by emphasizing the importance of individual states of mind and feeling, may subvert the concern for relationships. This, indeed, appeared to be one of the counter-culture's central dilemmas: its promotion of individual self-awareness and extended consciousness through mysticism, drugs or contemplation at the same time as its preoccupation with community and relationships.

The eighth value is, indeed, the extension of the sense of community and sharing which finds its fullest expression in the commune. Other values described above also find expression there. The commune is an attempt to establish community without power – especially the exploitative power which is thought to characterize the traditional monogamous family. The commune is a rejection of the 'nuclear family' not only on the grounds of its sexual exclusiveness, but its centralized exercise of power.

The commune may or may not be in a rural setting; but the values of the counter culture lead not only to political activism, and revolutionary Marxism or anarchism, but to bucolic retreatism. The value placed on handicraft, the distaste for urban life, the consumer-society, pollution and technology find expression in the rural commune. The deepest ambiguity of the counter culture centres on activism-retreatism.

The ninth complex of values concerns work. There is a rejection of the 'work ethic', a redefinition of human dignity and significance without reliance on work, ambition, and 'success' in orderly, linear careers. Begging is not inconsistent with dignity; 'stability' has no special virtue, and life should be episodic. Leisure is highly prized (although the boundary between (redefined) work and leisure is a matter for regret). A shifting, fluid life is the ideal. The only essential property is a sleeping bag.

These nine value-clusters interlock, and also conflict, in complex ways. Either singly or in combination they may explain particular behaviour: thus the rejection of the nuclear family may arise from a belief in emotional emancipation, or the social emancipation of women; drug-use may arise from a quest for aesthetic or mystical experience, from a rejection of scientific-rational modes of experiencing the world, or even an attempt to reach the worlds of those labelled insane. While the nine relatively distinct value-clusters appear to have a loose overall coherence or consistency, they appear to polarize around activism and an interest in power at one extreme, and aestheticism and concern for 'expressive' behaviour and spontaneity at the other. The inquiry reported below was an attempt to discover the underlying structure, the unity and division, among values which appeared *prima facie* to characterize the contemporary counter culture.

Eight statements relating to each of the nine value-areas were taken from 'underground' publications such as *The Berkeley Barb*, *Oz*, *The Los Angeles Free Press*, *Mole Express* and *Grass Eye*, as well as from American social-science students' interviews about the counter-cultural 'scene'. The concern about uncontrolled technological advance and its effect on the environment was expressed in such statements as: 'The earth's natural resources are being unnessarily depleted to satisfy artificially created cravings'; support for student activism against power structures by such statements as: 'Protests and sit-ins are desirable means of exposing injustice and corruption.' Some statements were presented in reverse form to prevent 'response-set', for example: 'Hippies live parasitically off the society they oppose', 'Legal marriage must be preserved', and 'Self-fulfilment can be found in working hard to be a success in our jobs'.

The seventy-two statements were presented for agreement-disagreement on a five-point scale to 150 university students selected from all academic areas. (Thirty-two of the seventy-five males were from science areas, thirty-three from arts, and the corresponding numbers for the seventy-five females were thirty-three and forty-two.) Forty-eight statements effectively discriminated (at the one per cent level) between the 25 per cent with the highest, and the 25 per cent with the lowest scores. The items correlated highly with each other and all forty-eight at the one per cent level with the total score. The scale was very reliable: the split-half correlation was 0.955. This analysis indicated a high degree of coherence among the forty-eight statements, which were used as a scale of counter-cultural attitudes.

The scores obtained by the 150 students on this forty-eight-item scale were factor-analysed using a second order five-factor Varimax solution. (All five factors satisfied Kaiser's criterion of an eigen value greater than unity.) Three factors were relatively 'pure': one was in favour of the fun ethic and uninhibited relationships and against organizational hierarchy and constraints;[5] the second was for a simple, natural life and against boundaries;[6] and the third was a 'commune' factor': against organizational regulation and authority, in favour of pop art, mysticism, handicraft, and the communal rearing of children.[7]

The remaining two factors were more complex, they accounted for most of the variance, and they were used in further investigations as sub-scales. Sub-scale A was labelled the 'Ruskin-Southey scale' because it reflects concern with runaway technology, a polluted and defiled environment, depersonalization in regimented, industrial work, and the suppression of spontaneity in bureaucratic organizations. It is an aesthetic scale, and it supports mysticism and a simple life in a pure and natural environment. But it is neither anarchistic nor activist; it is retreatist. It rejects careers but not work: work should allow self-expression, but it should not be undertaken for 'success' in a bureaucratic career.

There were sixteen items in the Ruskin-Southey scale. They are given below (with the factor-loadings in brackets):

*Sub-scale A: Ruskin-Southey*

The earth's natural resources are being unnecessarily depleted to satisfy artificially created cravings (0·599)

The good effects of technology are outweighed by its disadvantages (0·382)

Poets and mystics are of more value than scientists and engineers (0·604)

We are generally too inhibited in our personal relationships (0·401)

The really essential requirement of a job is that it allows for freedom of expression (0·474)

We all need vivid, exciting and exotic experiences which expands our minds (0·365)

Whatever party is in power, Government is corrupt (0·466)

To climb the social ladder is to collaborate in our destruction (0·545)

The contemplative Eastern life has many attractions (0·356)

We should try to develop simpler forms of life (0·411)

We are in danger of letting technology run away with us (0·692)

Life and work today are so inhuman that private life is ever more important (0·492)

People generally spend to much time at work, too little pursuing leisure activities (0·453)

Self-fulfilment can be found in working hard to be a success in our jobs (*reverse scoring*) (0·455)

People who want to hold positions of high authority are disgusting (0·388)

Too much of our lives today is ordered by faceless bureaucrats (0·349)

Sub-scale B is centrally concerned with power. It was labelled the 'Godwin-Shelley Scale'. It is non-deferential, anarchist, reformist, activist; it is opposed to rules and law-enforcement agencies; it is critical of the family because of its power structure. It is against boundaries. It rejects the work ethic. It supports obscenity, drug-use and communal living.

The sixteen items in this scale are given below:

*Sub-scale B: Godwin-Shelley*

The present family structure is outmoded (0·456)

It should be clear in any organization who is superior, and superiors should be respected (*reverse scoring*) (0·390)

Large gatherings can regulate themselves perfectly well without direction from on high (0·566)

Boundaries between teachers and students ought to be diminished or removed (0·391)

Everyone should be able to do just as he likes provided he doesn't hurt anyone (0·342)

The best justification for doing anything is because it's fun (0·375)

It's pitiable that people need artificial stimulants to 'turn on' (*reverse scoring*) (0·440)

Work should only be done when it's fun (0·399)

Education should be unending gaiety (0·646)

Obscenity is a legitimate means of communication (0·435)

We must have respect for authority (*reverse scoring*) (0·406)

The danger in outlawing 'pot' is that you make criminals of the most intelligent and sensitive people in the country (0·608)

Legal marriage must be preserved (*reverse scoring*)          (0·397)

Hippies live parasitically off the society they oppose
(*reverse scoring*)          (0·543)

Police violence and brutality in handling protest
marches and sit-ins is generally overstated (*reverse
scoring*)          (0·593)

Communal living, in which children belong to all,
is a highly desirable form of social organization          (0·488)

The structure of attitudes obtained from the factor-analysis was
based on the responses of a cross-section of university students. It
was assumed that this same attitudinal structure (but not the same
degree of support) would exist in other populations. And in fact,
when other subjects responded to the scales, as detailed below,
scale A and scale B were clearly tapping different attitudinal dimensions within the general complex of counter-cultural attitudes.
Thus scale B discriminates between age levels, but scale A does not.

*The extension of the inquiry*

The attitude scale was completed by 596 people: 311 males and
285 females. Of this total 473 were between the age of 16 and 25
(average age 20), 60 between the age of 26 and 35 (average age 30),
and 63 between 36 and 65 (average age 52). Respondents in the
age-range 16 to 25 were all full-time students selected to cover the
main areas of academic specialization. All the boys in the upper
sixth of a single-sex suburban grammar school completed the scale,
and second or third year groups in the following areas: in a polytechnic, the students of fine art (painting and sculpture); in a university the students of music, drama, trainee teachers of the deaf,
computer science, other sciences (physics and chemistry), and arts
and social science (English, history, sociology); and in a college of
education, all second-year students.

The older respondents (all with full-time work experience) were:
the 'mature students' in a teacher-training college; the company of
an experimental theatre; a group of American social planners
attending a summer school in a British university; a small group
of skilled mechanics in a car factory; and the members of four part-
time extra-mural classes in fine art or drama.

Counter-cultural attitudes were strongest among the polytechnic
and university students of fine art (painting and sculpture) and of
drama, weakest among the adults (average age 52) taking extra-

mural classes in fine art and drama. Among the students, the weakest support for counter-cultural attitudes was given by females taking science subjects and those taking a course leading to a degree in the education of the deaf.

Unexpectedly weak support was given by university music students and by the members of the experimental theatre company. The results for all groups of respondents are given in Table 1. The range of the scale was 48 to 240, the mid-point 144. The average score of all 596 respondents was 147 (s.d. 23·4).

*Table 1* Scores on a scale of counter-cultural attitudes

| Group | N | Av. Age | Score | S.D. |
|---|---|---|---|---|
| Fine art (polytechnic) : males | 22 | 20 | 169·9[1] | 18·9 |
| Drama (university) : males | 15 | 20 | 169·9 | 21·2 |
| Drama (university) : females | 11 | 20 | 167·3 | 18·3 |
| Fine art (polytcchnic) : females | 15 | 20 | 161·3 | 23·6 |
| Arts (university) : males | 28 | 21 | 160·7 | 23·5 |
| Social planners (U.S.A.) : females | 14 | 27 | 158·8 | 14·1 |
| Skilled factory workers : males | 6 | 30 | 154·8 | 9·3 |
| Science (university) : males | 29 | 21 | 151·9[2] | 21·9 |
| Arts (university) : females | 44 | 21 | 151·9 | 20·7 |
| Trainee teachers : males | 88 | 19 | 149·3 | 24·6 |
| Social planners (U.S.A.) : males | 23 | 32 | 147·6 | 15·9 |
| Music (university) : males | 13 | 20 | 147·0 | 21·3 |
| Theatre company | 9 | 30 | 145·8 | 14·3 |
| Computer science (university) : males | 16 | 20 | 145·6 | 22·9 |
| Trainee teachers : females | 89 | 19 | 142·2 | 17·3 |
| Sixth formers : males | 50 | 17 | 140·9 | 24·1 |
| Music (university) : females | 8 | 20 | 140·1 | 13·8 |
| Mature teacher trainees : males | 5 | 32 | 138·8 | 16·3 |
| Mature teacher trainees : females | 17 | 32 | 135·4[3] | 17·1 |
| Trainee teachers of the deaf (university) : females | 13 | 19 | 135·2 | 16·2 |
| Science (university) : females | 31 | 21 | 131·4 | 20·9 |
| Fine art and drama (extra-mural) : females | 45 | 52 | 130·0 | 16·0 |
| Fine art and drama (extra-mural) : males | 9 | 50 | 128·4 | 22·2 |

| | | | |
|---|---|---|---|
| Difference between 1 and 2 = 18·0 | t = 3·1 | P< 0·01 | |
| Difference between 2 and 3 = 16·5 | t = 2·7 | P< 0·01 | |

The scores of males were generally higher than those of females. Thus 29 male science students obtained a mean score of 151·86, 31 female science students 131·39 (t=3·68, P < 0·001). But among students of drama and fine art there was no significant difference between the scores of males and females. The American course of social planners provided the one case of actual reversal: the women were more counter-cultural than the men (with a mean score of 161·50 compared with 143·73: t=2·13, P < 0·02).

There was no relationship between students' social class and counter-cultural scores. The occupations of students' fathers were classified as professional, routine clerical, skilled manual, and unskilled manual. The mean score of male students of drama, music and fine art from the first two 'classes' was 162·81, from the second

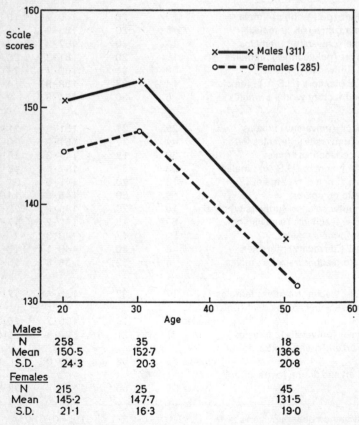

| Males | | | |
|---|---|---|---|
| N | 258 | 35 | 18 |
| Mean | 150·5 | 152·7 | 136·6 |
| S.D. | 24·3 | 20·3 | 20·8 |
| Females | | | |
| N | 215 | 25 | 45 |
| Mean | 145·2 | 147·7 | 131·5 |
| S.D. | 21·1 | 16·3 | 19·0 |

Diagram 1 Counter-cultural score and age

two classes, 163·56. The corresponding mean scores for females were 158·40 and 158·11.)

There was an apparent tendency for students who had grown up in London and the south-east to obtain higher scores than students who had grown up elsewhere in Britain. Students from London and the south-east who were taking music, drama, fine art, science and arts obtained a mean score of 157·26; those taking the same subjects who had grown up elsewhere obtained a mean of 153·13; but the difference is not significant.

Scores were related to age. The significant divide for both men and women was around age 36. The mean score of men (N.258) between the age of 16 and 25 was 150·5; of men (N.35) between 26 and 35 was 152·7; and of men (N.18) over 35 was 136·6. The difference between the first and second is not significant; between the second and third it is highly significant (t=4·1, P < 0·001). The mean score of women (N.215) between the age of 16 and 25 was 145·2; of women (N.25) between 26 and 35 was 147·7; and of women (N.45) over 35 was 131·5. The difference between the first and second is not significant; the difference between the second and third is highly significant (t=5·6, P < 0·001).

When the scores were categorized as high (163–240), medium (126–162) and low (48–125)[8] 25 per cent of the 596 respondents were high, 59 per cent medium, and 16 per cent low. The corresponding percentages for males aged 16 to 25 were 30 per cent, 56 per cent and 14 per cent; and for females of the same age, 16 per cent, 70 per cent and 14 per cent.)

## The sub-scales

The 'expressive-environmentalist' Sub-scale A and the 'anarchist-activist' Sub-scale B were scored separately for all 596 subjects of this inquiry. Scores on Scale A were consistently higher than scores on Scale B – respondents were more inclined to support spontaneity than they were to oppose power. The two scales are, nevertheless, closely related. When the scores of all subjects on Scale A were correlated with scores of all subjects on Scale B, the relationship was highly significant (product-moment r=0.53, df=594). But while some 40 per cent of the younger males were high scorers on Scale A, only 16 per cent were high scorers on Scale B.[9] The corresponding percentages for young females were approximately 24 per cent and 8 per cent. High scorers on Scale B – which can be regarded as

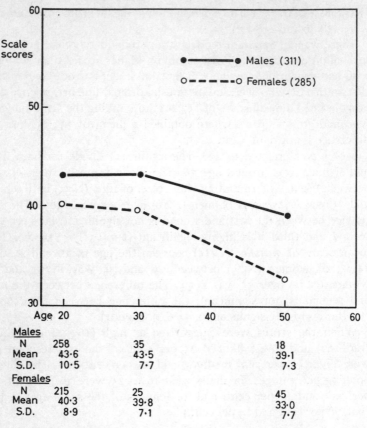

Diagram 2 Scale B (activist-anarchist) and age

the activists' scale[10] – were 12·5 per cent of the combined total of younger males and females.

The subjects divided at age 36 over power; they were united over spontaneity. On Scale A the mean scores of the 'youngers', 'middles' and 'olders' (both men and women) did not differ significantly;[11] but on Scale B, while youngers and middles did not differ, in the case of both men and women middles differed significantly from olders.[12]

## Discussion

With the exception of a small group of skilled mechanics, the populations studied in this inquiry were middle class either in terms

*Table 2* High and low scores on the attitude scales

|  |  | Low | Medium (*per cent*) | High |
|---|---|---|---|---|
| Younger males | Main Scale | 14·0 | 56·0 | 30·0 |
| (16–25) | Scale A (Ruskin-Southey) | 16·2 | 44·3 | 39·5 |
| N.258 | Scale B (Godwin-Shelley) | 44·2 | 39·6 | 16·2 |
| Younger females | Main Scale | 15·3 | 69·4 | 15·3 |
| (16–25) | Scale A (Ruskin-Southey) | 26·9 | 49·4 | 23·7 |
| N.215 | Scale B (Godwin-Shelley) | 58·0 | 34·0 | 8·0 |

of their prospective careers or, in the case of non-students, in terms of their own or their husbands' occupations. It certainly cannot claim to be a national cross-section. But it taps educated middle-class opinion which American research suggests is most likely to support counter-cultural values. Strong support for the general complex of counter-cultural values is found among a large minority of male students, especially if they are studying fine art, drama, or arts and social science subjects. (Trainee-teachers in a college of education, on the other hand, whatever their particular area of academic specialization, give generally weak support to counter-cultural values.) There is much stronger support for the 'expressive' than for the 'activist' aspects of the counter culture. The extremist, activist component finds strong support among some 12 per cent of the entire range of students in this inquiry.

This is strikingly similar to the results of extensive American survey research carried out in the late 'sixties. Lipset has summarized this as follows: '. . . approximately 10 per cent . . . show up as "radical", "alienated", or "dissident" in the surveys (of students) completed from 1968 to 1970 . . .' (The dubious concept of 'alienation' used in this connection will be examined in a later chapter.) The evidence presented here from the various national opinion surveys . . . generally indicates that the alienated include a relatively small proportion of the student population (10 to 15 per cent).' Surveys show that some 10 per cent of students regularly use drugs.[13]

One English survey of the late 'sixties shows student support for 'activism' of a similar order of magnitude. Hatch conducted an inquiry in 1969 among a sample of 1,000 students selected from three English universities. This was not a study of student protest, but attitudes to activism, and correlates of these attitudes, were investigated in conjunction with a study of student residence. The extent of approval of student sit-ins was ascertained by asking respondents whether they would support them 'in no circumstances', 'in very few circumstances', or 'in several or many circumstances'. Fourteen per cent could be categorized as strongly in favour, 49 per cent as moderate, and 37 per cent as strongly against. There was no relationship between support for protest and social background, but there was the familiar relationship with field of study: '. . . overall the social scientists do show a distinctly higher level of support than the technologists, with arts and science in between.'[14]

Hatch found other correlates of support for activism: 'Protesters show more tolerant attitudes, greater permissiveness and a higher valuation for ideas and culture.' There was clearly some relationship between activist and expressive values. Hatch concludes with the suggestion that:

> . . . the source of tension between a younger generation seeking to implement general principles and an older generation necessarily compromising between ideals and the realities of a technological, bureaucratic society will not grow any smaller. If this is true, the disaffection of students today may have a more fundamental and long-standing source and the possibility should be entertained seriously that these students may be bearing the germs of an alternative society.

The bifurcation of the counter-culture scale along the two dimensions, anarchist-activist and expressive-retreatist, suggests that the two main emphases of nineteenth-century Romanticism – associated on the one hand with Godwin and Shelley, on the other with Ruskin and Southey – are still present. (The actual number of factorial 'dimensions' is a function of the technique of analysis. There are other 'dimensions'. The two isolated in this study appeared to be the most prominent and plausible.) These two relatively distinct but nonetheless overlapping value-systems have been suggested on intuitive grounds by many observers of the contemporary counter-cultural phenomenon. Lipset calls them respectively 'radical' and 'renunciatory', claims that many individuals 'shuttle back and forth between these two incompatible positions', and suggests that while the former is forward-looking, '. . . the renunciation tendency is a conservative tendency in that it wants to protect the individual and the individual imagination against the crush of the economically expanding, collectivist industrial society . . .'[15]

The truth is more complex; but certainly the pattern of correlations (whether from factor-analysis or more simple observation of clustering round marker-items) which emerged from the analysis of scale scores, indicates that those who have misgivings about modern technology are also suspicious of modern bureaucracy, inclined to mysticism and place a high value on more privatized lives in a simpler setting. The activist scale is more combative, thrusting, concerned essentially with power and authority. But it also favours communes – less, perhaps, because of their apartness, than for the new principle of authority on which they are based.

One of the most surprising results of the attitude survey was the low counter-cultural scores obtained by university music students. The counter culture is an aesthetic culture (and Nietzsche had made much of music as a Dionysian art). Follow-up interviews with the music students confirmed the picture provided by their responses to the scale items. The interviews were focused on the nature of a university education in music. Their vocabulary was the vocabulary of the Puritan ethic – of *Pilgrim's Progress*. The words they used most frequently were 'perfection', 'striving', 'competition', 'ambition' and 'discipline'. They discussed a musical education in terms of intellectual accomplishment, without reference to feeling and emotion. They regretted that much of their education in music involved non-thinking activity, mindless memory work. They wanted it to be more intellectually critical. But they were dedicated to unceasing effort towards forms of perfection. They regretted that a career in music was a 'rat race', but were resigned to this fact. The only music student who obtained a high score on the counter-culture scale intends to become not a musician but a social worker.

The cut-off point for counter-cultural attitudes at around the age of 36 was also surprising. (The significance of this for the concept of a 'generation' will be considered in chapter eight.) A recent *New Society* survey of readers' attitudes to the recent past, the present

The cut-off point for counter-cultural attitudes at around the age The respondents were divided into the age-range 16–24, 25–34, and over 35. Gaps appear between the second and third age ranges only, and the topics which give rise to 'gaps' are marihuana use, perceived bureaucratization of the recent past, standards of honesty in the recent past and confidence in the future. Respondents over the age of 35 are less sympathetic to marihuana, perceive less bureaucratization, more honesty in the past, but more hope in the future.[16] Work by political scientists on political attitudes, which is reviewed in chapter eight, similarly suggests that a generation today is at least 36 years long.

The divide occurs around the age of 36 on the main scale – which includes a 'Fun ethic' factor, a 'Simple life' factor and a 'Commune' factor, as well as the 'Anarchist-activist' factor and the 'Expressive-retreatist' factor. There was no break with regard to this last factor. The generations divide essentially over power and work.

Communes do not receive overwhelming support even among the students of fine art and drama. Some 29 per cent think our present family structure is outmoded (11 per cent of those over 36 think so).[17] Communal living and rearing of children is thought desirable by some 18 per cent of the fine art and drama students (and by 9 per cent of those over 36).[18] These differences are significant: a gap is there. But when we talk about strong commitment to counter-cultural values, especially along the power dimension, we are talking about a small, if very important, minority.

# 6

# Openness and anomie

The counter culture celebrates openness. It is both a product and an affirmation of weakened social bonds, lighter constraints. This is also its problem. Adam Curle has rejoiced in an undersocialized conception of man. Durkheim was more fully alive to its side-effects. Curle applauds the counter culture because it is based on 'awareness-identity' rather than 'belonging-identity': it is not rooted in a sense of possessions and affiliation. It was this lack of a sense of society and binding relationships that Durkheim called anomie. But the counter culture is not simply a symptom of an anomic society: it is a solution. It explores viable ways of living with openness. Adam Curle is so impressed by its apparent success that he thinks we may have produced a 'new psychic mutation'.

Kenneth Keniston was less sanguine. He caught the first wave of 'the new generation' at Harvard in the late nineteen-fifties. He called them postmodern and diagnosed alienation. Their postmodernity he summarized thus: 'Their approach to the world – fluid, personalistic, anti-technological and non-violent – suggests the emergence of what I will call a postmodern style.'[1] Their alienation was expressed principally in distrust: 'Central to alienation is a deep and pervasive mistrust of any and all commitments, be they to other people, to groups, to American culture, or even to the self.'² It is not primarily an expression of individual psychology: it is a transaction between the individual and his culture.³ The culture was never more prodigal; the individual felt never more dispossessed.

Keniston's large book is based on twelve students. They were intensively studied for three years after selection on the basis of psychological tests, principally a series of eleven highly intercorrelated attitude scales. The twelve students were high scorers on these scales, which measured mistrust, pessimism, the sense of being an outsider, self-contempt, and related attitudes. There was among these students a deep sense of lack of order (they strongly supported such statements as: 'The notion that man and nature are governed by regular laws is an illusion'). Twelve low-scoring students were also selected for comparative purposes: 'Their style of life is committed or conformist, instrumental and practical; their ideologies are usually solidly and traditionally American . . .'

Salient characteristics of the alienated students were aestheticism, sincerity, and a quest for expanded awareness – the rejection of boundaries. One of them wrote: 'I think there is but one endeavour, and that is the struggle for infinite awareness, for total comprehension of all things and all events, of their origins, their evolutions, and their endings – the struggle to extend one's consciousness to the infinite limits of time and space, in all directions: a consciousness as large and eternal as the universe itself.' Another expressed similar Dionysian sentiments: 'I want to circumscribe my life as little as possible. I do not want to narrow my horizons more than absolutely necessary.' All twelve emphasized the cultivation of sentience and perceptiveness. They were in search of a breakthrough: 'The alienated value most those moments when the barriers to perception crumble, when the walls between themselves and the world fall away and they are "in contact" with nature, other people, or themselves.'⁴

Keniston was concerned with two problems: the reason for 'alienation' among the fortunate and the privileged and (in his later publications) the distinction between the alienated and the activists. He was perplexed by '. . . an alienation that has few apparent roots in poverty, exclusion, sickness, oppression, lack of choice and opportunity. This alienation is more puzzling in that it seems to beset youth most heavily, yet by the standards of an earlier generation, youth "has the most to live for" and has been given "every possible advantage".'

If Keniston had read Durkheim (instead of Merton) his puzzlement might have been less. What Keniston calls alienation, Durkheim called anomie; and he associates it with openness and opportunity. (Matza recaptures the original meaning of anomie when he refers, in his study of deviant behaviour, not to deprivation but to 'unlimited choice', 'which was the original meaning of anomie'. But Matza prefers to speak of drift.)[5] Merton perversely re-interpreted anomie as heavily restricted opportunity, '. . . an acute disjunction between the cultural norms and goals and the socially structured capacities of members of the group to act in accord with them.'[6] Anomie was linked with low social status, traditional delinquency, and frustration. Joseph Priestley knew more than a century before Durkheim that the problem of wealth and social privilege was 'a state of suspense and uncertainty what to do' which '. . . often becomes intolerable and . . . is perhaps more frequently the cause of suicide, from life becoming insupportable, than all other causes of it put together.'[7] Merton ascribes anomie to too little opportunity and choice; Durkheim (and Priestley) to too much.

Flacks was quite clear that the 'liberated generation' of students which he studied in Chicago were not protesting about lack of opportunity. The disaffected students had everything on their side: high status families, superior academic attainments and excellent career prospects: they were '. . . in a position to experience the career and status opportunities of the society without serious limitation.'[8] The key generational experience of 'the new generation' is not deprivation but affluence.[9]

The retreatism of the alienated suggested to Keniston that their values were crucially different from those of the activists. The latter were committed to change and adopted a public posture; the former withdrew into private behaviour. Keniston makes the distinction a sharp one:

'. . . most activists seem to me to possess an optimism, faith in human nature, belief in the efficacy of human action, and a capacity for co-operative endeavours that few alienated students manifest. Thus, on the whole, alienation as I have studied it, and the current phenomenon of student protest seem to me two quite distinct, if not opposed, phenomena.[10]

Adam Curle does not see mystics and militants as opposed phenomena, but as different stages or levels of development.

Militants, he thinks, have a developed 'awareness-identity', but mystics have reached a still higher level. But at the highest level of all 'the ways meet. Men like Gandhi have been both militant and mystical.'[11]

Curle sees 'belonging-identity' as the product and reinforcement of a stable and conservative society: 'We become what we belong to and what belongs to us: our civilization, our nation, region, family, church, political party, wife and children, school, university, neighbourhood community, house, land, books, profession, clubs and societies, social standing, investments, taste in music and literature . . .' This is a matter of profound regret. This is our dominant culture today, but the counter culture expresses higher forms of awareness – 'Higher supraliminal awareness: weak belonging-identity, increasing awareness-identity: weaker mask-mirage.' The supreme expression of counter-cultural values, thinks Curle, are to be found in the hippie commune.

Curle's notion of contemporary communes is highly romanticized: he describes the idealism of their origin (in the late 'sixties) rather than present realities. But his work has interest as a statement of the counter-cultural ideal:

> Although all persons who have reached a certain degree of awareness are proponents of the counter-culture, I associate it particularly with the supraliminal aspirants. It is in the communes that the construction of a new sort of society is being most systematically undertaken, and it is there that specifically spiritual objectives (through, for example, meditation or yoga) are most constantly pursued.

There is a wistfulness in Curle's contemplation of the new generation, and a keen sense of its profound differences from his own:

> I am constantly amazed that this generation has achieved, so collectively for all the exceptions, a level of awareness which has enabled it to cast off its belonging-identity and related material assets. I am also impressed by the rich diversity of the hippie type. It is not, of course, necessary to have dropped out to be a hippie – many are still 'in', in the sense that they are working or studying. But they are hippies in their rejection of violence, the anti-human qualities of society, and the belonging-identity, and their acceptance of love, of caring for each other, and, perhaps, of what the Quakers call 'that of God in every man'.

*Perceptions of generational differences*

High scorers on the author's scale of counter-cultural attitudes (see Chapter five) saw their world as superior to the world in which their parents grew up and in which their own children will grow up. They expressed satisfaction with many aspects of contemporary society, notably its comparatively light constraints; but they looked to the past with dismay and to the future with foreboding. They tended not to describe themselves in terms of their social attachments and relationships, and their self-concepts were negative. Satisfaction with the present co-existed with pessimism about the future; a belief in joy and spontaneity co-existed with profound self-doubt.

The literature on alienation and anomie is voluminous. The two terms are often used interchangeably. Either or both are thought to refer to 'powerlessness', 'normlessness' and 'social isolation'.[12] But when attitude scales are constructed for use in survey research, alienation usually means little more than dissatisfaction,[13] and anomie means pessimism. Alienation (dissatisfaction) relates to the present, and anomie (pessimism) relates primarily, though not exclusively, to the future. It is quite possible to be satisfied with the present but apprehensive and pessimistic about the future. There is no necessary correlation between alienation and anomie.

Anomie is properly a characteristic of societies; 'anomia' a characteristic of individuals. In the author's study anomie was investigated in this second sense, as expressed in the attitudes of individuals. A short scale was constructed which indicated pessimism, distrust of people, and a sense of the purposelessness of life. The items appeared to encompass the very general sense of anomie expressed by Aron, 'the absence of a system of values or of behaviour patterns which would at once impose itself with self-evident authority.'[14] The concept of anomie as uncertainty and mistrust is found in important papers by Srole[15] and by McClosky and Schaar.[16] The notion of uncertainty, unreliability and untrustworthiness run through the scale items of both researches. McClosky's measure of anomie (uncertainty) was positively correlated with a measure of pessimism. (It was also correlated with support for mystical beliefs.)

The anomie scale used in the author's study comprised the following three items which were presented for agreement-disagreement on a fivepoint scale:

1 Life today seems to have little purpose or meaning
2 People in general are basically co-operative (*reverse scoring*)
3 People will generally take advantage of you if they think they can get away with it

Scores on the scale of counter-cultural attitudes were positively correlated with anomie measured on this three-item scale (product-moment r = 0·30 df 594 P < 0·01).

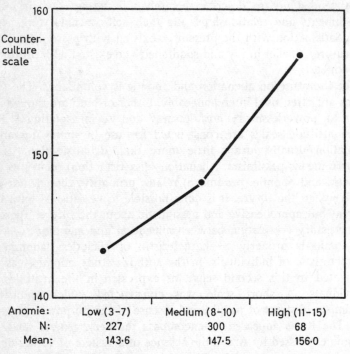

| Anomie: | Low (3-7) | Medium (8-10) | High (11-15) |
|---|---|---|---|
| N: | 227 | 300 | 68 |
| Mean: | 143·6 | 147·5 | 156·0 |

Diagram 3 Anomie and counter-cultural score

Anomie scores were very significantly correlated with scores on the total scale of counter-cultural attitudes and with scores on the expressive-environmentalist-retreatist Sub-scale A (r = 0·24 P < 0·01); but anomie scores were not correlated with scores on the activist-anarchist Sub-scale B. (On the other hand, they were not negatively correlated. The correlation was virtually zero: 0·04.) This, like the interviews reported in Chapter two, lends some support to Keniston's contention that activists and what he calls 'the alienated' have very different orientations. But there is overlap and interpenetration, too. Scores on Scales A and B are highly correlated, and there is no justification for supposing that they represent completely 'opposed' social and psychological phenomena.

When the subjects who took part in this inquiry were asked to write about the world they had grown up in, compared with their parents' world, they wrote overwhelmingly in praise of the present. In their perceptions of generational differences high scorers on the scale of counter-cultural attitudes were more favourable than the rest in their evaluation of the present; but they had more forebodings than the rest when they considered the future. When they look before and after, high scorers even more than the rest find few grounds for complaint about their world. They do not make the kinds of deeply dissatisfied statement we associate with 'alienation'. They feel at home in a world which is more just and tolerant than it ever has been or will be again. Less than a third of the high scorers look to the future with general optimism, but two-thirds describe the present in appreciative terms.

The statements made by respondents about the present (compared with the past) and about the future (compared with the present) were classified by three independent judges as 'mainly favourable', 'mixed' and 'mainly unfavourable'. Eight groups of respondents were selected for close study: two groups were high scorers among the younger respondents (the students of fine art and drama), and two were low scorers (the students of music and the trainee teachers of the deaf). Two groups were high scorers among the older respondents (the skilled factory workers and the American social planners), and two were low scoring groups (the actors and the women taking extra-mural classes in fine art and drama). The extra-mural women, who ranged in age from mid-twenties to mid-sixties, were not asked questions about the past, since 'the world their parents grew up in' might be any time from late-Victorian England to the nineteen-thirties. The question they were asked about the future was not in terms of the world their children would grow up in – since their children were often grown up at the time – but in the form of 'any important ways in which you think the next fifty years are going to be different from the world of today.'

Respondents tended to see the world of twenty, thirty or forty years ago as restrictive, intolerant, impoverished, war-like, hierarchial, authoritarian and limited in opportunity. It was a less spacious world, physically in the opportunities for travel, and intellectually and artistically in the world of the mind. Low scorers were in some instances inclined to see in their parents' world an enviable stability and accepted morality; high scorers often saw in the advantages and progress of today the seeds of future disaster. But the trend for high scorers to be more generally appreciative of the present was unmistakable.

*Table 3* Perceptions of the present (percentages in brackets)

|  | Mainly favourable | Mixed | Mainly unfavourable |
|---|---|---|---|
| High scorers (N.51) | 34 (66·7) | 8 (15·7) | 9 (17·6) |
| Rest (N.78) | 33 (42·3) | 26 (32·9) | 19 (24·8) |

Chi-square 5·98    P< 0·05

There was no apparent social-class difference in perceptions of the present and the past. Students from working-class backgrounds did not differ in their evaluations from middle-class students; and the small group of factory workers looked to the past with no less dismay than the students. A 29-year-old factory operative said:

> There was the debris of war, high unemployment, a Victorian-type discipline, and close-knit family life. All these things made it more difficult than today to visit other continents, to see for yourself, and communicate at first hand with people of other races.

A 32-year-old worker said:

> In the schoolroom twenty years ago discipline ruled. Today there is much more freedom. Parents today show the same tolerance, and the freedom of teenagers is limitless.

This theme recurs ('There was less freedom of expression and feeling'): today there is choice where formerly there was compulsion. A 37-year-old worker said:

> People of twenty years ago went for security of employment or professional security, as advised by their seniors. Today young people question more and want a more satisfying involvement with life.

. High scorers, whether students or workers, generally referred to today's more humane social order and the reduction of social distinctions. (When low scorers referred to a more egalitarian and tolerant society, it was usually with regret.) The strongest sense of flux, and discontinuity between generations, was expressed by a 22-year-old high scoring student of painting:

> The biggest single difference from my parents' youth is one of choice: there are far more alternatives open to me than there were to my father. Hence I tend to be less decided and single-minded, but at the same time less prepared to take a specialist attitude to anything. The rate of change in my parents' life-time has been staggering. When my father was born the Tsar was still the ruler of Russia. One effect has been to give me a great sense of separateness from my parents through history. And today there is scepticism about any form of faith. We differ greatly from our parents who believed in one commonly held faith or morality.

A high scoring American social planner, a 29-year-old divorced woman, also speaks of greater freedom and choice and similarly sees some of the problems this may create:

> The world my parents grew up in was one of restraint due to the Depression and then rationing along with traditional strict parenting. The world I grew up in was relatively free from these restraints, due to a growing economy and the over-reaction of my parents against strict discipline. I grew up to be independent, which is good to a certain degree, but I had difficulty in setting my own limits, which only maturity has taught me to do.

Unlike most high scorers, she sees hope for the future, chiefly because changes in child-rearing will promote better mental health:

> There is an increasing emphasis on the child's sense of self-esteem in American schools. The war in Vietnam has made many young parents stress verbalization of feelings instead of encouragement of aggressive behaviour.

More typically, high scorers see the benefits of the present turning sour in the future or provoking a back-lash.

The highest scorer among the drama students illustrates these different perceptions of the present and the future. (He is the 19-year-old son of a skilled manual worker who grew up in the southeast. He expects, after graduating, to become an 'unemployed creative', but would ideally like to be a 'self-employed creative'.) He

*Table 4* Perceptions of the future (percentages in brackets)

|  | Mainly favourable | Mixed | Mainly unfavourable |
|---|---|---|---|
| High scorers (N.44) | 14 (31·8) | 7 (15·9) | 23 (52·3) |
| Rest (N.104) | 43 (41·3) | 30 (28·9) | 31 (29·8) |

Chi-square 7·8    P< 0·02

made no adverse comment on the world in which he has grown up compared with his parents' world:

> There are more exciting experiments in the arts; there is greater availability of mind-expanding drugs, and in general there is a greater amount of freedom. The world is more classless, generally speaking, there is less differentiation between male and female, and less regard is paid to age. There are more flamboyant life-styles, and more importance is attached to pop culture and new ideas. There is more widespread criticism of society and 'the system'.

By contrast, he sees no redeeming feature in the world in which his children will probably grow up:

> It will be regimented, documented, systematized, organized, more confusing and insane. It will be full of files, technology, machines, and bureaucrats. It will be urban, crammed with factories, people, plastic, synthetic fibres and waste. It will be crammed with humans all acting like Pavlovian dogs; a uniform system which will be boring, deadening and inhuman.

A high-scoring music student sees the gains of the present carrying the seeds of their own destruction:

> Today there is less emphasis on possessions, social standing and position. There is more freedom of expression; the individual is left to decide for himself what to do, on the whole. There is less respect for those above, simply because they are above. Society is more permissive, at least things are more in the open now, e.g. homosexuality, drugs and pornography. Life on the whole is easier with regard to money and amenities. But there is more violence, and there are more individual 'hang-ups'. In the future, some of our present ills will be accentuated, particularly violence, racial discrimination, and lack of fixed moral standards.

There were very few political references in these statements about past, present and future. One very high-scoring female drama student, the daughter of a professional-class father, sees herself as 'very vulnerable, not an escapist, a believer in violent revolution'. Compared with the world in which her parents grew up, 'the world now is moving dangerously near the Fascism and depression of the 'thirties, which bound my parents down and forced them to sell out to middle-class values.' The only hope for the future lies in a rather unlikely revolution: 'I rather doubt that my children will grow up; but, presuming they do, I dread to think how – unless the Revolution comes.'

More typically, statements contain no explicit political references. They refer to social attitudes which have changed for the better and opportunities that have greatly expanded: 'There is more educational opportunity, easier access to the arts, greater ease of travel, a less enclosed and insulated life' (high-scoring drama student). High scoring students generally see the defects of the present outweighed by significant advances: 'There are more people, more noise, dirt and danger', but 'There is a more widespread acceptance of wider ideas, and a reluctance to classify things, as "mad" or "bad". Minds are less boxed in.' But they look forward to their children's world with unrelieved dismay: 'There won't be many children; there may be none. The world will be more radio-active, dirtier, emptier, sadder. There may be no world.'

Low scorers tend to see the present less favourably; their parents' youth was a golden age; but the future is promising, chiefly because of technological advance and medical progress. The low scorers are strong on discipline.

Even students of painting and sculpture, if they are low scorers on the counter-culture scale, lament contemporary laxity: 'Children are given a much freer hand today. It is detrimental that they have things too easy – so much is simply handed to them that they are discouraged from any real effort' (21-year-old female student of painting). 'It is much more free today, there are no standards to go by. There is little to rebel against, so it is difficult to find a discipline for oneself. Some kind of discipline is necessary for the young. My children will find it very hard if discipline is abandoned in school and college' (20-year-old female student of sculpture).

Low scorers regret a decline in moral standards and respect for authority: 'There has been a decrease in respect for authority and all sorts of responsibility' (24-year-old low-scoring American female social planner); 'There is an unfortunate lack of patriotism in our present generation' (low-scoring female trainee teacher); 'The church unfortunately has less impact on life' (low-scoring 25-year-old actress). But this actress, like many low-scorers, looks to the future with optimism: 'There will be scientific advance to combat disease and also to explore space, resulting in a new awareness of the outer world. Overpopulation can be solved – even, perhaps, by colonizing other planets. There will be greater co-operation between world powers, both technically and socially.' A low-scoring 46-year-old American male social planner expressed a similar faith: 'The future will be an era of cooperation rather than competition, an age of abundance rather than scarcity, a re-cycling spaceship-earth economy. The future has all the potential of realizing the ideal of brotherhood.'

A low-scoring male student of music saw his parents' youth as a golden age. (He is the son of a professional-class father, grew up in Wales, and hopes to become the conductor of a B.B.C. orchestra.)

The world in which my parents grew up (despite such things as poverty, which still exist today), was a slower-moving world, in which self-discipline and individuality were respected and encouraged. There was more time to 'stop' and contemplate on things in general. I feel, possibly illogically, that it was a much nicer place. Today, there are more opportunities to do all sorts of things, but quite often they are misused. I think that since the turn of the century Western civilization has steadily degenerated: the decline of culture, the rise of unthinking socialism for socialism's sake without any consideration of reality.

Unlike may low scorers he sees little hope in the future:

I look forward to the future with horror – to an overpopulated, underfed and very much polluted world, torn apart by racial strife and animal instincts which are already being allowed to run wild – the so-called permissive society. There will be a steady increase in crime and mindless vandalism. I am utterly pessimistic. I doubt whether my children will even have the opportunity to grow up.

Other low scorers have similar forebodings: 'There will be fewer natural open spaces and trees to enjoy; many natural resources will be used up; there will be more and more noise; shop assistants will be even less courteous than they are today; children will be even more undisciplined' (42-year-old woman member of an extramural class). 'I hate to contemplate the next fifty years unless everyone exercises greater self-discipline. Thank goodness I shall be reposing in the ground long before that time has passed' (50-year-old widow). But more typically low scorers have a sense that the future is under control and that the advantages of technology far outweigh its defects.

A 70-year-old very low-scoring woman:

There will probably be a cure for cancer and other diseases which are at present incurable. Population will be regulated and pollution controlled. People will have more leisure and know how to use it to the best advantage to themselves and others. Hunger and world poverty will be abolished.

A 54-year-old low-scoring woman:

There will be more leisure through increased automation; national, social and colour barriers will break down; there will be still more rapid travel and the development of food from such things as plankton and wood.

A 28-year-old low-scoring single woman:

Conscientious people are taking notice and becoming worried by our social and environmental problems. Consequently, over the next fifty years, we shall see a cleaner world. People will become concerned about the future and what kind of world they are creating. They will consider the wellbeing of their children and consequently take measures to limit the size of their families. Education must play an important part in this. Age limits in education will vanish: the structure of schools and colleges will change completely. Classes like W.E.A. classes will be the general structure: a local authority publishing a syllabus of classes at the beginning of the academic year and students of all ages choosing and signing for classes which they themselves wish to take. Age would be no barrier: an 8-year-old prodigy could be at the same stage as an 18-year-old remedial pupil. Industry will allow time off for education. This will answer the unemployment problem, and the excess leisure-time problem felt by many people.

Society will become more tolerant of itself. Class barriers, already largely imaginary, will completely disappear. Reprocessing will be the chief occupation of research scientists. There will be many communes consisting of people who have developed a way of life for themselves. Rather than being dependent on society as a whole, they will be a safety-valve for the socially maladjusted: a child who wishes to leave home to get away from his parents might find sanctuary there, or an elderly person wishing for company. There will be tensions, personal grievances, seekers for power, just as now. More international exchanges of workers and a more cosmopolitan society are inevitable, but in face of world survival problems the human race will probably pull itself together more than ever before in an effort not only to survive, but to improve and develop a worthwhile future.

Like this low-scoring single Englishwoman in her late twenties, a low-scoring single American male in his early thirties also looked forward with apparent approval to radical changes in the relations between the sexes and the structure of family life. He thinks there are already signs of profound change: 'The family is no longer the primary unit of society to the extent that it once was. More variant family forms are now acceptable.' There will be still greater change in the future: 'There will be a number of ways to express himself (or herself) sexually that are now unacceptable. There will be a number of acceptable forms of marriage or cohabitation. Group-care of children will be more prevalent. Parents will have a smaller part to play in the socialization of children.'

The commune in some form seems to be the answer to a wide variety of personal needs and dilemmas. Both the single English woman and the single American male described themselves in terms of very weak attachment to society. The Englishwoman's self-concept is dominated by a sense of transience ('I am one of millions of parasitical specks crawling about this earth; I am only flesh and blood and therefore temporary: something that will vanish and be forgotten very easily with time; a frustrated being, unable to find an outlet for my ideas . . .'). The American similarity shows little sense of rootedness:

I am an affluent, middle-class, single male in his thirties who has an affinity for living life without making long-term commitments to individuals or groups; with regard to religion, I am more agnostic than believing, a fact which I regret; I am a person who has difficulty in forming close, trusting relationships; I am a lover of womankind but incapable of fathoming their emotional make-up.

For the lonely the commune is the millennium.

## Anchorages for identity

Adam Curle claims that 'If we ask ourselves the existential question, "Who am I?" . . . we have to admit that we respond largely in terms of belonging.'[17] This is not generally true of high scorers on the scale of counter-cultural attitudes; it is generally true of the rest. Curle recognizes that those who don't define themselves in terms of belonging may simply be selfish, egocentric or narcissistic, but considers that they probably have a higher form of awareness: they are not seeking to shore up their inner deficiencies through possessing and being possessed. Schon has a livelier sense of their problems: he recognizes the difficulties involved in finding new definitions of self in a world of change. He also claims that people generally answer the question: Who are you? in terms of their occupation, community and family. 'When one of these institutions becomes unstable, its theory and ideology are threatened, and the anchors for identity which they provide are loosened. The net effect contributes to the assault on the stability of the self.'[18] The higher scorers on the counter-cultural scale are not only without a belonging-identity; they also have a very negative conception of themselves.

The subjects in the author's inquiry were asked to write ten statements in answer to the question: Who are you? These statements were classified in two ways: first as positive, negative or neutral;[19] second, as 'consensual' or 'subconsensual'.[20] Consensual statements related to membership of groups and social classifications – they placed an individual in a social system ('I am a student', 'I am from London', 'I am a Baptist'); subconsenual references would require further information to place the respondent relative to other people ('I am bored', 'I am too heavy'). Detailed analysis was made of the respondents in the eight groups referred to above – four groups of adults (the factory workers, the extra-mural women, the American social planners and the theatre company) and four groups of students (of fine art, music and drama, and trainee teachers of the deaf).

*Table 5* Self concepts of high scorers and the rest (percentages in brackets)

|  | Positive | Neutral | Negative |
| --- | --- | --- | --- |
| High scorers | | | |
| N. (statements) | 102 (25·5) | 180 (45·0) | 118 (29·5) |
| Rest | | | |
| N. (statements) | 345 (34·5) | 490 (49·0) | 165 (16·5) |

Chi-square 32·01  P< 0·001

High scorers often expressed a sense of loneliness, isolation and confusion. Three high-scoring students of fine art simply answered the question as follows: 'I haven't found myself yet. I am very confused'; 'I am finding out all the time. I hope I don't find out'; and 'This is too difficult to answer. I feel confused about everything, including myself, and I change my views every day. I feel that gradually, over the next few years, I shall be able to sort myself out.' Loneliness is a recurrent theme among high scorers: 'I am a single girl of twenty, an art student studying sculpture, not very intelligent and very lonely.' A 19-year-old male student of sculpture said:

> I don't place anything like enough value on human life, either my own or anyone else's; I have little desire to be anyone in anybody else's opinion: my idea of a person is not built enough from relationships with others. I lack self-respect and care little and feel less for others. I lack courage and try to avoid anything unpleasant: I refuse to face what is hard to face, despite its necessity. I am lacking in self-belief and unwilling to take part in life.

Two low-scoring female students of painting see themselves quite otherwise:

> I am a normal girl, totally unambitious, who can adapt to most situations. I am an art student and happy to stay one as long as possible. I am an only daughter; I have three brothers; I shall go home to live after I have finished being a student: I shall be happy and so will my parents.

The second low-scoring art student said:

> I am an art student who realizes that the term 'artist' is never likely to apply to me, but I am a successful teacher in the making.

I am hopeful of making a success of marriage, but I am somewhat unambitious careerwise. I am rather unrealistic but possess incredible patience; I am willing to work hard, but only at things I consider worthwhile. I am willing to give up things for people who mean a lot to me, but I am too soft-hearted for my own good. I try to get the most out of living through experiences and relationships.

High-scoring American social planners were similarly distinguished from their low-scoring colleagues by the extent of their self-disparagement. A high-scoring 26-year-old woman was uncertain, self-doubting and a would-be bucolic retreatist:

I was married at twenty-five. I haven't the self-discipline to sustain my chosen career. I am appalled at Americans' refusal to adapt to living together. I am doubtful about feminism and how it will affect me. I am wondering how my intention to work for a law degree will affect my career; I am wondering, in fact, whether I have chosen the right profession after all, or whether I have been attracted by motives far too idealistic to be workable. I am looking forward to renouncing acquisitiveness (once I am in a position to be acquisitive) in pursuit of a simpler life. I love nature, the forests and the sea, but feel I have lost touch with these roots. I don't like modern music, I don't smoke or take drugs; I don't approve of government censorship of films, books, plays or publications of any form.

In comparison, the low-scoring American social planners are strikingly self-congratulatory. A 45-year-old very low-scoring divorced woman said:

I am a somebody. I am the mother of a daughter who returns my love and affection; a career woman who excels in a job that reaches many people; a journalist who enjoys the confidence of many important people. I am the sister of two brothers and daughter of a fine gentlewoman who has worn herself out to make this a better world. I am the aunt of two fine nephews who love to have me around and seek my advice. I am the sister-in-law of one brother's wife and for twenty years we have been very good friends. I am a public but also a private person who shows a sense of strength, and a sense of loyalty to myself and to my friends. I am fair, with a sense of objectivity; I am generous in providing thoughtful acts for people; but many times I am critical, demanding of myself that I be better.

Two very low-scoring American male colleagues wrote as follows. The first is a 28-year-old married man, a community planning consultant:

> I am a civilized human being, a husband and father, a professional planner, a friend to others, and a citizen of the United States. I am a dedicated person: strong-minded. I am a student, a member of the naval reserve, and a country boy with a strong penchant for directness.

The second very low-scoring American planner is a 29-year-old married man:

> I am a man, ambitious, conservative. I am patient, a man of principle, trustworthy, proud, flexible, opinionated and nationalistic.

High scorers do not describe themselves in terms of social categories and relationships. The statements they make about themselves are typically philosophical, metaphysical and scientific.

*Table 6* Consensual and subconsensual self concepts (percentages in brackets)

|  | Consensual | Subconsensual |
| --- | --- | --- |
| High-scorers | | |
| N. (statements) | 113 (25·0) | 336 (75·0) |
| Rest | | |
| N. (statements) | 481 (49·0) | 506 (51·0) |

Chi-square 69·32  P< 0·001

One might expect that older respondents, married, established in careers and neighbourhood communities, would in any case see themselves in terms of social relationships more commonly than students. But the difference between high scorers and the rest holds up if we take the four student groups together, and the four adult groups. There is, of course, a much lower proportion of high scorers in the older groups, and the proportion of subconsensual statements is correspondingly low.)[21]

The most subconsensual self-concepts were found among the

students of drama (79 per cent of their statements were subconsensual) and among the students of fine art (75 per cent); the least subconsensual self-concepts were found among the trainee teachers of the deaf (29 per cent), the women in university extra-mural classes of fine art and drama (48 per cent) and the theatre company (48 per cent). (The first two groups were the highest scorers on the scale of counter-cultural attitudes, the last three groups among the lowest.)

The social attitudes and self-concepts of the theatre company were among the most surprising findings of this inquiry. This small group of avant-garde actors and actresses were dominated by the work ethic, pre-occupied with achievement and success, defining themselves in terms of status-conferring social relationships. A 36-year-old male homosexual described himself:

> I am a northerner but not particularly proud of the fact; a creature of infinite whims and fancies; a dedicated actor; I am most myself when playing a part. I am very egotistical, hidden by a million tensions and pretensions, ambitious for worldly success. I am not a family man; I am made and destroyed by the opposite sex. I am nothing without my work.

A younger actor (25 years of age) described himself wholly in terms of 'belonging identity', possessing and being possessed:

> I am a man, a son and relation to other members of my family, a boyfriend, an employee of the theatre and a colleague of fellow actors. I am an entertainer. I live in a particular house in a particular street; I am a British citizen, a taxpayer, and the owner of records, stereo, pictures and furniture.

The success theme runs through their self-concepts: 'I am sick that my work doesn't get the recognition it deserves' (23-year-old man); 'I am a long-distance runner in the sense that when others have had quick success, I have taken longer; but I have tended to outlive them. In primary and secondary school I was a failure; as an adult I have been a success' (30-year-old woman). And there is an acute sense of social status and origins. A 43-year-old man referred to his being 'A working-class person who has moved into the middle class. I am a late maturer, aware of my potential, which may never be realized because of the accident of birth and background.' A 24-year-old actress of superior social-class origin is well aware of this fact:

I am a young woman, a potential wife and mother, and a thinker. I am the woman behind a potentially famous actor. I am my mother's daughter, and a snob – intellectually in particular. I am intelligent and was educated at a boarding school, where I learnt nothing. I am honest and hard-working, old-fashioned (I get it from my mother), but over-affectionate – to men in particular.

Low-scoring factory workers are not pre-occupied with success and failure, but have a strong sense of social involvement. A 28-year-old married man describes himself:

I am an active member of my union, a very sexy husband (my wife thinks so), an engineer centre lathe turner. I am a Christian, a provider, and a member of various union committees. I am a strong Labour Party follower, the organizer of family activity, and a general dogsbody at home.

A high-scoring factory worker is far less securely embedded in social networks:

I am the worker, 37 years old, with a wife and two children, who juggles with resources to make ends meet, who lives outside his means in trying to provide a better outlook for his family. I can be inconsiderate and arrogant: I seek the sweet life. I am the dreamer of fantasies rather than the doer. I see insecurity around each corner. I am the extremist. I wonder whether my ideas of fair dealing are the results of the constraints of society. I am someone who seeks the truth but is not always prepared to accept it. I wonder whether my boss is really as insecure as I believe he is. I have difficulty in understanding how some people need continual change and others, though not wanting change, adjust themselves to it. I am the individual who loves life and its people, but has difficulty in diving in.

The same differences in social rootedness hold up among students who score high or low on the counter-cultural scale. A low-scoring student of music says she is: 'A female aged twenty and unmarried, a student of music, the daughter of my parents, a Yorkshire lass, a would-be teacher, and inhabitant of Earth, from Rotherham, a flat-dweller, a friend of my friends, the sister of my brothers.' By contrast, a 20-year-old high-scoring female student of drama says she is: 'A particle floating in a galaxy, a mixture of environment and social conditioning, an oppressed woman fighting for liberation, a chemical reaction, a mind, capable of anything.'

A very high-scoring mature university student of drama, aged thirty-eight and married, described himself almost wholly in scientific and metaphysical terms:

I am an animal who can reason on a small scale, a part of nature but separated from nature, a piece of matter floating with other pieces of matter on the planet, earth. I believe in an evolutionary creative process: a struggle between idealism and ever-present painful reality. I am a seeker after self-knowledge and revelation, occasionally glimpsing light through the wall of my being. I am a believer in human equality, a seeker after alternative means of economic exchange. I am an optimistic pessimist. I am just a chromosome different from a female.

Perhaps the least consensual and most confused sense of identity was that of a very high-scoring 22-year-old woman, a student of painting:

I am a female human being, and so quite unlike other forms of life, e.g. animals. I am childish and hope to remain so, but I have the sensitivity of an adult. I am shy and reserved, but sometimes I can be noisy and extrovert. I have had confused ideas of my status: because of social repressions I have thought I didn't belong to my own sex. I am discovering myself as a woman. I try to give a true projection of myself: I try not to be false. I find myself behaving according to my conditioning: I wonder where the person in me comes from. I am part of everything and everyone. I am a completely unique individual. I belong to myself.

The most consensual self-concepts were found among the low scoring trainee teachers of the deaf and the women attending university extra-mural classes. High scorers in any group seldom claimed membership of a Christian church; often they proclaimed themselves atheists or agnostics. The low-scoring trainee teachers of the deaf usually made reference to church membership. The low-scoring extra-mural women claimed elevating social connections.

A low-scoring 53-year-old widow describes herself:

I am a housewife with my own home, the widow of a professional man, the mother of two children, both married. I have my elderly parents in my home: my father is a retired clergyman. I am a grandmother, a voluntary worker at a girls' hostel (on the committee), and ex-chairman of various committees and a member of extra-mural classes. I enjoy company and have good friends. I have a liberal outlook.

Another widow (aged 58) said:

I am a widow with four sons and the mother-in-law of four daughters. I am the only daughter of an aged mother and the grandmother of eight children. I am a voluntary worker in the citizens' advice bureau, a student in a university extra-mural department, a committee member of the local social club, a member of the A.A. and a householder.

The third low-scorer who illustrates the highly consensual self-concept was not a committee woman, but enjoyed high-status connections. She is 48 years old and married:

I am the daughter of a retired professor, the sister of a professor, the sister of a colonel and the wife of an engineer. I am the mother of a banker, and a tall Nordic type. I appreciate beauty, kindness and honesty. I am right-wing. I am neither an atheist nor agnostic but a somewhat doubting Christian. I like argument. I have had little formal education.

The low-scoring trainee teachers of the deaf are more inclined to mention their sinfulness and church connections; but they, too, are deeply embedded in the web of kinship. Their self-descriptions tend to be succinct and non-evaluative. A 19-year-old said: 'I am a Christian, a member of a family, a student, a girl, a daughter, a sister, a British citizen, a member of a group running a playgroup, and a member of the Christian Union.' Another 19-year-old: 'I am a Christian, a young woman, a university student, a sister, a daughter, a room-mate, a prospective teacher, a person very comfortably situated in life compared with many, a person in my late teens, British.' A 20-year-old said: 'I am a Christian and a member of the Methodist church, a daughter (though not always a very dutiful one), a prospective teacher of the deaf, a lieutenant in the Girl Guides, a singer in an up-and-coming pop group, a university student, a member of the Labour Party, a very modest and unselfish person and a pacifist.' The final example, another 19-year-old girl, again illustrates the low scorer's rootedness in Church, family and locality: 'I am a follower of Christ: a member of the Christadelphian Church. I am a Sunday School teacher and a university student. I am looking forward to going back to Devon. I play the guitar and piano, I do not take part part in politics, and I am a conscientious objector. I believe that suffering should be alleviated where possible. I am very attached to my home and family. I try not to be racially prejudiced. I am a sinner.'

## Discussion

Mary Douglas brackets hippies with pygmies and anchorites and gives them a social location which allegedly breeds optimism. She distinguishes between the social constraints of group and grid, 'two independent variables affecting the structuring of personal relations.'[22] The grid consists of ego-centred social categories such as age and sex which do not necessarily give rise to groups. When the group is strong but the grid is weak, she claims, we have puritanism, caution and restraint. When the grid is strong but the group is weak, we have a markedly secular outlook. When both are weak we have secular and joyous abandon.

When both group and grid are weak, '. . . where social relations are structured to a minimal extent, the social world of anchorites, hippies, or pygmies, the cosmos is experienced as benign, sufficiently to justify faith in the inner purity and goodness of the human individual. There is little sense of sin; little interest in crystallizing states of mind in ritual form, little sense of opposition between inside and outside or obligation to impose an inwardly perceived pattern on the external environment, or vice versa.'[23] The truth is more complex. The scale of counter-cultural attitudes can be roughly equated with a 'hippie scale'. Our high scorers certainly show every sign of experiencing weak grids and groups; but they do not experience the cosmos as especially benign. While appreciating the openness of the present, they are pessimistic about the future. They are not alienated. They are anomic.

It is true that they show little sense of sin and have rejected ritual. (The counter culture is as unChristian as Nietzsche would have wished.) Anti-Christian attitudes of student activists have been shown in numerous surveys in Britain and America.[24] Those who are low on the counter-cultural scale clearly experience stronger grids and groups; and they are as self-righteous as they are boring. But the high scorers have self-doubts and acute problems of identity. They have a weak sense of boundaries either of the self or of society. They face, and attempt to solve, the characteristic problems of outsiders.

Like Keniston's Harvard dozen in the late 'fifties, the high scorers tend to have negative self-concepts[25] and to see themselves as outsiders. Keniston informs us that his dozen '. . . accept and sometimes enjoy the image of themselves as outsiders.'[26] They had read Colin Wilson's recently published book, *The Outsider* (1956), and Keniston constructed an 'outsider scale' based on its themes. These outsider items were enthusiastically endorsed by Keniston's 'alienated' students. In a world which will, for structural reasons, contain a steeply rising proportion of outsiders, the contemporary counter-cultural young are experimenting with alternative and viable values and life-styles. They are facing the problems inherent in a heightened awareness-identity and a weakened belonging-identity.

But it is far too simple – indeed, it is simply wrong – to regard the contemporary counter culture as a 'Bomb culture'. Roszak interprets the counter culture in some measure in these terms: 'We are a civilization sunk in an unshakeable commitment to genocide, gambling madly with the universal extermination of our species.'[27] Similarly Jeff Nuttall: 'It (the Underground) was simply what you did in the H-Bomb world if you were, by nature, creative and concerned for humanity as a whole.'[28] This is not how the high scorers on the scale of counter-cultural attitudes see it: quite the contrary. One of the major themes running through their comparison of the present with the past is the pacific nature of the contemporary world and the war-torn world of their parents' youth. The counter culture is the product not of a less, but of a more humane society: it flowers with affluence, openness and opportunity. It explores not the problems of deprivation and despair, but the problems and possibilities of a future cyberculture of unprecedented opportunity.[29]

# 7

## At the micro level

At the micro level life in the counter scheme is gritty. The next meal is uncertain. 'The scene' is shifting and formless, fragmented, without unity or cohesion. There are solitaries in insanitary attics, and groups constituting communal households. Social action groups concerned with purely local problems shade into activist groups with wider political aims; writers for alternative magazines may be marketing health foods and involved with community music or theatre groups. But the mystics stand apart from the rest and are isolated from each other.

All have the following in common: rejection of regular paid employment, ritual smoking of pot, search for intense experience, and contempt for bogus counter-cultural manifestations which are spurious because they are in some sense commercial. The Divine Light Mission is as contemptible as with-it university students and their own members who have become 'careerists', out for the ego-trip, self-glorification, and possibly highly remunerative work in the overlapping world of entertainment and the mass media. Within the counter culture there is charge and counter-charge of dereliction from the high standards of commitment and renunciation that mark the authentic member. And an eddy of derelict inadequates, drug-bemused drifters invade, confuse and pollute the picture. As one of our interviewees said: when you look at the counter culture in the urban north-west, 'it is difficult to put a structure on it'.

This chapter will attempt to meet one of the prime requirements of the counter-cultural ethic, which is 'to say it like it is'. To this end, those interviewed in the course of some thirty 'field-trips' in the urban north-west during 1973 will be allowed to speak for themselves. More than a hundred individuals talked to the interviewer;[1] they were involved in three main areas of activity – social and political action (including writing for 'alternative' publications); mysticism; and community music and drama. It is not possible to claim that the interviewees were 'representative'. Chain-interviewing was carried out, and conversations were held with groups as well as individuals in their 'pads' and meeting places. Some individuals talked about their activities, experiences, perceptions, relationships, philosophies and motives. Some interviews and conversations were more guided by the interviewer than others. The main prompt that was given, when possible, was to ask 'how they had got in', and whether there had been any particular turning points. There were no turning points: only the recollection of long personal histories of attitudes which explained 'where they were at'. 'Significant experiences' tended to be of openness, looseness, social isolation, chaos and disorder, rather than particular, dramatic incidents of oppression and restraint.

## Anarchists and political and social activists

Anarchists and social and political activists congregated – and undertook unpaid duties as shift-workers – at the Northern Alternative Aid and Information Centre.* Conversations were held with them there on some twenty occasions during 1973. Contacts were also made through the Centre with other anarchists and activists who were interviewed in their own accommodation. None of them had paid employment: all lived principally off social security. They smoked pot.

The Centre was busy. Shift-workers worked hard: they manned the telephone round the clock, dealt with the emergencies of people who came in often desperate for help, kept a log and an efficient filing system. The files contained names, addresses and telephone numbers of persons and organizations which could be called on to give help to people in crisis. Crises ranged from destitution, near-

* This is a fictitious name. The Centre has now closed down.

starvation and mental unbalance, to eviction and drug addiction (being 'smashed'). The files contained a crashpad blacklist, a list of 'teachers' who would give free lessons in communal living, bread-baking, flute-playing, meditation, even languages and mathematics 'for radical reasons'. A note on the file-card on 'Community Transport' illustrates one of the Centre's central dilemmas: 'Very straight. Main function seems to be to save the social services money by undercutting commercial firms.'

The shift-workers ranged in age from mid-twenties to mid-thirties. Men were more numerous than women. They discussed whether they were 'freaks' helping other freaks, or whether they were providing more general social aid. A girl said despondently: 'Most of the people who phone up are old people, now.' A man replied:

> 'The Centre should be for freaks. We should be a lot more radical. But people ring up and you have to meet the needs that are presented to you. It's hard to politicize when someone's desperately in need of a place to stay.'
> 'But who are these freaks?'
> 'Well, just look round this room. We're all freaks!'
> 'I think you've got a rosy view of what freaks are.'
> 'No, I don't think I've got a rosy view. I mean, I've spent a few years sitting round and smoking dope and doing nothing. I can't have that rosy a view or I'd still be doing it. No, I mean young freaks, who've just about got their heads together enough to realize it's not just their heads that matter, but that something political needs doing.'
> 'Yes, the freak scene is a sort of alternative. The fact that one stereo will do for eight ears is what capitalists find hard to understand. The freaks' life-style implicitly undermines things like "work" and "marriage" . . . And then there's the cultural unity. I mean, that's like nothing else. Not even the diggers. The life-style's the same all across Europe and America. I mean, banal though it sounds, we've been into Europe a lot longer than they realize. Anyone of us with the knowledge we've picked up here at the Centre could go to any European city and make out.'

Another shift-worker saw things differently:

> 'But political struggle is only one strategy for changing things. There are other ways you haven't considered. Perhaps some kind of radical social work achieves more.'

On another occasion another shift-worker gives his views of the Centre's function:

> It isn't really a simple split between the 'politicos' and the 'social workers'. The issues are mixed. I suppose we help two kinds of people, mostly. There are those who have dropped out consciously, wanting to do something different – the so-called 'alternative'. Then there are people who have dropped out because they have been forced to. They had no choice: circumstances or some handicap forced them. We try to deal with both kinds, though there are individual preferences among the shift-workers. I suppose I'm more interested in the political thing – helping people set up an alternative society. Perhaps because most of my time is spent helping the other kind, the homeless – people who can't even claim social security. They don't know how to approach the S.S. in a manner that will make them acceptable. The S.S. is like all the rest of capitalism – the consumers do not control the producers. I suppose the Centre really is 'alternative' in that sense. It answers the needs that are presented to it, rather than dictates what sort of needs people should have.

The Centre tries to give help wherever it is needed – to the homeless, the drug-addicted, the mentally ill:

> 'We used to get more people coming in who were smashed. You have to know what to do with them – laying them down on their side, and that. Sometimes we have to talk people down off bad trips, but that doesn't happen as often now. Last year we did the festivals, setting up bad-trip tents and that. I expect we'll do it again if there are any more festivals.'

Another kind of 'client' is discussed: Jane, who has been under treatment in a mental hospital:

> 'She's the most distressing person I've ever met. She's eighteen. Nice girl. I've got right into her head and I feel just angry, really angry at what's been done to her. She's completely withdrawn. But there's nothing I can do except be angry.'

Workers at the Centre are 'into' drugs but deeply concerned with the drug problem. They distinguish sharply between 'dope' (marihuana) on the one hand, and heroin, barbiturates and L.S.D. on the other. They know that 'barbs' do not enhance, but destroy, personal relationships. One reflects on a conversation between two 'clients' who were into barbs:

'They were talking about "scoring" and "jacking up" and "rolling" their friends. It's really different from the dope scene. I remember going around with a crowd who smoked, talking and dressing the same, and feeling that the rest of society was against you, but feeling great with your friends. But with barbs you've got to watch your friends as well as your enemies. You really have to start from scratch and teach people how to relate, that it's not on to roll your best friend.'

This view is shared by the shift-workers:

'There's not really the social lubricant thing with hard dope. You smoke with friends, but you jack up on your own. People like other people around when they're smashed, but they're not really experiencing each other. It's a funny sort of communication.'

The editor of an underground magazine who had dropped into the Centre explained why he was writing an article against drugs ('Mind you, it won't necessarily be dope that gets denounced, more likely L.S.D.'):

'Most of the people I know who are really into L.S.D. just aren't good for anything else afterwards. They just wander around with their minds totally scrambled. They're just totally irrelevant. If anything actually needs doing, any hard work, they're not the people to ask.'

There is a deep contempt for the 'sixties-style hippie. One shift-worker observed:

For me there's a good and a bad use of drugs. There's a lazy way of using them. Like when I went to visit my sister, she had some of her friends round and they were all smoking joints. There was one girl there who kept saying – 'Oh, far out, man, far out, oh wow!' – all evening. I mean, there was a girl so completely taken with the image of herself smoking a joint, that she wasn't really doing it. But if someone smokes not from habit, but now and then with expanding his consciousness in mind, then I think that's all right.

There is concern at the Centre with their 'social worker' image, but doubt how to dispel it. (Some have been professional workers

but have left out of disgust with the system.) They discuss the way
'straight' social workers treat drug-users:

> It seems like it's more important to have case records than to
> know people. You're judged on how good your records are. I
> know. I was a probation officer, I hate to say. I had to leave, I
> mean, I chose to leave. People are sometimes brought to us now
> by social workers. They talk about 'the case' with the person
> standing there . . .

A shift-worker expresses his misgivings about voluntary aid
organizations which accept substantial public finance:

> Basically, they're out to integrate people back into the system. At
> this Centre, we're not just trying to help people, but hoping to do
> something more – like making them think that the system needs
> changing and is wrong. These publicly financed organizations
> just want to produce good system people again.

On another occasion talk turned to the East:

> 'Has John gone to India, yet? I thought he was going.'
> 'Oh, yes, he's going, but he hasn't got it together yet. He's trying
> to sell his stuff. If he gets enough bread he'll be off.'
> 'What's he got to sell?'
> 'He's got records. And a really good stereo player for £60, that's
> all hand-made and worth a lot more. He's going to live in a
> village and go to one of the sitar schools. He's a pretty good
> player. Like if you want to play classical stuff you have to train
> for years. They reckon it's the highest form of prayer. The
> universe began with a song, they say. But he doesn't fancy being
> a music monk for fifty years.'
> 'Wat's this about you going to Morocco?'
> 'Yeah, I'm going.'
> 'Where do you get the bread from, man? Didn't your parents
> pay for you to go to India?'
> 'No. They were going to. I went to live at home for a while.
> Started arguing again, you know. Didn't feel like taking the
> money off them. Because of all the obligations it meant. So, what
> I did, I forged a rent book, crashed for a few weeks, and claimed
> on social security, and saved up enough for the air fare. I'm doing
> the same for Morocco. It won't cost me a thing when I'm out
> there.'

Thus conversations at the Northern Aid and Information Centre revolved around the problem of providing aid which, instead of paving the way to the alternative society, propped up a corrupt social system which all were committed to undermine. Talk revolved around the problems of drug-use, organizing and financing journeys to the East, the barbarities of 'straight' psychiatric treatment and the harm done by 'labelling' the mentally afflicted, tenants' legal rights and the law of trespass, projected vegetarian restaurants, debased commercialism of the Divine Light Mission, the absurdity of Jesus Freaks, the autocratic power of some local anarchist leaders committed in theory to an egalitarian ethic, the silliness and perfidy of bejeaned, pot-smoking university students, and the alternative's work in the cause of gypsies and local inner-city working-class street cultures and communities. In the English alternative gypsies and traditional working-class communities have the sanctity which Black culture and the North American Indian culture enjoy in the American alternative. In rejecting the middle-class social structure and culture of the dominant straight society, the English alternative seeks, rather sentimentally, close links and even 'integration' with the obsolescent cultures of picturesque minorities and the underprivileged.

There were anarchists and political activists in the area who were uninvolved in the Centre and tended to despise its activities as 'mere social work'. One was in his mid-twenties, recently returned from America, living on social security, and reading ecclesiastical history in the university library for a book he is writing on 'The Just War'. 'I was a university student but got chucked out – you remember the files business. I was the proposer of a sit-in motion: I'd done two years of my degree course. I went to America and worked for the Farmworkers' Union over there. I find I can live better here on social security than if I were a student. I get £16 a week because I'm married. I come in here and read books. It's O.K., you know.'

He is organizing a food co-op and a craft centre. He says of the former:

The vegetarian restaurant group really exists only in embryonic form. The idea is to get the stuff in bulk – rice, and so on, and parcel it up in pound and five-pound packets. We would take sacks of the stuff and sell it to people who want to buy in bulk. I am sure there are thirty or forty communally occupied houses in this city that would like to buy a whole sack of rice now and then instead of little bags every week. We wouldn't make a profit, or anything . . .

With regard to the proposed craft centre, he says:

We want to start a craft centre. There are a lot of people around who can make things. All there is now is that Northern Craft Centre place opposite Habitat. A right bourgeois affair that is, and the stuff costs so much. We want to start somewhere where people can sell stuff and perhaps make enough to live on.

But his real interest is ethics:

What I'm really interested in is ethics, which is what really matters. Whether they exist or not may be a problem for some people, but it doesn't matter one way or the other to me. What I'm working on now is a book on arguments for 'The Just War'. That's why I'm reading all this church history. It seems that the early Christian movement was pacifist, but they decided to drop the idea when Constantine became a Christian, him being a soldier. From then on you get ever more sophisticated arguments to justify the occasional war and killing. It's fascinating. Augustine and then Aquinas – fantastically closely argued things about the ways people can be justifiably killed in. It's amazing. Right up to the Professor of Ethics at Princeton University using verbal syllogisms to justify the Vietnam war. It's done by imparting falsely restricted meanings to words, and forgetting what they really mean in usage. And this guy's supposed to be a professor!

He reflects on the alternative scene in America, compared with Britain:

It's a lot more diverse over there. It ranges from people like Charles Reich who think that everything will turn out right if everyone turns on and goes to Grateful Dead concerts, right through to hard core left organizations and specific issue groups. But everything's a lot clearer cut over there – the issues are clearer. There's the draft . . . but that's ending soon, thank God. Then there's the clinics. Like in America, if you've no insurance, you can't get treatment . . . so there are people's clinics opening up in Boston and elsewhere. There's more street people, too. People who just drift around from city to city getting jobs now and then. It just doesn't seem to happen much here. Maybe it's because there is only so far you can go in England. You soon come to John o' Groats. But I suppose over the whole of Europe you could say it was happening.

He does not think the mystical scene is so developed here:

'You see a few Krishna Consciousness people on Market Street, but in Boston, say, where I was, there's this street that goes across the river to Cambridge, and every five yards there's a weird group of some sort, yellow robes, black robes, chanting – it's fantastic. I miss America very much . . . The Farmers' Union, too . . . trying to get Mexicans and Indians to join . . . I've never been into mystical things myself, I suppose because I feel reasonably happy, apart from living in the wrong country. If I felt there was a huge emptiness in my life, I suppose I would join up.'

Unlike most interviewees, he sees the local 'alternative' as quite coherent and integrated:

'Like in any big city, there's a core of people who make up the alternative scene. It just happens that someone may be in the Information and Aid Centre and the Gypsy Liaison Group, for instance, or into community action and the restaurant group. It works out like that. They all interlock.'

But he did not see the mystical scene as interlocking with the rest.

A 'situationist' was interviewed at his flat. He is a 27-year-old former university student who writes for the underground press. (When he was interviewed, he was writing a review of an anti-student pamphlet which presents the dope-smoking student as a regrettable role produced by the student's position in capitalist society.) He spends four or five hours a day typing, arranging the magazine's lay-out, and trying to get contributors to meet deadlines ('I take a pretty professional attitude to the magazine now'). He live on social security ('The S.S. is pretty good, really, because it leaves people free to do all sorts. Like you can start a shop or something, and you don't have to live off it yourself'). He is against work. He tried it once ('I quite enjoyed it'). But the trouble with work is, 'it fucks your mind'.

In the flat there was a pile of records, mostly fairly old progressive rock with the odd classical thrown in. There was an unmade single bed along one wall and in the bay an old brown leather settee on its side, so the back now served as a seat. On a chest of drawers there was a copy of a thick, white publication called *The*

*Monday Club: A Danger to Society*. A book-case had two full rows of books. Otherwise the room was in an untouched, 'furnished flat to let' state, with wallpaper and worn carpet. There was one hard chair.

Interviewer: *What is a situationist, then?*

Well, it's kind of hard to put a structure on it, just like that. There isn't really a group or an organization here, it's just me. I helped to produce a situationist magazine a few months ago, but it didn't really get off the ground financially. It's a marxist thing that sees two essential elements that are fundamental to society – commodity and spectacle. Commodity is the economic substructure, and spectacle is the image of illusory needs, desires and lifestyles that capitalism needs to generate in order to perpetuate itself.

*What do you do to free yourself?*

Well, you become a revolutionary.

*Does the idea of a local 'alternative society' mean anything at all to you?*

Yes. There are shops, you know, like some of them are alternative and some like to think they are. One down the road is alternative, not because of what it sells, but because it is organized as a co-operative and gives money to other alternative groups. But The Food House isn't. It's good food, mind, but it's just a hippie capitalist affair. They employ freaks, but that's because freaks will work for less than anybody else – they don't get much more than on social security. Then there are alternative bookshops. The economic structure has to be alternative for something to be alternative. There are various institutions like this, and then the political groups, that make up a sort of society. But it's very hard to come out with a formula and say that this is the alternative.

*The whole thing seems to be getting more organized and hard-headed?*

Some of it's beginning to be, thank God. People are beginning to realize the practical importance of organizing to do particular tasks, or to work out particular pieces of theory. I don't like pragmatism as a political philosophy, but it seems the best way to get specific tasks done. There's still the anarchist strain who won't have organization at any cost, but it seems stupid to me to have a theoretical belief against organization. Yes, it's true things are becoming more oriented to specific tasks – sectional groups like Women's Lib are all much stronger and more inspired than they were . . . But about five years ago everyone seemed to know everyone else, and everyone was into dope, acid, politics and black magic all at the same time and seemed to be able to keep it all together in their heads, and everyone else had the same interests. Now the heads and those into mysticism and the politicals hardly know each other. But it's all got bigger – it's more fragmented, but more organized and stronger . . . The hippie thing's dead – that was pretty useless, really: love and peace and all that. Have you read *Fear and Loathing in Las Vegas?* That's pretty good for telling you how it all collapsed in America . . .

*There seem to be historical parallels, in periods of technological change?*

Well, that's a lot better than what a lot of people around say – that what's happening is totally unique, like they look back to 1966 as the beginning of the world. A cult book that's just coming into fashion – well, there's no cult yet – is Cohn's *Pursuit of the Millennium*. About all these really way-out groups that were into counter culture, I mean really into it. Like they killed all the bourgeoisie and burned their houses and proclaimed a revolution all mixed up with these religious cults. Marx could have given them lots of good reasons why they hadn't a hope in hell of succeeding, but still . . . I've just been reviewing a book called *Art and Industry in the Nineteenth Century*. There's a great quote there about work being used as an instrument of repression. A quote from this cotton mill owner about how he'd better pay his workers less so they'd have to work more hours and have less time to kick up trouble.

*What about communes?*

I don't like them, but they are trying to make their actual lifestyles match up to what they believe, which is good. That's the big problem . . . But it's just not my thing . . . It's hard enough getting me to share a flat.

Another political activist was interviewed in his home. He is in his late thirties, married, with children. He is a former labourer, with a long history of subversive activity. At the time of the interview he was a mature university student reading for a degree in anthropology; but he is contemptuous of students, whom he considers servile. He has served various periods of imprisonment. He is a vegetarian; he has rejected work. He is contemptuous of old style hippies but considers that they were, in their time, genuinely and beneficently revolutionary, because they went on the dole without shame. He has travelled extensively in the East, and he has worked for the interests of gypsies and evicted tenants.

Interviewer: *What's the idea of the group you're with now?*

Well, we set out to try and fracture the structure of society, as it exists now, in any way that we can. We work fairly carefully and methodically. We set out on specific issues, where we can see an injustice, and try to get something organized. Like the gypsies . . . We're revolutionary socialists, but not of the doctrinaire kind. The other more orthodox marxist-anarchist groups would probably say we administer 'social aspirins' – that we just reduce injustice at small points and so hinder the revolution. We just think you should always enjoy what you're doing and the world you live in. The old marxists tend to postpone the happiness.

We work quite openly. That's why we don't like to be called the underground. In a country where you haven't got the secret police on your backs, you should work openly and enjoy what you're doing. But then there's the Stoke Newington Eight* – I don't know . . . I suppose they haven't got much to be happy about . . . We work through non-violent means . . . most of us. But the others must work for their violent revolution, too, in their own way. If you want to know roughly what our ideas are, read *The Second City*. It's about the exhaustion of consumer society, the future of a wasteful, throwaway society. It says we must build a second city fit to live in.

*Have you always been in the movement, as you call it, or was there some turning point in your life?*

No. There was no turning point. I've always been like that, I suppose. I was brought up in the East End. It's a really good area. Working-class background. My family came from Russia. My grandparents used to print subversive literature in London, ship it to Russia on the Black Sea ports, and try to distribute it. That's the sort of background I've got. I've always done labouring. I worked as an agricultural labourer near Cambridge for five years. I tried to get labourers to join the agricultural union. They were all scared . . .

* Anarchists of the Amherst Road commune, four of whom (John Barker, James Greenfield, Anna Mendelson and Hilary Creek) were sentenced in December 1972 to ten years' imprisonment for anarchist activities.

Well, suddenly I got this job, working for this mad professor. I was earning two-and-a-half thousand a year. I mean, that was huge, unprecedented. That's how we managed to get this house together. Then this mad Professor lost the grant and there I was on the dole with this huge mortgage. So I signed up as a mature university student. I'm in my last year now. I've had a great time.

*Were you involved in things before you came north?*

Sure. I've been to prison several times. Three month sentences for civil disobedience. One six-monther for refusing to fight their colonial wars for them. We were living in South London before we came here: but people don't really live in those dormitory places . . . Things are more definite in this city. It's just a series of villages. The issues are definite: tenants, gypsies, housing and so on. We're not really a group. It's always been very informal. We meet every Monday, but there's no regular membership. The gypsies is what is happening over this weekend. We always said we wanted to support the gypsies in what they wanted to do – but not to lead them, or interfere with their culture in any way. And this patently hasn't worked. With the gypsies, unlike the tenants, things haven't worked out. They're so scared of authority.

Then there was Operation Omega. I expect you heard about that . . . a group of us here, during the Bangladesh affair, decided we wouldn't just stand by and do nothing while people starved to death. So we organized this great overland trek to Bangladesh, and publicized each city on the way, telling people to join us and bring food. It was mad, really. Anyway, some people are still out there, helping the Bengalis – victims of collaborators. But during the war they risked their lives daily smuggling food across the Pakistani lines . . .

*Is the counter culture getting more diverse and more organized?*

I think things have developed. The hippie movement did two things that were really important. First, they went on the dole and social security without shame. Now I regard that as really a great historical development. The second thing was that they lived all together in houses. That idea has been developed into purposeful communes – people living together.

I don't know about pot. I really don't know enough about it. I only had it once, or it might have been L.S.D. There were these two hippies staying here once. It turned out they were quite famous.

Anyway, they were up here for some reason, and when they left they left a note saying: There's a present for you in the kitchen. And there were all these cookies! Anyway, I said let's have a go, so I ate two of these buns. I nearly went off my head. I'd just been reading a book about L.S.D., and I nearly went out of my mind. I don't know if it was L.S.D. or pot – but anyway, never again!

About food: you'll find that most of us in the movement are vegetarians – for various reasons, you know, and none of us perhaps thinks that it's that important. I became one because of what one of the judges said at my tribunal. He said: So you don't believe in killing people and that wars never solve anything – well, what about killing animals? It was a red herring, really, but I thought: perhaps he's right.

*Does the university play a big part in the 'alternative'?*

No, not really. Someone had a theory that it's because this is becoming such a high status university. It's felt to be enough just to have got here. It makes people complacent – they think they've made it. But I've found the university course tremendously exciting. But the way some of the lecturers talk, they've really no idea of what's going on. It's tremendously middle class. There's old Bernstein's rubbish about elaborated codes of language. That's still taught as standard, you know – that only middle-class people can use elaborated codes and deal with the abstract. I mean, it's just bullshit. You should hear the level of discussion at a tenants' meeting. These people are deeply versed in the subtleties of trade unionism. I mean, what I've felt throughout is that there were people who I'd trimmed hedges with around Cambridge, who would have been far better students than me on this course. I'm not a good student – I just go in when I'm interested in something.

But it's really hard to get a discussion going in seminars. I'm always afraid of saying too much. This young lecturer always comes in and says he *likes* people to talk. The others are so deferential. I have standing arguments with this Professor. He maintains that sectional and minority groups play no part in revolutions. But the resistance to the invasion of Czechoslovakia, that was started by the hippies. They were the first to climb on to the tanks and hang flowers over the guns. He had to agree with that, but said it was an exception.

I read a lot of anthropology – the Nuer, Azande sorcery, and

Epstein's stuff on India. I was actually with the swats for a while. I was bumming round India. Funny how that book of Barton's brought it all back. Epstein said a lot of good things, but there was a big mistake in it. I wrote this in my anthropology paper. A certain organization, she said, was an agent of government land reform. That was wrong, because I went out to join that organization. It's a Gandhian outfit, very anti-government. I don't know how she came to make a mistake like that . . .

## Mystics

Anarchists and political activists showed considerable interest in Eastern matters, including Eastern philosophy and religion; but they were not, as a rule, 'into mysticism', and were deeply contemptuous of the Divine Light Mission, Jesus Freaks, the Festival of Light and the Children of God. An anarchist at the Aid and Information Centre spoke of the Divine Light Mission:

They aim at anyone who's got money. Mostly it's people who are on L.S.D. or who've been taking stuff like that, and are looking for a new trip. A lot of people I know who have been into it are already on the way out. Some just go along because they like to belong to something. It's a social thing. One guy who was always trying to get me in – 'When you gonna take knowledge, Jake, it's great, man, great' – is now actively against the whole thing and talking about anarchism instead. It usually only takes a few months to get over it.

On another occasion a shift-worker at the Centre referred to the Jesus Freaks:

There's thousands of the bastards. There's some living in a house in this row. They're the only people who've never been in here to use the phone. Either they've got a phone of their own or they use a phone box. They probably regard this place as the gateway of hell.

Other freakish religious groups were discussed at the Centre in no more flattering terms:

'The people who really give me paronoia are the Children of God.'
'Yeah, the home-grown variety of Jesus Freaks is mad enough,

but their leader, "Moses", is really sinister. They don't even know what country he's in. Sometimes he just sends orders and whole groups pack up and leave for Abyssinia or somewhere.'

'But they're into communal living, aren't they?'

'Communal living with sexual segregation! I don't call that very revolutionary. They've been doing that in the British army for years.'

The mystics, for their part, were apolitical. They were less interested in social issues than the anarchists, and generally less socially involved. They meditated alone and tended not even to know one another. Their social isolation made them difficult to locate and contact.

One mystic who was interviewed is a university drop-out now in his late twenties. He was notable for his nonpolitical stance and for his social unrelatedness ('We are outside society'). His room (where the interview took place) was small and square with yellow walls, various cupboards and sideboards painted bright red, an unmade double bed, cushions on the floor around an electric fire. On the walls were posters and drawings and a cartoon entitled 'Mystics at Work' showing two people without faces. The Egyptian sign for life was written large in a number of places.

Interviewer: *What's the wikka group about then, in a word?*

In a word, it's hard to say. Here we teach meditation, do rituals and study texts and encourage people to adopt a new way of life, which follows on.

*How long has the group been going?*

It's in its fourth year.

*Is it a university group? Are you a student?*

No, I'm not a student, though I was at the university. There are some students and some ex-students, like me. And there are some people who have never been to the university. I'm the oldest: I'm twenty-seven. But it's not really a group.. It's more a scene. People go off and do other things in other places, perhaps get into something else ...

*Did you have any teachers you learned from?*

Yes, I've got an Egyptian teacher, a Buddhist teacher and a witch teacher. I go and see them now and then.'

*What led you to this?*

Well, I came into it from witchcraft. Then some of us felt it wasn't getting us anywhere – the rituals weren't getting us on fast enough. And it didn't go deep enough, either. So we decided to take up Egyptian teachings.

*What are the Egyptian teachings?*

They're taken from the pyramids, the scrolls, the 'Book of the Dead'. We also study hieroglyphics.

*What is the substance of the teaching?*

Well, it's a way of knowledge based on meditation. It has to do with achieving mental health, absolute mental health, and longevity, and the strengthening of the personality, until it becomes something indestructible. But it may take twenty or thirty years.

*You mentioned witchcraft. Was it instrumental witchcraft, where power is summoned up as in African witchcraft?*

We never did anything like that. Oh, no, it's not that, it's a more interior thing, inside the mind.

*Have you read a book by Castaneda called 'The Teachings of Don Juan'?*

Yes. Don Juan certainly knew what he was talking about – the discipline and the long time taken over everything to become a man of knowledge. There are a lot of systems in the world, all basically trying to do the same thing – arrive at knowledge. Don Juan's system is all right, but he can only work under drugs. You can't stay under the influence all the time. With meditation, I find I can be in the right state of mind all day long – it gets you places much faster than either drugs or rituals. We have specialized in the Egyptian teachings, and there's no other group in England doing the same as us, as far as I know. The texts have only been translated this century – in fact, we have been doing our own translations. There are different systems within the Egyptian corpus – the different periods of the Empire each had their own slightly different way of expressing things. It's best to perfect one system. It's a question of which powers you meditate on.

*Do you think these powers are out there, to be tuned into through meditation? Castaneda came to believe that Mescalito, the god he saw in his visions, objectively existed.*

The powers are there, but they are all inside the mind – but they're not unreal or imaginary because of that. Castaneda was bound to see Mescalito because he followed Don Juan's system.

*Do you have any connections with any other mystical group?*

No. There's no one in this city doing what we do better. There's no point in knowing about them or they us. To achieve more knowledge you have to stick to your own system – and go outside this city when you exhaust what's here. Most of the other groups, like the 'Seed Centre', are doing what we're doing, only in a different way. Some we've no time for at all, like the Divine Light Mission.

*So there isn't a mystical scene, like the political one?*

No, there isn't a scene, because everyone seems to adopt this same philosophy of sticking to their own system, and following a fairly narrow discipline, to achieve most knowledge.

*You mentioned Buddhism. Does what you are doing link up with Buddhism in any way, or is that just a personal connection you have made?*

Yes, that's just a personal connection, but we tend in that direction. Tibetan Buddhism is very highly regarded. We tend away from most Hindu things because they are concerned with social morality. We have no social morality. We have no society to work for. We are outside society.

*Does being part of the group make you stand anywhere in particular politically speaking? Do you have contact with the political alternative scene?*

No, not really. There are people of all political persuasions in the group – working-class conservatives, and I'm a sort of communist I suppose. I've been in political groups in the past, but I've never known Wikka change anyone's political opinions.

*But you did say that a completely different way of life was involved – doesn't that have any political implications, if only at the level of personal revolution?*

It does, perhaps, for those that way inclined. The new way of life is a kind of liberation. We liberate ourselves from mental blocks through meditation, and that certainly enables you to make truer political choices. The results of meditation are many.

*But it's hard to say what meditation itself is, is that right?*

Well, you can sometimes isolate particular liberating experiences. People-Not-Psychiatry interests me a lot, though I've never been to any of their meetings. I'd like to work with them, but I've never got round to it. I think it would be hard to persuade them in to what I thought was a going idea. There are many of us who support and work for 'the alternative' way of life, but I'd never lay one particular view on to people. Basically, one political opinion is as good as another.

Another mystic is a university drop-out in his mid-twenties living on social security. He produces a magazine devoted to mysticism. He was interviewed in his tiny room which had a single mattress by the door, cardboard boxes full of rubbish, and another mattress. The walls were papered but one wall had been half covered with dark red emulsion paint. The mystic was short, with long, unkempt hair, wearing very old jeans. He spoke quietly but with determination.

Interviewer: *I'm looking into the 'alternative' in this city.*

I don't know whether this is part of the alternative. We're just doing our own thing. I mean, the political scene – they're all right and getting along fine – except for the 'bombers' – but the mystical revolution never happened, somehow.

*Is there like a mystical scene in this city?*

Well, it's very hard for people to co-operate. There's not much help anyone can give anyone else. It's a very individualistic thing. You're on your own and the answers to your difficulties come from yourself. I've come to the conclusion that you've just got to sit down on your own and start meditating.

*Does your magazine take a political stand of any sort?*

When we started out we had a lot of political aspirations, but we seem to have dropped them. I don't want to be called a 'left-wing mystic'. I don't want people to reject my mysticism with my politics. I mean, I don't see why fascists shouldn't meditate. It might make them less fascist if they did.

*Are there any mystical teachers in the city?*

Yes. But the real ones don't advertise. If it's your destiny to have a teacher you will find one. But if it's your destiny for things to come from inside yourself, then that's that.

*The idea of destiny seems to be important to you. I've been using the 'I Ching' a bit lately. I suppose that's what its about. What do you think of the 'I Ching'?*

I use the 'I Ching' a lot, though I've been trying to use it less. I use it to lean on, I think. I reckon there's more chance of misinterpreting the 'I Ching' than of making an error of judgement.

*I reckon I need a lot more knowledge before I can begin to understand.*

I used to think that . . . that I had to be let into some big secret, to be initiated into a coven . . . I spent pounds on books, but they don't get you any nearer. It's got to come from within. You've just got to sit down and start. At one time I was desperate to get into a coven . . . but there are so many people going around calling themselves witches, who really can't do anything. You know, 'Two vacancies in a coven for girls, blonde, 36–29–36.'

*What do you personally do? What techniques do you use?*

I meditate – concentrate on the psychic centres of the body.

*But can people just start without a starting point?*

Well, teachers aren't much use. There's very little they can do beyond giving you advice if you get into difficulties.

*What sort of difficulties?*

Well, a few weeks ago I got into a state . . . like the idea is to get into a higher level of being, where all the needs we have now will just drop away – like we've lost tails. They won't be important any more. Well, to do this you need energy. I had these nervous energy difficulties. I had all this nervous energy, shooting out all over the place.

*Have you got over that now?*

Not entirely.

The Divine Light Mission offers inner peace in a troubled world. In spite of the disparaging observations of both mystics and militants, some devotees who spoke at the Mission's meetings appeared to have looked hard for serenity and to have found it. It is true that there were in attendance men in three-piece suits with short, well-groomed hair. But a girl in her early twenties, wearing a duffle coat and jeans, with long unkempt hair and face untouched by makeup, rose and spoke: 'I've just come back from India from a meeting of the Western devotees of Guru Maharaj Ji, and I find it difficult to talk about anything else.'

At this point an Indian aged about thirty, in a neat black suit and tie, short hair and polished appearance, walked into the room. He went up to a picture of the Guru, bowed, and sat down in a chair with a white cloth on it. He smiled and the girl continued:

It was really, really beautiful. It's really strange, being back here – for there we were in the village of the devotees, everything was there, and we had no need to go outside it. There is nothing to compare with what we were experiencing. Everyone was seeking for the same thing, and you could really feel it. The love. It was just love, you know. When people got down to sleep, it was all close together, side by side. And the medical tent – just people working together non-stop, because lots of people were sick because of the climate and the food. Perfection was there – and Guru Maharaj Ji is so perfect. More and more people will turn to him because things are getting worse – the vibrations are getting worse, more and more confused. By their fruits ye shall know them – and Maharaj Ji bears such good fruit.

Her style was unrhetorical and free-flowing. She was serene. She finished with a bow to the picture.

*Community music-makers and actors*

Among the more expressive-artistic manifestations of the alternative in the urban north-west are groups which make music and drama in inner-city working-class communities. They are uncommercial, their music and drama are strong in social criticism, they are concerned about creativity and spontaneity, they are not seeking personal fame (though they are concerned to show that the north can 'make it' as well as London). They work hard. It was in interviews with the community musicians and actors that class-based statements were made. It is not only the north that can 'make it'; the working class can 'make it', too.

At the headquarters of Music Group a member explained their aims: 'We're a musicians' collective. It's for people who are fed up with the commercial scene. And we're trying to get through to people that there are things happening up here, and there's a lot of talent. Because up to now it's all been in London.'

He expressed the group's rather ambiguous relationship with left-wing political organizations: 'Well, we're an alternative. We've done things with the Socialist Labour League. But their motives weren't . . . creative . . . you know. But it's very much community music. I mean, the musicians think of themselves as part of the community, not different from it.'

Another member explained:

> Some of us are into working with political groups. We went to a Socialist Labour League Rally in London. There were groups, and street theatre people doing little plays. The musicians and the people in the plays were working-class lads, and they were really glad, you know, that a thing like that was being got together. But the people who were running it were all middle-class drop-out types . . . You know . . . like most of the people around on the scene. But the people in the bands are definitely working-class lads. There's no doubt about it, somewhere the right music is being played by the right people.

They see themselves as 'rock musicians, basically', but they're not interested in promoting themselves and trying 'to make the Big Time'. 'I feel I just want to go on writing my own songs. I don't want to go in for revivals of 'Blue Suede Shoes' and all that. I mean, it's all right, but it's not very creative.' They claim to have 'a lot of contact with the underground press – anything that takes a knock at the commercial thing . . .' They work hard: 'I haven't been out of this city for five years. Except for a weekend in London to see some friends, and that was taking some equipment to try to sell it. Musicians don't have holidays.'

The Community Drama Group consists of five actors in their twenties. They are a registered charity. The three men and two girls live communally and work a nine-to-five day. The commune has strict rotas for cooking and cleaning ('otherwise nothing would ever get done').

Their activities are principally in the form of street games and street theatre. They go into the streets with a loud-hailer, gather children around them and take them, 'pied-piper style', to the park and start a game going. The games are strictly non-competitive, in effect a form of socio-drama. Their street plays range from ten-minute sketches to hour-long presentations followed by discussions with the audience. The themes may be a local soldier's experiences in Northern Ireland, or life on the dole. The focus is on the communities embedded in particular networks of working-class streets. The drama group does not claim close contact with other alternative activities in the city: 'Not much contact, really. Like we see ourselves as working with the community here, not as some sort of alternative society . . .'

But the drama group (even though four of its five members are former university students) shows the characteristic contempt for university students that runs right through the counter culture. In May 1973 the group presented a play at mid-day in a central city square. The theme was the career of a student through university: harshly satirical, mocking, finally dismissive.

Twenty or so curious, smiling, somewhat embarrassed and sheepish members of the general public sat on benches in the square and watched the drama unfold. The student arrived at the university, visited the Union, and there met Hairy Harry.

'Hey, man, want to score?' said Hairy Harry. 'Smell this, this is Afgani brown.'

'What do you do with it?' said the student.

'Like this, man, like this.'

They roll a joint and suck vigorously.

'Hey, crazy, man, far out,' said the student.

And so he progressed to L.S.D., returning to Hairy Harry to declare:

'It's crazy, man.'

With his improved consciousness he visits parts of the city where working-class communities are being destroyed to make room for office blocks. 'It ought to be stopped; it shouldn't be allowed.' So he joins Community Action and goes on a soup run, 'but the soup ran away with him.' And then he's a demonstrator, shouting slogans. But when he's approached by a political organization and asked to join: 'No thanks, I'm a loner, man. I don't want to belong to no organization.' He's interested, but not too interested, which is just what the university wants.

And now he's within three weeks of finals and has done no work for two years. So off he goes to Hairy Harry:

'I need something to keep me awake.'

'You need some speed, man, you need some speed.'

He buys a hundred for five pounds and stays awake for two weeks and gets a 2.2.

The next scene is in the University Appointments Office:

'Personnel management at £2,500 a year.'

'I'll take it.'

And now there he is with the new car his mother has bought him, beating down the unions and sacking the workers. At the end he is phoning his wife:

'Sorry, darling, I shall be late tonight. The train's not running. Those bloody unions are on strike again.'

## Conclusion

For all the squalor, the in-fighting and the bathos of ecstasy that has gone off the boil, the counter culture observed at the micro level is intent, in Illich's phrase, on the celebration of awareness. Its quest, along divergent pathways and often cul-de-sacs, is ecstasy. Illich rightly proclaims that 'All of us are crippled', but sees the possibility of delight, joyfulness and dignity, if we recognize that 'a striving for seal-realization, for poetry and play, is basic to man' and if we 'end the use of coercive power and authority: the ability to demand action on the basis of one's hierarchical position.'[2] But, 'We can only live these changes: we cannot think our way to humanity.'

In the grittiness of the counter culture there is a genuine, difficult, and often very courageous attempt to live the changes which may make us human. The paradox of counter-cultural life is that its hallmark is material poverty and squalor, but it is an experiment that is made necessary by the promise of plenty. As Illich rightly suggests (in his manifesto which mirrored the mood of 1967): 'We believe that a human adventure is just beginning: that mankind has so far been restricted in developing its innovative and creative powers because it was overwhelmed by toil. Now we are free to be as human as we will.'[3] At present the experiment has to be made on social security.

The counter culture rejects human triviality for ecstasy. And ecstasy is the capacity to stand outside the obvious. This, as Peter Berger maintains, is the source of the richness of human life: 'any openness to the mystery that surrounds us on all sides.'[4] *Ek-stasis* is the privilege and the problem of the outsider – who stands outside the normal routines of living, taken-for-granted values, the conditioned reflex, the programmed response, received opinion, the hard edge of definition. Ecstasy is irrelevance: it composes sonnets in prison cells and combs its hair before Thermopylae.

# 8

## Generational consciousness and the decline of deference

One important aspect of the counter culture is its attitude to power and authority. This is linked with a concern for personal dignity. Radical questioning of the bases of authority is represented by the anarchist-activist sub-scale B described in Chapter five. This questioning appears to be more widespread among people under, rather than over, forty years of age. This chapter looks at other kinds of evidence for the decline of deference, principally in the recent work of political scientists; and it explores through interviews the outlook and experiences of members of three contemporary protest movements in the field of education: the National Union of School Students, the teachers' movement, Rank-and-File, and Free Schools.

All people who today question the legitimacy of bureaucratic and political authority and are suspicious of the operation of law-enforcement agencies, are not necessarily committed to the entire complex of values which constitutes the counter culture. But they will tend to have sympathy with the expressive and aesthetic values of the counter culture, and they will tend to have misgivings about modern technology. None of the three movements selected for study could be described as 'alternative' or counter-cultural in the same way that most communes are. But in varying degrees, they have counter-cultural affinities – teachers in Free Schools most, and N.U.S.S. members least, of all. The N.U.S.S. is probably the least 'way out', a reformist movement clearly within the system; Rank-and-File is probably more radical, but clearly 'within'; teachers in Free Schools are probably the least deferential of all, and more obviousy 'alternative', challenging the system from outside.

Clive Bell maintained that 'the mere exercise of power, the coercing of others, will tinge a man with barbarism'. The former schoolmaster now living on the dole and teaching in a Free School expressed a similar view of power when he said in one of our inter-views: 'I didn't want to stay in a job which would force me to be a bastard for the next forty years.' He knew that roles are as coercive as persons and that to coerce is as degrading as to submit. In the counter culture no one wants to be forced by his 'role-obligations' into being a bastard; all want to renounce power and become artists. They have rediscovered Clive Bell's recipe for civilization.

The rise of the counter culture is one symptom of the decline of deference. For the counter culture all power and authority is con-ditional, contractual, on trial: it must constantly explain and justify itself. The rational-legal authority of bureaucratic office is in no better case than the traditional authority of birth and breeding. The decline of deference is a demand for dignity. Subordination is ever less acceptable when there are so few subordinates left – when the social landscape has been transformed by the disappearance of domestic servants and the virtual elimination, or at least the effec-tive concealment, of children. Today some 15 per cent of the population is under ten; in pre-industrial England 30 per cent. This quantitative change, this narrowing of the base of the age-pyramid until it is virtually a column, has profound consequences for the quality of our society: there is simply a higher proportion of socially and intellectually autonomous people around.[1] Formerly, a very large minority of the population were sub-persons: they didn't count (quite literally – they were not enumerated in records and chronicles). In the seventeenth century '. . . nearly half of the whole community (was) living in a condition of semi-obliteration.'[2] Today, when comparatively few are obliterated, everyone wants to count.

The decline of deference is technology's child. Highly industrial-ized, technologically advanced societies have two outstanding characteristics which are relevant in this connection: not only do they have a relatively small proportion of juveniles who 'do not count', but they are highly urbanized and the urban population lives, in the main, in one-class districts. One-class residential areas are a powerful safeguard of human dignity. Deference is eroded in one-class estates, where a man can walk his neighbourhood streets without having to pull his forelock. Titus Salt knew the value of a small, multi-status residential community which replicated and reinforced the hierarchy of the work-place. Working-class voters in southern England are more politically servile (and inclined to vote Conservative) than working-class voters in the north: Parkin accounts for this, in appropriate sociological language, as arising from the southerners' lack of access 'to a normative sub-system which provides the necessary buttresses against the dominant value system'.[3] They are likely to live as well as work in small, servile, multi-status communities, whether as domestic servants in large houses or agricultural labourers in small villages. But the trend throughout this century has been towards large urban concentrations and one-class areas in which a man can escape from the boss. Multi-status communities are now rare outside military camps, new towns and new universities. Deference (and 'social control') are secure at Cranwell, Cumbernauld and Keele.

The decline of deference raises, perhaps, fundamental problems of social order. All ages have feared that a decline in deference would bring chaos. Bagehot saw deference as the cake of custom and believed that cabinet government was impossible without it. The seventeenth century believed that 'Without degree, unquestioning subordination, and some men being privileged while all others obeyed, anarchy and destruction were inevitable.'[4] Reasoned explanation is often a good substitute for autocratic power; but it is probably the case that we must learn to run our affairs with less predictable and reliable, and far more 'disloyal' behaviour.

The counter culture is not a delinquent teenage pop culture. It is neither specifically teenage nor is it 'pop', at least in any simple sense. Indeed, it is probable that people deeply committed to counter-cultural values actively reject 'mainstream pop' as represented by Englebert Humperdinck, Val Doonican and Frank Sinatra. But it is almost certainly the case that they find meaning and a message – even inspiration and confirmation – in 'underground pop' as represented by the Rolling Stones, Led Zepellin, Donovan, Bob Dylan and John Lennon. The music of underground pop has more substantial and subtle intellectual content, sharp social criticism, and references to sex and drugs, than 'wholesome' and vacuous mainstream pop.

Pop culture is not unified and homogeneous. Pop culture A (Humperdinck) and pop culture B (Lennon) are in fact deeply opposed. Pop culture B is not embraced by working-class youth as a response to academic failure and rejection, but by middle-class youth as a response to academic success.[5] It is subversive. Working-class failures and rejects do not turn to pop culture B, very seldom, even, to pop culture A (which is the pop culture of the straight, adult middle class); they turn to the traditional culture of the streets.[6]

The counter culture is not a youth culture. The decline of deference is not teenage impertinence and disrespect – although Bryan Wilson appears to think that it is. In a facile and wholly unwarranted equation he makes student activists equal the 'youth culture' and brackets football vandalism with university protest about power. 'Only long after the street brawls of the Teddy boys and the *Halbstarken* of the mid-1950s, and the beach-fights of the Mods and Rockers, and the football hooliganism, have the universities experienced the same generational discontent.' This youth culture, says Wilson, which embraces student rebels and football hooligans, is a 'pop culture' which challenges the traditional values of the university. Students now think of themselves as a 'class'. This is part and parcel of the phenomenon of '. . . youth as a separate stratum of modern society with values and a life of its own.'[7]

Many issues are confused in Wilson's analysis. Student protest is put in the same class of action as juvenile delinquency. The counter culture is neither juvenile nor delinquent. Neither the counter culture in general nor student activism in particular is delinquent in this conventional sense. The delinquent breaks the rules but accepts their legitimacy. The counter culture questions the legitimacy of the rules and the concept of legitimacy itself.

There is no evidence that students think of themselves as a 'class' or that student activism is one aspect of a teenage youth culture. The author's studies of students' 'reference groups' and sources of identity indicate that only a small minority – perhaps an eighth – of first-year students think of themselves primarily as 'one of the younger generation'. It is true, and hardly surprising, that they think of themselves as students; but already they are thinking of themselves primarily as prospective members of particular professions or vocations.[8] The counter culture in its various manifestations is not a teenage phenomenon. (Full-time members living on social security are typically in their late twenties and thirties.) But Wilson is undoubtedly correct in giving student protest a generational base. What he needs is a more sophisticated concept of 'a generation'.

## The new generational consciousness

Student unrest in the nineteen-sixties took the sociologists completely by surprise. They had argued that the 'function' of a generation was integrative: it bound the young to society. When a significant proportion of the young were clearly failing to be bound to society, functionalist sociology had no explanation. Mannheim was hastily resurrected.

After surveying the American scene in the 'fifties – and especially the spinelessness of American prisoners of war in Korea – Edgar Friendenberg wrote his book, *The Vanishing Adolescent*. Young people could still be troubled and troublesome, but spineless, supine and plastic adults were successfully raising correspondingly spineless, supine and plastic successors. Adolescence was becoming rare: 'Few youngsters really dare to go through with it . . .' Indeed, '. . . adolescence as a developmental process is becoming obsolete.' Friedenberg can scarcely be blamed for lacking foreknowledge of the courage, tenacity and commitment to values at odds with orthodox adult society, which characterized Berkeley's Battle of People's Park.

The functionalist argument found its fullest expression in the work of Eisenstadt in the nineteen-fifties. His comparative study of age-groups, age-grades and age-regiments in some fifty traditional African societies seemed to support the view that age-grades emerge and perform important adaptive functions when social integration and solidarity are not achieved by descent- and kinship-groups. This apparently held true of 'segmentary', non-centralized tribes equally with centralized chiefdoms. When lineages, clans and descent-groups determined 'role-allocation' (whether among the segmentary Tallensi or the centralized Ashanti), age-groups or regiments were not needed; they arose when 'important integrative functions remain to be fulfilled beyond these (kinship) groups', as among the segmentary Masai and the centralized Swazi.[9]

Age groups did not promote social disharmony; their function was to do precisely the opposite, to bring about adaptation and adjustment. They did not cause social division; they arose to prevent it. On the basis of his comparative anthropological data Eisenstadt concludes with confidence that '. . . age groups provide integrative mechanisms which contribute to the continuity and stability of societies which are not organized solely on the basis of descent groups and over-all kinship relations.' Age-groups united potentially divided societies: 'The age groups serve as important educational institutions through which the common values of society are inculcated in the members before they set out to engage in competitive and contractual relations. Thus they are important 'reservoirs' of solidarity and identification with the society'.

Eisenstadt proved nothing. He had made the wrong comparisons. He did not compare societies which were integrated with those that were not. One can see his difficulty. This was only exceeded by the difficulty of fitting modern industrial societies into his integrative thesis. Even in the nineteen-fifties youth groups in Europe and America were not notable as means of promoting social harmony, continuity and solidarity. But Eisenstadt persisted. By extending youth-groups to include schools he could claim that they 'inculcate the first dispositions to identification with society, its general values and norms of behaviour and collective symbols'.[10]

In an important and influential paper on American student protest Richard Flacks has completely misunderstood the functionalist position. He imagines that his inquiries support it. They do not. Flacks, like Eisenstadt (and Parsons) recognizes that in many respects the gap between the modern family and society is getting wider: its values are collectivist while those of society are competitive and individualistic; it is particularistic when society is universalistic, diffuse in its functions when the functions of the institutions of society are specific. It is, in short, a thoroughly bad preparation for life. It is precisely in these circumstances that age groups should arise to put things right, to provide the preparation, and promote the adaptation, that the family cannot. Flacks thought that the functionalists had argued that 'The greater the disjunction (between family and society), the more self-conscious and oppositional will be the youth culture . . .' That is just what he found. Instead of supporting the functionalist argument, he had refuted it.[11]

Functionalism has been unhelpful in understanding the 'new generation' which has emerged since the late nineteen-fifties: student protest, the counter culture, the decline of deference.

Sociologists have turned to Karl Mannheim for a more illuminating approach to generations. 'Mannheim's historical-consciousness theory goes beyond structural-functional theory by relating generational change to the broad context of social and cultural change'.[12] A generation is what it experiences.

Mannheim saw a generational position as analogous to a social-class position: both a class and a generation '. . . endow the individuals sharing in them with a common location in the social and historical process, and thereby limit them to a specific range of potential experience, predisposing them for . . . a characteristic type of historically relevant action.'[13] Life is not cumulative: its experiences are 'dialectically articulated' – its later stages are reactive. 'Early impressions tend to coalesce into a natural view of the world. All later experiences tend to receive their meaning from this original set . . .' We are the prisoners of our generation for life.

A generation is a world-view produced by particular historical events; the length of a generation is the interval between historical events of requisite potency. A new biological generation must experience some trigger-action or catalyst in order to become a social generation. 'Whether a new generational style emerges every year, every thirty, every hundred years, or whether it emerges rhythmically at all, depends entirely on the trigger action of the social and cultural process.' Biology is merely potentiality: 'The biological fact of the existence of generations merely provides the possibility that generation entelechies may emerge at all . . .'

Mannheim's theory accomodates the variability of generational characteristics. Not only do generations vary in length, but, in a complex society, a generation is unlikely to be homogenous in values and outlook. Even within the same age range, people experience the same historical events differently: 'generational units' are the internal subdivisions which may form along political or social class lines. As Bennett Berger pointed out in a very perceptive essay, the temporal and structural characteristics of a generation must be sharply distinguished: ' . . . it is essential, when using the concept of the generation in a cultural sense, to specify generations of what . . .' There are literary, political, musical and athletic generations. These various generations differ in length.[14]

The danger with Mannheim's theory is that, in accommodating everything, it explains nothing. In their flight from functionalism, sociologists (and others) have turned to Mannheim in an excess of zeal. Thus a spirited but unconvincing attempt has been made to explain changes in artistic style in fifteenth-century Italy in terms of generational consciousness precipitated by 'generational events' (the fall of Constantinople, the French invasion of 1494, the sack of Rome).[15] The bifurcation of the immigrant Russian community in Minneapolis has been interpreted in terms of generational units (which started from the same base-line and had identical historical experiences!);[16] preferences for rock music in Vancouver have been explained in terms of generational consciousness.[17] Wherever differences within or between age-groups are observed, Mannheim is thought to have been vindicated.

Lewis Feuer has applied Mannheim's concepts to generational conflict and student movements over the past two centuries and has concluded that generational consciousness first appeared with the Romantic movement.[18] But we have not been short of generations since: they have proliferated, the interval between them reducing as historical crises have multiplied. 'Rapid social change' would appear to require nothing less; but it is unclear why the Armada and the execution of Charles I lacked potency as trigger mechanisms. Berger has concluded the opposite: that generations are getting longer. He is undoubtedly correct. It is not enough that events occur. They must be experienced as uniquely problematical.

The generation is really less important in Mannheim's theory than the generation unit. 'The generation unit represents a much more concrete bond than the actual generation as such.' This argument runs the danger of robbing the concept of generation of all meaning. If units may be irreconcilably antithetical, it is difficult to see in what sense except the purely temporal they constitute a generation at all. Feuer finds no difficulty in this. Class-based generational units are usually without shared values, he thinks, and 'Generational consciousness . . . is generally not strong enough to bind students and workers of the same age.' Ortega y Gasset, whose theory of generations anticipated Mannheim's in a remarkable way, had a surer historical vision and made the appropriate comparisons: 'The reactionary and the revolutionary of the nineteenth century are much nearer to one another than either is to any man of our own age.'[19] We can speak of the new generation of the nineteen-sixties without requiring that all who were then twenty years of age held identical beliefs, but without denying distinctive characteristics which mark it off from earlier generations.

Generational consciousness is not simply the product of events; it is the product of problems. Mannheim made this point clearly:

'We are directly aware primarily of those aspects of our culture which have become subject to reflection; and these contain only those elements which in the course of development have some-how, at some point, become problematical.'[20] Personal dignity and a sense of worth have become subjects for reflection in the new generation; and the denial of dignity is seen in the exercise of bureaucratic authority, and the imposition of bureaucratic cate-gories on experience, not least in educational institutions.[21] Dignity and humiliation have always been problems; they have led to duels at one social level, and to mutinies at another, but never before to social movements. Ralph Turner has argued that the problem of personal worth has become the focus of new social movements with a generational base. The new generation defines itself through its claim for dignity and refusal of personal belittlement by persons or systems. Prominent among its targets is the educational process: '. . . the passive, routinized, hierarchical, and continuous nature of the passage through schooling and bureaucratic employment will assuredly be a continuing target in the developing movements.'[22]

Political scientists have (unwittingly) provided the best confirma-tion of Mannheim's theory of generations and (knowingly) the most impressive support that we have for the decline of deference. Their studies of the changing incidence of 'cross-voting' provide some of the most systematic evidence that we have for differences in genera-tional consciousness.

Deference is not a simple concept and its indicators are often ambiguous and invariably imprecise. Even Bagehot recognized that deference may be multi-dimensional: that the English were not equally deferential about everything – that they were actively hostile to enacted legislation (as distinct from natural or common law), which they regarded as artificial, arbitrary and alien.[23] (In our supine acceptance of statute law over the past century we have become more deferential rather than less.) Runciman's studies of the English sense of 'relative deprivation' in the early nineteen-sixties[24] have been taken as evidence that we are still highly defer-ential. In fact, we are simply not very envious. We are not only not prepared to see others as our 'betters', but even as significantly better-off.

The terminology and definitions used in this debate, as well as the 'measures' used, are shifting and often shadowy. Bagehot's 'decorous dulness' and 'dignified torpor' are probably poor indicators of deference – which is the acceptance of authority not for its actual efficiency, but for irrelevant attributes of the person who wields it (such as 'birth', accent, divine descent, age, sex, personal style or academic qualifications). American political scientists conclude that England is a 'deferential civic culture' apparently because we are prepared to concede that our civil servants and policemen are useful.[25] Cohort analysis of voting behaviour brings a semblance of rigour into the debate.

Butler and Stokes conducted extensive surveys of voters in the mid-'sixties,[26] McKenzie and Silver made intensive studies;[27] both focus on the working-class Conservative voter, and both show that working-class deference has declined. 'Deviant' members of the middle class who vote Labour have received less attention: they have been observed only in passing. But even middle-class deference may also have declined.

Butler and Stokes surveyed a random national sample of voters in 1963 and followed them up in 1964 and 1966. They distinguished between four cohorts: those who were qualified to vote before 1918, in the inter-war years 1918–35, in 1945, and post-1951. Almost half (48 per cent) of the earliest cohort of working-class voters supported the Tories in 1963, 34 per cent of the inter-war cohort, and 27 per cent of both the post-war cohorts. If working-class support for the Tories is a sign of deference, the younger members of the working-class were markedly less deferential than their elders.

McKenzie and Silver made an intensive study of 600 working-class voters. Twenty-nine per cent were Tory supporters. McKenzie and Silver distinguished between 'seculars' and 'deferentials' – the former supported the Tories for pragmatic reasons, their commitment was highly conditional; but the deferentials supported the Tories in the belief that they were uniquely qualified to govern by virtue of birth and breeding. When classified in this way, the deferentials were 26 per cent of the working-class cross-voters, the seculars 38 per cent (the rest 'mixed').

But the interesting differences relate to age. In the age-range 25–34 only 6 per cent of the cross-voters were deferentials; in the age-range 55–64, 42 per cent. 'Taken together, these results suggest that at present the ideological base of working class Conservative voting is moving away from deference towards secularism. The younger generation in this sample (those under 44) include only one in ten of the deferentials but one in two of the seculars.'[28]

It has been persuasively argued that any vote for Labour is a 'deviant' vote, and any vote for the Tories a deference vote. Parties of the Left challenge the dominant institutional orders of our society: the Established Church, public schools and universities, the élites of the military establishment and the institutional complex of private property and capitalist enterprise. 'Socialist voting in general can be regarded for analytical purposes, as a symbolic act of deviance from the dominant values of British capitalist society, whilst Conservative voting may be thought of as a symbolic reaffirmation of such values.'[29] In these terms, while the reduction in cross-voting among the working-class is a sign of declining deference among the working-class young, the increase in the amount of cross-voting in the middle class is a sign of declining deference among the middle-class young.

The evidence of Butler and Stokes is that such an increase has occurred. In the pre-1918 middle-class cohort, only 15 per cent were Labour supporters, but 25 per cent and 21 per cent in the 1945 and post-1951 cohorts respectively. The trend is much more pronounced if middle-class men are considered separately: '. . . among men of the 1945 cohort . . . middle class electors were more likely to be Labour than working class electors were to be Conservative.'

But the evidence on middle-class traitors has to be treated with a good deal of caution. The non-deferential middle-class is mainly (perhaps three-quarters) of working-class origin.[30] Social mobility introduces into the middle class a Trojan horse. The majority of those who rise from the working class to the middle class remain politically non-deferential. But longitudinal data on social mobility and associated voting do not exist which would show whether the non-mobile middle class are declining in deference. There is, however, some indication in studies of the social and political attitude of schoolchildren that this may be so.

A recent study of the 'political socialization' of a national sample of 14- and 15-year-olds in all types of school provides little evidence for political deference, especially among middle-class children. This questionnaire study indicated an extensive rejection by young people of our major social and political institutions. 'It is hard for us to interpret our data and conclude that we have either "a stable democracy" or a "deferential civic culture"'. There was very deep scepticism about our system of government, '. . . and it is interesting that the most intense suspicion of governmental responsibility is centred in the upper middle class category.' 'The picture we have is one of middle class hostility to the status quo combined with working class indifference.'[31] The picture is only a snapshot in time – no trends were established. But there was little evidence that the young were being effectively socialized into a deferential culture.

Both the Butler and the McKenzie studies relate shifts in voting behaviour and political outlook to 'generational experience'. Changes in political behaviour in the younger, post-war generation – even 'the progressive conversion of the working class to the Labour Party' – are not the product of deprivation and embittered social class relationships. Quite the contrary: the changes are closely associated with growing affluence and opportunity. It is one of the major findings of Butler and Stokes that the conflict image of politics has declined among postwar voters. This is a central paradox explored by Butler and Stokes: 'The intensity of the class tie may have declined at the same time as its extent became more universal . . . The first ground for our supposition lies in factors that broadly condition the electorate's view of class and politics, especially the visible change in British conditions of life. The affluence of the postwar world is much more than an illusion of the party propagandists. Real incomes have risen steadily to levels far above those of the prewar world.'

Others who have tried to interpret postwar values and generational differences similarly point to a major discontinuity in the rate of social change around 1950, notably improvements in living standards: 'The period 1945–1950 marks the shift from industrial to post-industrial and technological society; from moderate abundance to spectacular affluence . . .'[32] This was written of America; similar changes occurred in Britain. Butler and Stokes conclude that to understand political attitudes and behaviour, 'We must ask not how old the elector is, but when it was that he was young.' Political generations find their explanation in Mannheim's concepts of generational events and historical consciousness.

## Three educational protest movements

In 1973 we carried out six extended interviews with prominent members of the N.U.S.S. in the north-west; with six teachers prominent in Rank-and-File; and with eight teachers in Free Schools in widely separated parts of England.[33] These twenty individuals cannot be regarded as necessarily 'representative' of their respective movements: each was prepared to invite us to his home and talk to us at length after we had made contact with the organization, and then to introduce us to other people whom they saw as 'mainstream' in their movement. The interviews are reported below to provide insight into their problems and the way they perceive themselves and their world. All were concerned primarily with 'power relationships' and the problem of being human in formal organizations. All but one explained their present involvement by referring to a lifetime of predisposing values. The one who did not was a teacher in Rank-and-File who had experienced something akin to a conversion while on an industrial vacation job during his time at Cambridge. The teachers commonly referred also to pre-cipitating experiences in their schools; but the school pupils appeared not even to have had precipitating experiences, or were at pains to describe them as irrelevant if they had. They explicitly rejected 'clash of personalities' explanations of conflict with authority. (Official accounts of conflicts in schools, as given to us by officers of local education authorities, were in these terms: there was nothing basically wrong, there just happened to be a clash of personalities in particular schools.) Members of the N.U.S.S. and of Rank-and-File rejected the thesis that there was nothing basically wrong and all was explained by the accident of personalities. The confrontation was between their pre-existing values and 'the system'.

The National Union of School Students was established in the wake of the May–June rebellion in France in 1968. It was at its most visible in demonstrations in London in the summer of 1972; by the middle of 1973 it had an estimated membership of 10,000, but was heavily in debt to the National Union of Students. Its own members feel that the movement is precarious: as they leave school they wonder whether they will have successors. But a survey of 500 pupils in 1972 indicated that as many as 60 per cent strongly support the movement's aims, that 'In no sense can the growth of their (pupils') critical awareness be regarded as a purely parochial phenomenon related solely to their immediate situation . . .' Contemporary pupil action is not a mutiny but a movement. 'There appears to be little reason to suppose that this process of politiciza-tion will be reversed.'[34]

Two schools of high academic standing in the urban north-west have a reputation for providing strong support for N.U.S.S. activi-ties. One has experienced some internal unrest, the other none. Three well-known N.U.S.S. supporters were interviewed in both schools. Their attack, essentially, was on the power and position of head-masters: 'the mere fact of his position is a form of violence'. But they do not necessarily have anything personal against their own headmaster: 'We all like our headmaster – you can't help it.' Their attack is not on assistant teachers (although they would like more informal relationships, particularly in the upper school); indeed, their campaign is in the cause of assistant teachers, and the consequence is, as one interviewee said, that: 'More radical groups, like Rebel, accuse us of being teachers' "Uncle Toms".' The N.U.S.S. is not a revolt against teachers' power and brutality, but the interviewees have despaired of finding effective allies among teachers:

> I'm not saying that teachers in our school are violent. When they are, occasionally, it's just taken in the course of things. There's a teacher in our school who'd like to get rid of all school compulsions, but he realizes he's got to stay within the system. That's why I personally give up the idea of trying to work through teachers. They've got a job at stake so their hands are tied. You can't work with teachers to get democracy in schools. There's no teacher in our school prepared to sacrifice his job.

All the interviewees saw their movement (somewhat apologetically) as mainly middle class, with strong support in liberal schools of good academic standing. The parents of the active members were usually in professional occupations and generally supportive. The N.U.S.S. campaigned less for themselves than for the less privileged: 'Pupils in tough schools in slum areas don't join. They have no time to think or read or reflect. Members of the N.U.S.S. are mostly from good homes and schools – they have a good school life and they want others to have a good school life.' Another sixth-form interviewee explained reasons for joining as follows:

> I think a lot of people join not because anything specific has happened to them; it's their background, really. Most of the kids who are in now are sort of middle-class intellectuals. With me it was a gradual realization of what education is all about – it's a system to exploit people. We're trying to make things better for the poor underprivileged working-class kids. But they're so apathetic. It's difficult to get through to them. They're conditioned to accept what they're given.

All the interviewees saw themselves as academically successful (two said: 'You could say I was a model pupil, until I began to question the system'). A recurrent diagnosis was: 'You could say it is in liberal schools where there is an atmosphere conducive to questioning and thinking and argument that you get a lot of N.U.S.S. members.' Middle-classness was also a recurrent theme: 'The Schools Action Union has basically the same style of leadership in terms of middle-class parents, but they're more childish – they made long hair essential. I suppose we like to be thought of as fairly studious people. We probably have a middle-class image, which is mainly but not entirely accurate'.

They recalled loneliness and a sense of social isolation to account for their present beliefs and actions. One said: 'I was always a loner. I was a model pupil in the lower school. But I began to question things. First of all, I kicked religion. But I decided I'd got to get in with others if I was going to change things.' He has considerable interest in a commune: 'There are six or seven in it – anyone can go in for a night, or a month. One guy has a farm, which provides most of the food. They're vegetarians. The main idea is helping each other – sharing. But they're not wholly alternative: some of them work, and there are marriage-type arrangements in the commune.' He is very sympathetic to the commune ideal, but 'It wouldn't suit me for long – I prefer being alone more.'

In the other school a sixth-former dwelt at length on a disordered childhood (in an upper middle-class home) to explain his present attitudes. Periods of his earlier youth were spent with his family abroad:

> I've always, since childhood, had long periods of isolation. I was very much a recluse at times. I felt very isolated from academic things and also from other people. I've always had periods when I've felt I had nothing I could associate with. My surroundings and the people around me didn't mean much to me. I've never felt part of things. My childhood was very confused. I had great periods of isolation and confusion and never felt I could express myself properly. I feel even now that there isn't anyone I can really talk to. I've probably got about a dozen good friends, but no one I can really express myself to.

He was the most articulate of the interviewees and at seventeen one of the most prominent and effective leaders of the National Union of School Students.

Power and authority are the preoccupation of the teachers' movement, Rank-and-File. As R. G. Gregory, the Head of Drama at Market Drayton Comprehensive School said, when he was sacked after a bitter two-year struggle with the head: 'Ring your own bloody bell.'

Here, in a phrase, we have the essential concern of Rank-and-File with power, ritual, bureaucracy, and people-processing. (Mr Gregory's drama teaching was, by his own account, very open and unscripted indeed.)

Mr Gregory was a member of Rank-and-File. He published his story in 1971 in a pamphlet entitled *The Grove*.[35] This gives an account of very spirited, courageous, vigorous, non-deferential action against a headmaster whose concept of a head, we are told, 'was that of a squire, for whom others worked loyally and without question.' 'He hated meeting the whole staff and sometimes got his underlings to go around pleading that he found it difficult to face more than six teachers at once ... But he believed that real decision-making was his prerogative only.' But Mr Gregory was at pains to argue that the trouble was not, as officially diagnosed by the education authority, just a conflict of personalities: 'Throughout the troubles ... in 1970 and 1971, it was frequently suggested that the root cause was the clash of personalities between (the headmaster) and myself. This explanation was absurd ...' Mr Gregory gives us a long history of his 'prior values', which had been forming throughout his non-linear career since 1952, when he graduated in English from the University of London and became a labourer, subsequently teaching in various schools, leaving the profession for a time for full-time authorship, and later spending a period in East Africa. In the stormy years 1969–71 Mr Gregory was no teenage rebel facing an adolescent crisis of identity. He had been shaped twenty years before, in the 'fifties.

All members of Rank-and-File do not engage in such open, spirited and sustained conflict with the headteacher; they don't all get sacked; indeed, many are very cautious, fearing reprisals. We have found them fairly difficult to investigate. But we have, by invitation, attended their meetings, where the discussion was at a high level of intellectual sophistication, and all but one whom we approached agreed to be interviewed. Rank-and-File is in effect a splinter movement of the National Union of Teachers. Its members, who appear to be mainly under thirty and disproportionately female, feel that the N.U.T. is dominated by headteachers and interested only in salaries. They want to discuss more fundamental issues – the nature of the educative process, the relationship between education and the wider power structure of society, the basis of authority and personal relationships in schools – and their own personal problems, notably 'discipline'.

Members of Rank-and-File are very critical of examinations and all forms of grading and classification, but they say, in despair, at their meetings: 'But I've really no choice about marking and grading their work when I go into school tomorrow.' And they are strongly opposed to the autocratic power of headteachers. They blame the system rather than individuals: conflict is a basic structural fault.

One interviewee – a very deeply committed member of Rank-and-File – explained how the system makes bastards of us all. She reflected on one school in which she taught:

> People don't like to be awkward; they like peace; they don't like to be rude. But to fight you've got to be prepared to be rude. The headmistress in that school was generally respected and liked – she was very humane. But when the fight came (over comprehensive reorganization) and the staff was very polarized, she acted more and more like a head. She was forced into a position by the stress and rigours of her job. At one stage she reduced one of us to tears: at a staff meeting she harangued us publicly – in the end she was talking about extremists and Hitler, and she really stirred it.

This particular member of Rank-and-File showed remarkable insight into the headteacher's position: 'He faces upwards to the local authority, and one of his jobs is to soften and mediate between points in the hierarchy. Their behaviour is not just a personal thing – the head is forced into that role by the position.' But this does not make the lot of teachers any less humiliating: 'Because of the pressures teachers work under, because of the system, they find they have no real control over how they teach and how they carry out the job. And this is a very degrading experience.'

Another Rank-and-File member described the circumstances of her joining:

> Well, I started teaching, and I found my first term shattering. Discipline was such a problem. You had all these wonderful ideas on teaching, and discipline was so hard. And you were given very little support. So I went along to a N.U.T. meeting – I thought they were going to talk about teaching, you see. But they didn't: they talked about finance and the minutes and so on. Later I went to Rank-and-File: there were lots of sympathetic people there, and we talked . . .

Rank-and-File teachers are humiliated by the power of children and by the power of headteachers, and feel degraded and brutalized by exercising power themselves. The real enemy is 'the system'. Another member explained how a headmaster's liberal intentions were defeated by the pressures of his role-obligations:

> In my old school we used to have a lot of staff meetings because the head had ideas in the beginning about being democratic – he didn't want to impose his ideas on us, he said; he wanted to discuss things. But you found that people tended not to want to do the things he thought best, so he did what he wanted, anyway. He was just letting people have a say and ignoring it.

The head is as big a problem as children and she appreciates the predicaments of both. Examples of victimization have influenced her deeply. She told the story of one boy who was systematically humiliated:

> He was very disruptive in class, and the head's solution was just to isolate him, to withdraw him from every single lesson. He sat in the hall for a whole term by himself, everyday. At first teachers took work down to him, but then he was forgotten. And he'd just come back from a Child Guidance Clinic, and it said in his report: 'This child feels neglected'. So the school went even further, and the head actually read the report out loud, at a staff meeting, with tongue in cheek. I just couldn't get over it. And I used to say, 'What are we going to do about this boy?' And they all said, 'What *can* we do, it's the head's decision.' And what's more, he publicly humiliated that boy by announcing that he was a thief. And he put another boy on the stage and shook him by the shoulders when he tackled him over something. That really sickened me. I think that heads are always on the look-out for scapegoats. They don't care as long as they can pin the blame on someone and be seen to assert their authority.

Concern with dignity and degradation runs through the interviews. These teachers realize that if they refuse to humiliate their pupils they will be considered ineffective. A member rather older than the average – a man in his late forties (who has also lived a somewhat episodic life, with periods in journalism and some years in India), who is not displeased to be called a 'middle-aged hippie', reflected on teaching:

> It is really very hard work. I find discipline very difficult. I don't like to use the methods necessary to attain it. I love talking with

the kid and we have a marvellous relationship. I feel I am meeting their emotional and social needs, but not their intellectual needs. When a child told me to 'fuck off', I thought, Yes, he's quite right. I *should* fuck off. Why should I force him to study all sorts of subjects that the curriculum demands?

Although they recount incidents of degradation and humiliation in their schools, they account for their membership of Rank-and-File in terms of long-standing values: 'I'm a revolutionary socialist – that's the key to it, I think. I was in the International Socialists before I was in Rank-and-File. I became rather left-wing at university – I had a left-wing pal with whom I argued far into the night'. Similarly another interviewee:

It's my politics, I suppose. I am left-wing, and at Rank-and-File meetings I have found lots of sympathetic people, the sort I wanted to meet. It was the same at the meeting last night. I thought there were some very intelligent and articulate people. I'll probably join the Communist Party sooner or later.

A young Cambridge science graduate explained his militancy in terms of the social and political values that had matured before he began teaching, but were precipitated by an experience of degradation on a vacation job. His values appear to have made him incapable of coping with the school system. His twin problems, too, are discipline and the headmaster:

I am an International Socialist, and I'd be a militant in any union I joined. It started long before I started teaching. When I was at Cambridge I took a vacation job in a bean factory. We had to sit down by the conveyor belt, watching the beans go by; and if you saw a bean with a stalk, you had to take the bean, remove the offending stalk, and put it back on the belt. It was very boring, and one guy fell asleep with his head on the conveyor belt. So the foreman made us take our chairs out and we had to stand. This led to protest and a strike. It was my political awakening. Before this I'd accepted everything. I went to a direct grant school and didn't question a thing.

Teaching in a comprehensive school has raised acute problems of dignity and deference:

I had trouble very early on because I had all sorts of ideals which just didn't work in practice. I refused to hit the kids, unlike all the other teachers, who were bumpers. I tried to reason with the kids. I think if a kid starts shouting in class it *can* lead to consultation, not confrontation. So my class got a bit out of hand from time to time, but we had some sort of relationship going. But in the head's terms, I had a discipline problem. All the teachers are so conscious of scale posts and promotion prospects that they toe the line. And they bump the kids so they can be seen to be in real control. I have to protect the kids against the head, who fetches them out and canes them. If a kid breaks something in practicals – an old mirror or a test-tube – I always pretend to have done it myself, to save the kid a beating.

Attending meetings of Rank-and-File and interviewing members, one had a strong impression of anxiety and of loneliness. One interviewee said: 'I don't mix much: I'm just sorting myself out. I had psychiatric treatment at the Maudsley for quite a long time. I was quite mature in years when I got away from my mother, if you see what I mean.'

Another young man was interviewed in his attic flat, where he lives alone: a small, dark, untidy and badly furnished room with a tiny kitchen on one side. There were no windows – a door led to the fire-escape and its glass panel was the only source of light. The young teacher switched on a table lamp made from a sauce bottle. There were one or two posters on the wall – 'Remember Derry', and a picture of a Spanish revolutionary facing a firing squad. He was near the end of his probationary year and feared that he would not be confirmed in his post:

> One of the complaints the head made about me was that I didn't talk to members of staff. I did talk to them at first, but I realize now that I've nothing to say to them. All I say to them is 'Good Morning', and I don't really mean that.

'Free Schools' are in the disreputable, experimental margins of society. The teachers meet one critical test of 'alternativeness' in that they have given up paid employment and live on social security in order to teach in these schools. (But they certainly have not rejected work, even if they have rejected careers.) Although they are in the margins of society, they are deeply concerned to establish close relationships with the local community and even to merge with it. (They tend to be somewhat sentimental about 'street culture'.) These teachers have the characteristic concern of the counter culture with authority and hierarchy; they are especially concerned about the constraints of the traditional teacher role. The eight who were interviewed in three schools came from very 'straight' middle-class (even upper-middle-class) homes, but some had experienced a very disorganized upbringing. All recalled the inadequacy and triviality of their university degree courses with horror.

One young woman felt bereft of humanity in her first job in a secondary modern school:

> It was awful, right from the start. I just couldn't be myself. I felt I was acting a part that was alien to me. I couldn't get used to being called 'miss'. I'm not 'miss' – I'm Mary. They expect you to sit on a pedestal and preach to the kids. That's not what educa-tion's about. It's about learning from one another because we've all had different experiences. Even a six-year-old has had different experiences, which I can learn from. Anyway, I talked to some-one involved and decided I'd teach in a Free School full-time. I gave up my job and went on the dole. If we set up as a school for truants they'd pay us £1,600 a year each. But we'd have to re-adjust the kids to go back to an ordinary school. We don't go along with that, of course. So we're on the dole. We could get into trouble. So we all have to pretend to be looking for jobs.

She, too, recalls long-standing if ill-formulated attitudes which were finally crystallized by her first classroom experiences:

> I don't think I thought too much about the system beforehand. Lots of people just drift into teaching. I think my present ideas had been floating around in my head for a long time – it just took the state school experience to make me realize them.

She does not reject conventional school in its entirety:

> Kids still need to learn to read and write. The difference is that they learn how and when they want. The kids choose what to do at any particular time. This doesn't mean that we take a sub-missive role, either. We try to create a community where the autonomy of each member is equally respected. We want to break down the barriers between kids and teachers, older kids and younger kids. Also between the school and the community. Lots of parents are already very much involved. And it doesn't just stop at education: we hope that other community projects will develop, such as playgroups, community transport and

holidays, bulk-buying and legal aid, and so on. Ideally, there should be a whole network of community-based Free Schools.

A former journalist teaching in a Free School said:

I don't have any actual teaching experience, but I've done a lot of work with children, though – I've seen what schooling does to them. My editor wouldn't let me write about it as I wanted. That is why I left journalism. I couldn't write about such a meaningless experience except to say it was just that.

He hopes the Free Schools will not be for ever 'alternative' – that the 'straight' system will be infiltrated, converted, and fall into line.

Another former journalist had had a brief experience of teaching (six months). This had marked her for life:

I was in a slum primary school. This was a most shattering experience. It really was a case of death at an early age. I couldn't stand it – seeing five-year-old kids having all life taught out of them. I had to leave. I think you have to have such an experience to know what it's really like.

A teacher in a Free School in a town in the south-west explained her present position by referring to her experience of university study:

I was at Manchester University. I hated the place. It's such an unwelcoming place if you don't happen to come from there. And my course was awful. I was reading English and the stuff we had to read was really medieval. So I failed my first-year exams and they threw me out. That was nine years ago – things may have changed. I did an external degree at a poly. I do a bit of F.E. teaching, which gives me enough to live on. I'd lived in this town before and liked it. The trouble is that the local education authority is so reactionary. But I think the Chief Education Officer is a liberal man. I don't think you can blame anybody. It's just gone on so long that the system's too big to change.

A second interviewee in this school is a graduate who failed his postgraduate's teacher's certificate. He said:

I got a degree in English then did the education year and failed. And I know why I failed. It was because the headmistress of the school where I did my practice was such an old bat and treated the kids so badly – like heads of cattle – that I wrote an appendix to my dissertation saying exactly what I thought of her and quoting what the kids had said about her. I've enjoyed teaching in a Free School but I'm going back to take the teacher's certificate. I don't think you solve the problem by escaping. You've got to fight within the system.

In the Free Schools they are wrestling above all with the problem of personal meaning and dignity for teachers and pupils. But nobody thinks they've found final answers. It is all frankly exploratory (and some Free School teachers are anxiously aware that it may be dangerously exploratory). In one Free School the teacher was very firmly in charge, and this was pointed out to her. She replied:

This is a problem we've thought about a lot. But when you think about it, hierarchy is based on information: most hierarchies are based on a sort of information gap. We initially had the information on how to set up the school, because of all the research we did. We didn't like it, but it was a question of our assuming charge or the thing collapsing. Now we disseminate information to everyone as it comes in, and in this way we're overcoming what is, I agree, a problem. In real hierarchical structures information is withheld – it's the basis of power, and ignorance is their security.

There is a sense of dislocated upbringing and loneliness running through the interviews with Free School teachers, as there is in the interviews with members of the N.U.S.S. and Rank-and-File. One Free School teacher explained her present outlook by recounting graphically her peripatetic youth:

I went to eleven different schools between the age of eleven and university. I didn't stay at any one long enough to become involved. I ended up at eighteen with the girls I'd been with at eleven at a girls' public school. I felt absolutely shattered by the way my contemporaries had developed – or rather, hadn't developed, compared to the way I'd grown up. I felt very isolated and different. They accepted everything I wanted to question – I just couldn't believe it. I went up to London University to read philosophy. It was awful: so badly thought out and badly taught. I spent most of my time at the Royal Academy. It was such an escape, playing music.

One young woman graduate (a trained and qualified teacher) was interviewed in her small attic room. The Free School in which she had been a full-time teacher had recently closed down. She was wearing a yellow vest, a long cotton skirt, open sandals on bare feet, and no make-up. She smoked cigarettes hungrily throughout the interview. She lived alone in the small room with sloping ceiling, walls painted bright yellow and ceiling dark blue with yellow stars. There was a record-player in one corner, a large mattress covered with an Indian bedspread, vases of dried grasses and peacock feathers, a row of books (mainly Penguin Education Specials), clothes hung on the back of the door, and a poster of Angela Davis on the wall.

In answer to the question: 'What led to your becoming a teacher in a Free School?' she gave the story of her academic life from the time when she was a pupil at a girls' private school in Bournemouth. ('I tried to rebel at first, but then conformed. I tried to find someone in the school who didn't believe in corporal punishment, but there wasn't a soul. So I gave up'.) At the university she read sociology: 'It was really a bad course. We had this professor who insisted that we put both sides of every argument in our essays. He didn't let us take a stand on anything. I learned very little.' Her education year was traumatic: 'I hated the teaching practice. I felt so inadequate.'

Her Free School teaching experience has not brought reassurance. The school closed down partly because it was infiltrated by hippies:

> They had no real commitment. Some gave us real trouble, like the guy who was a real acid head. He was always high and he confided in one of the parents what he was doing. It got around, and soon everyone was saying that we were all on drugs. And then one tried his hand at sex education without telling anyone. We heard about it from the kids and we got really scared wondering what he'd done to them.

She is disconsolate and lonely in her attic: 'I keep thinking that maybe I've fucked up those kids' lives.'

## Conclusion

The members of the N.U.S.S., Rank-and-File and the Free Schools were not arrogant and defiant: they were typically somewhat diffident, anxious, lonely and disturbed – but they were taking a stand, often at considerable personal risk and (in the case of Free School teachers) genuine material hardship, to rescue dignity and humanity in circumstances which they felt were intrinsically dehumanizing and degrading. They were all minority movements,[36] but their devotees are intelligent and articulate, and certainly more important than their numerical strength suggests.

The teachers had often found particular experiences at their schools intolerable, but they were intolerable in relationship to personal values with deep roots in individual histories. These personal histories were not, at least in their earlier phases, records of defiance and rebellion, but, on the contrary, of docility and conformity. Typically the background was high-status home, high-status school, and high-status university. It was in 'good' backgrounds – if often somewhat unstable – that the new generation had characteristically come to consciousness that humanity was inhuman. And rather lonely, timid, anxious and perhaps overly-sensitive people had decided they would fight. They had decided not to be made bastards by the system.

# 9

## Work and the fun ethic

### Work, service and uncareers

The counter culture rejects work but is devoted to service. Thus redefined, work becomes leisure and the whole of life. This is an aristocratic concept. Members of the counter culture work hard at traditional arts and handicrafts because they are means of self-expression; they give personal services simply because we are human. These activities are not contractual obligations. The counter culture rejects as immoral the idea of society based on 'exchange relationships'.

Even the great social contract theorists never wrote work into the social contract. It finds no mention in Rousseau or Hobbes; in Locke it is found in the small print with reference to property rights. (Locke foreshadowed the labour theory of value.) It was Luther and Marx who gave work its portentous character. (Aquinas had given it no particular spiritual significance.) In Marx work is exchanged for sustenance; in Luther it is traded in for salvation.

The counter culture offers service because we are men; it does not offer work as part of a social bargain. It takes service out of the morality of the market place. It rejects work and, on different grounds, it rejects careers. Careers have connotations of power and personal aggrandisement; and orderly careers bind us tight to society. This is the evidence of history and of contemporary socio-logical inquiry.[1] A career in the sense of a succession of related jobs arranged in a hierarchy of prestige fosters long-term perspectives and a rational life-plan. It is even better than a house or a wife. The counter culture logically rejects careers, houses and wives.

Work is no longer a dance; it is a confidence trick. It would be foolish to romanticize work in pre-industrial, seventeenth-century England, or in pre-Reformation Europe. In cottage industries toil was long and arduous; a twelfth-century steward meticulously regulated a peasant's work on the lord's domain. And yet, as Have-lock Ellis maintained in *The Dance of Life*, in simpler, peasant societies, to dance was both to work and to pray.[2] The cathedral choir was a dance floor (in Roussillon right up to the eighteenth century); and dancing expressed the rhythms of work and converted work into art. Dancing expressed the essential unity of life; it arose out of work, love and religion, it penetrated all spheres of life and bound them together. 'It was the dance that socialized man.'

It was Luther, rather than the steam-engine, who gave a new meaning to work. He, and later the Puritans, gave it dominance, a centrality, which it had not had before. They spiritualized work and robbed it of gaiety. Work took the place of repentance as a sign of grace. The beggar lost an honourable place in society. Under the late-Tudor poor law his penalty for a third conviction was death.

The original attitude of the counter culture seven or eight years ago was purist on the question of work: it rejected it in all its guises. In practice this was very difficult to do. And it was profoundly boring. The boredom of 'spectacle' was replaced by the greater boredom of idleness. Purposeful activity – provided its goals are not too far in the future – is no longer a betrayal of counter-cultural morality.

In the rhetoric of the counter culture, work in industrial societies is condemned as 'alienated'; but it is also fraudulent – not because it pays too little, but because it pays too much. It is not really very demanding (although it may ask for high qualifications); it is seldom uplifting; much of it, seen in context, is positively harmful. The counter culture sees clearly that work is unworthy of the solemnity and reverence with which we commonly regard it, and that we grossly exaggerate the talents and training required to perform it. It is no longer needed for salvation. But it impudently claims to dominate our lives. And outside the counter culture it is remarkably successful in doing so.

The economists have begun to share the counter culture's scepticism about the pretensions of work. Does it really 'need' all the qualifications it asks for (and for which it is even prepared to pay)? Ten years ago economists wrote confidently about education as the creation of 'human capital'; now they often speak of education as 'filter'. They are less confident that the extra earnings of the highly qualified represent a real net addition to national income; they may merely, or largely, result from pushing the less well educated into ill-paid jobs.[3]

Employers are often prepared to pay for high-level qualifications: this does not necessarily indicate the need for high-level performance. An employer's tastes may be more important than his needs.[4] The narrowing pay differentials between the 'qualified' and unqualified may indicate that employers in recent years are less willing to pay a tax for qualifications.[5]

Industrial productivity has not been shown to bear a very close, if any, relationship to the qualifications of senior personnel.[6] Layard and his colleagues are deeply sceptical that the senior occupations they studied in more than sixty factories engaged in electrical engineering really 'needed' the qualifications of the men who occupied them.[7] The indications of Dael Wolfle's studies of American talent are that the economy 'needs' the high qualifications of only the most intelligent 10 per cent of the age group.[8]

Work has displaced death and the dance as centres of life. We do not need the prophetic visions of control engineers who write about automation to suggest that work for more than a small minority (perhaps Wolfle's highly intelligent 10 per cent) is unlikely to sustain indefinitely the burden of meaning and significance that we now require it to carry. The counter culture may teach us to treat work and careers with appropriate irreverence and to explore centres of life and meaning in other forms of experience.

The paradox is that the morality of work was never so strong. In our hierarchy of moral values it is almost certainly higher than charity and now probably higher than chastity. The obligation to engage in productive labour is probably stronger and more inclusive than at any time in the past four centuries. Fewer social categories are exempt. Non-work is earned by fifty years of unremitting toil. Idleness is no longer reprehensible only in the poor, even gentlemen are expected to engage in regular, gainful employment. And what is still more to the point, they no longer pretend that they do not, as they commonly did when making their census returns in the nineteenth century. Gainful employment was by definition discreditable and incompatible with the status of gentleman.

In democratizing the world ethic and including within its imperative all except the young, the old, the sick and the maimed, we have strengthened its hold. Two world wars which subjected everyone to call-up, and periods of ensuing scarcity, have helped to make the concept of a leisure class, however appointed, immoral. The overriding work ethic, appropriate in time of total war, or in the early stages of a new economic take-off, is ever less necessary in peace, and increasingly dysfunctional in an automated economy. We probably evaluate our fellows more often in terms of their ability, reliability and endurance as workers than in any other terms. In this sense at least we are now one-dimensional.

The counter culture rejects work as the centre of life. It does not reject activity (although the mystics may try to achieve non-doing as their path to truth). It rejects work with its accretion of meanings acquired over the past four centuries. It squarely rejects 'careers'. Karl Mannheim viewed careers in a similar light and, like the counter culture, made no sharp distinction between 'real' work and leisure. Bureaucracies, said Mannheim, provide a 'chain of assured possibilities of success which, taken as an entity, we usually term a "career".'[9] Such careers twist the soul, principally, thought Mannheim, 'because of the predominance of relations of personal dependence in the bureaucrat's life . . .' Moreover, bureaucracies ration and graduate success, they under-utilize talent and set limits to what the personality can achieve. They create artificial scarcities of human resourcefulness. Success is mapped out in advance, the stages by which the individual proceeds are pre-ordained. Politicians do not have careers: they create their own place for themselves. So do artists and craftsmen. For Mannheim, 'true' work, which is not mutilating, appears to be what self-employed artists, craftsmen and businessmen do. They do not need to escape into a leisure sphere marked off from their work. Work *is* leisure. 'The true artisan and the true tradesman and the true scholar do not really have "spare time" as such.' The poor twisted career-man needs leisure but can't use it: 'He rests – but he does not enter a new world in his spare time.' The crippling nature of his work has made him unfit for anything else.

'Uncareers' is a Birmingham organization which produces *The*

*Directory of Alternative Work.* It advertises activities available in the loose, unstructured margins of contemporary society. Many of these activities are in effect (very badly paid) social work conducted outside the bureaucratic structures of the social services. There is work in residential communities which help people passing through a mental crisis. The directory explains that hospital treatment may be quite inappropriate and advises potential applicants to read R. D. Laing's booklet, *Intervention in Social Situations.* There are a few jobs on organic farms and with work groups making hand-made things – leather-goods, candles, shoes. But most of the work is with associations like the Simon Community which helps vagrants, alcoholics and the homeless and rootless; 'workers usually get £1.50 or a little more per week and their keep.' The directory emphasizes absence of structure in the work situations listed: 'Don't be put off too much by the fact that most things in the directory are fairly informal and non-institutional.' This is the directory for people seeking an uncareer.[10]

The directory lists communes, 'alternative' newspapers, Free Schools, and a variety of art and theatre projects among the opportunities for uncareers. Art, drama, sculpture, community living and social action projects overlap in their concern to provide therapy, more tangible forms of welfare and aid, and opportunities for new and more satisfying forms of self-expression. But the proportion of the population seeking uncareers is certainly small and probably concentrated in the age-range 25 to 35. They represent an anticipatory drift to the margins of society, an exploration of meaningful activity in the absence of work carried out primarily for the production of wealth. They are the counter-cultural young, rejecting ambition and work as a means of personal aggrandisement.

## Satisfaction with the unsatisfying

Social theorists say modern work is alienating and dehumanizing; empiricists, who have actually investigated work experiences, say most people actually like it. 'Job-satisfaction' is widespread and high. The theorists say that modern work devitalizes – either because of technology or bureaucracy or both – but despair of finding an answer in leisure, even though this may become more abundant. Empiricists tend to see work, whatever its intrinsic character, as 'symbolic of a place among the living'.[11] What is alarming is not that we have a high degree of 'alienation' (we don't), but that so many people invest meaningless activity with meaning, trivial work with high significance.

Prominent French sociologists are united in their view that work in industrial societies is anti-human. Friedmann sees routine, mechanized work leading to either apathy and withdrawal or to a feverish hedonism. We have produced a devitalized 'after-work man'. Work and 'time spared' are now sharply distinguished: 'This sharp division of time is not natural to the human species.'[12] Dumazedier is similarly concerned about the unnatural rhythms of modern work and sees the popularity of fishing as 'reaffirming in leisure time the value of those natural rhythms that involve wasting time in the traditional way.' This is compensatory activity which supports the contemporary structure of work by making it tolerable, it plays 'a stabilizing role in modern industrial organization by allowing some aspects of traditional work to survive or be reborn . . .'[13]

Dumazedier thinks satisfactory leisure makes unsatisfactory work tolerable; Ellul thinks it would make it impossible. Only unsatisfactory leisure makes unsatisfactory work bearable. Unsatisfactory leisure is 'functional', it supports the system: 'Man's leisure must reinforce the other elements of this culture so there will be no risk of producing poorly adjusted persons.' The system can stand unassailed because modern work has mutilated man, made him incapable of refreshment in leisure and hence of rebellion at work. 'The melancholy fact is that the human personality has been almost wholly disassociated and dissolved through mechanization.'[14]

Aron is not trapped in the circularity of functional analysis: he thinks that in the long term the answer to dehumanized work will be found in leisure. He sees little possibility of self-realization in work except for a very small minority of top managers who will be involved in decision-making which is 'synthetic and venturesome', interesting and exciting.[15] For the rest, necessarily depersonalized and rational work systems will drive them to weekend cottages as 'compensation for the deficiencies of industrial civilization.'[16] He thinks 'there is reason to fear that in the foreseeable future the feeling of autonomy and responsibility will be reserved for a minority alone.'

Only Fourastié sees the great benefits conferred by mechanized work. He sees through the historian's eye that 'le progrès technique libère les hommes du travail servile; il accroit la durée de leur vie; il augmente leur autonomie par rapport aux besoins physiologiques et par rapport au milieux extérieur; il autorise le passage d'un stade

végétatif de vie à un stade spéculatif . . .' [17] But Fourastié is less
concerned with the personal experience of work in an advanced
technological society than with its general social consequences.
The rise in the standard of living over two centuries is scarcely in
doubt.

Neither Dumazedier nor Aron sees any intrinsic virtue in work:
if leisure can confer a sense of significance, it will do as well or
better. Indeed, Aron concedes that 'we can conceive that men will
find in non-work their reason for living.' This would be progress: 'In
this way industrialization would, so to speak, rise above itself.'
Ellul's plight is that only work will do: 'Work is an expression of
life. To assert that the individual expresses himself in the course of
his leisure . . . is to accept the suppression of the human personality. History compels the judgment that it is in work that human
beings develop and affirm their personality.' But Ellul is at one with
a host of social theorists on both sides of the Atlantic in claiming
that work today is not good enough.

It is curious, therefore, that countless studies of job satisfaction
show such positive results. The conceptual and methodological
difficulties that arise in measuring job-satisfaction, especially by
using poll-type questionnaires, are enormous. But there is a remarkable consistency in the results even when more subtle and indirect
methods of inquiry are used. There is now even considerable doubt
that the car assembly-line worker, who invariably comes at the
bottom of any poll, is as 'alienated' as was once commonly supposed – although the boredom of the job has probably been further
intensified rather than alleviated by technological advance.

It is shameful in Western industrial societies for anyone to con-
fess that he hates his work, dislikes his boss, and has often changed
his job. This is surprising, since work and steady application to a
calling have lost the spiritual characteristics ascribed to them by
Luther and the Puritans. The concept of vocation has been secularized: work is not a religious commitment. It is not associated with
salvation and asceticism, but with prestige and consumption. But
Whyte's 'social ethic' is still a work ethic: 'it rationalizes the
organization's demand for fealty.'[18] Its emphasis on rationality is its
only obvious link with the Puritan work ethic.[19] It is anti-indi-
vidualism: the path to salvation is through the boardroom. Max
Weber's ascetic Puritan entrepreneur experienced 'a feeling of
unprecedented inner loneliness.' He followed his path to salvation
alone: 'No one could help him.' But Weber is wrong in his con-

tention that: 'The Puritan wanted to work in a calling; we are forced to do so.'[20] Work has lost its spiritual meaning but has been invested with deep secular significance.

There is now a very strong cultural bias toward expressing contentment with work. Blauner recognizes this, and the consequent problem of knowing what men 'really think' about work, but nevertheless concludes his survey of research with the claim that: 'The studies of job satisfaction reviewed in this paper further question the prevailing thesis that most workers in modern society are alienated and estranged.'[21] The horrific reports of Chinoy and Dubin from the industrial front in America in the immediate post-war years have not been matched in subsequent research.

Dubin studied the 'central life interests' of industrial workers and concluded that only one in four could be classified as mainly job-oriented. Only some 10 per cent of his 491 relatively low-skilled workers in small midwestern cities saw the social world of work as an important source of satisfaction. Dubin concluded: 'All the communication effort and group dynamics in the world will not alter the basic drift in our society away from a central life interest in work.'[22] Dubin was out to rebut Elton Mayo; everyone since has been out to rebut Dubin. And they have mainly succeeded. Chinoy's classic study of automobile workers preceded Dubin. It was based on long interviews with sixty-two workers. They wanted to get away. Even when they saw pay and conditions as good, 'workers frequently complained that they could see no "future" in the factory and they displayed feelings about their work which can best be summed up in the concept of alienation.'[23]

But they did not reject work. Indeed, their very discontent made them value it more highly: '. . . talk of leaving the factory, particularly when focused upon traditionally sanctioned goals, serves to reinforce the worker's identification with the dominant success values of American culture'.

The difficulty in comparing studies in this field is the variety of concepts and measures employed. What is being measured is variously called satisfaction, involvement, attachment, identification and alienation; moreover, the precise source of satisfaction varies: sometimes it is simply the task, sometimes the job in a more embracing sense, and sometimes the career. Task, job and career may yield quite different levels of satisfaction. Measures of satisfaction, involvement and alienation have become increasingly indirect and sophisticated. But if their validity is suspect – perhaps they tell us little about absolute levels of satisfaction or alienation – they are useful in making comparisons among various occupational groups.

What is remarkable is not variation between 'social classes' and occupations involving different levels and kinds of ability, but overlap and convergence. American studies usually show that lawyers, professors and scientists would try to get the same type of work, if they could start all over again; unskilled workers generally would not. But middle-class white-collar workers would opt for the same kind of work less often than skilled manual workers.[24] In England, Parker found differences of involvement among middle-class occupations, but considerable overlap with manual workers. Twenty per cent of bank employees thought they were using most of their abilities on the job, 40 per cent of manual labourers, and 60 per cent of youth employment and child care workers.[25]

Wilensky defined alienation as 'the feeling that routine enactment of role obligations and rights is incongruent with prized self-image.' In a sample of more than a thousand workers drawn from all occupational levels in the Detroit area, he investigated the extent to which 'prized self-image' matched corresponding attributes of the work situation. His index of work alienation-attachment comprised six items for comparing work with self. Less than 1 per cent proved to be alienated on three or more items. At any occupational level, alienation was negligible. 'By our stringent measures, relating work role to prized self-image, the incidence of alienation is low: only 177 of our 1,156 employed men score "alienated" on even one of the six possible attributes of the work situation; only 51 are alienated on two or more attributes, eleven on three or more.'[26] Social class was a poor predictor of work satisfaction (and more generally of life-styles).[27]

Work not only confirms prized self-images, but may be a central life interest after all. It certainly was for 150 American nurses who were investigated along the lines employed by Dubin. While they tended to prefer a non-work location for informal group participation, they wanted relationships in formal organizations and general activities giving personal satisfaction to be centred on work. At least in terms of the research techniques employed, 'work appears to be a major, if not dominant, interest of the professional nurses who constituted our sample.'[28]

We really have no adequate word to describe the attachment of English industrial managers to their work – unless it is addiction or obsession. They are as 'privatized' as affluent factory workers in that they sharply mark off their work from their homes lives: their wives are very little involved in the social world of the firm. But work infiltrates the home, seeps into their leisure, preoccupies their most private hours, and generally dominates their lonely lives.

In the late 'sixties Sofer studied attitudes to work among executives and technical specialists in an English science-based chemical firm and in a mass production car manufacturing firm. Work was very important in giving significance to their lives; their careers structured time in a meaningful way, dividing their lives into sequences and phases, giving them form and shape.[29] When they placed their jobs on a scale ranging from 'a dominant factor in one's life and a primary source of satisfaction' to 'a source of demand that threatens other activities', the majority were at the former end of the scale. They were heavily dependent on their jobs for a sense of personal worth and made heavy and probably unrealistic demands on work as a source of satisfaction:

> I was struck by the amount of reward, satisfaction and concern for themselves the men seemed to want from their job. They seemed to me (and this is a personal judgment) to be placing more in the way of expectation on their employing organization and seniors than these could reasonably be expected to bear. The picture of the ideal employing organization is so idealistic as to be quite unrealistic.[30]

They were pre-occupied with promotion although it was not of the magnitude to make any marked change in their standard of living, and the outside world would be unable to appreciate the subtleties of organizational rank. In a celebrated paper Davis and Moore argued that the function of social stratification was to ensure that men strove for important and onerous positions.[31] But these executives and technical experts were not playing to an external audience which would applaud their success: 'The men we studied made little or no reference to the implications of their advancement for status in the eyes of a conceptualized wider society.'[32] Organizational rank was its own reward.

Dahrendorf says: 'For the bureaucrats, the supreme social reality is their career . . .'[33] The Pahls take Dahrendorf and Sofer severely to task and confirm the essential point made by both. Their error was to overlook the manager's home-life. When the error is rectified, it is only to show that home-life is completely overwhelmed by work.

The Pahls interviewed eighty-six managers and their wives, mostly in their thirties, but a third over forty. They were concerned to explore the relationship between home and work, and they succeeded in revealing the ambiguous attitudes to work which studies of work in isolation usually miss. The career in itself is not the supreme social reality: 'it is the tension between the conflicting value systems of home and work, of family and "career", which provides the dialectic of social reality for the middle class.'[34]

But work wins. The managers say that their 'greatest achievement' is work, but 'the most important thing' in their lives is wife and children. But they don't behave as if wife and children were especially important: 'These middle managers in British industry appear to be willing slaves to the system; only their wives complain and even they are not sure whether they ought to.'[35] As one wife said: 'His work is not only his hobby, but his life, and he has no spare time . . . he will never alter . . .'[36]

The managers were servile to higher authority, with narrow interests and restricted horizons, without friends and without culture. They obey the board without a murmur, 'happily taking more work home to the dismay of their wives.'[37] They have no outside interests: 'The men appeared to have few interests apart from their work, although we took considerable pains to probe this in the extended interviews.' They were apparently friendless: 'Few talked at any length about their friends, and few seemed to have really close friends.' They have no culture: 'This, then, is a work-dominated generation without capital or "culture", using the term in a restricted and elitist sense.' But they keep their home-life separate from the world of work and do little entertaining for business purposes.[38]

Like Sofer, the Pahls are puzzled why managers should work so hard. 'We have shown that the managers work very hard, but it is not clear why or what for.'[39] It is true that they have an idealized vision of the professions affording non-striving, relaxed and more leisured lives, which they themselves would have preferred. In future, managers may not work so hard, think the Pahls – principally because their wives won't let them.

The disturbing comment on contemporary civilization is not that so many are 'alienated' from their work, but that so many are not. The attitudes of Chinoy's car factory workers made good sense:

they wanted to leave. Sixty-three per cent of the assemblers in an English car factory investigated by Goldthorpe, had never thought of leaving.[40] Attachment to employment seemed to have little connection with task-satisfaction: dislike for unsatisfying work-tasks co-existed with appreciation of the firm as employer. It is true, the relationship was essentially 'calculative', but it was a strong and positive involvement: 'Thus, these workers are disposed to define their relationship with their firm more as one of reciprocity and mutual accommodation rather than as one of coercion and exploitation. And in this sense at least they are far from being alienated.'[41] More objective indicators, like rates of absenteeism and labour turnover, also suggested little alienation.

'Men have attached meanings to their work as wondrously varied as the meanings they have attached to sex and play.'[42] Goldthorpe's studies show the danger of ascribing to technology inevitable alienation from work: 'In brief, we reject the idea that workers respond or react in any automatic way to features of their work situation, objectively considered; and we emphasize the extent to which the "realities" of work are in fact created through workers' own subjective interpretations.'[43] John Cohen had earlier emphasized the importance of such a 'phenomenological' approach to 'the subjective side of work, what work means to the worker.'[44]

American advertising men find the very senselessness of their jobs gives them sense, the rat-race attributes of their jobs give them meaning. The irrationality, powerlessness and senselessness constitute a challenge to manhood: 'The challenge is "be crushed or survive" . . . The response is a Promethean challenge to the gods and the fates.'[45] And so it is that the apartment-building janitor invests his apparently menial and unattractive job with high significance. Apparently tied to his job so that he can deal with mechanical and human emergencies, apparently at the beck and call of tenants, he sees himself as the indispensable guardian of the building, carrying sole responsibility for life and property, 'training' the tenants to behave responsibly, and very much his own boss.[46] The subjective side of work is infinitely malleable.

Erich Fromm explains an unabated addiction to 'alienated' work as a refuge from unbearable boredom.[47] Berger does not think that the ideology of work can indefinitely remain out of line with structural changes. The division of labour has made it ever less possible for most men to 'realize themselves' in work, but they persist in looking for realization. Work is no longer a religious calling:

> At the same time, there persists an ideology of work that continues to present the individual with the expectation that he finds his work 'meaningful' and that he finds 'satisfaction' in it, an ideology that is institutionalized in the educational system (for instance, 'vocational counselling'), in the media of mass communication and, last but not least, in the various occupational and professional organizations.[48]

Berger regrets that modern society does nothing to prepare its members for meaningless lives. It is the argument of this book that the counter-culture is such an exploration of possible ways of meeting precisely this problem.

## A fun ethic?

It has been argued by Dumazedier in France, and more strongly by Roberts in England, that today leisure is 'autonomous' and is the basis of the self-consciousness of modern man. And we are constantly discovering a fun ethic which is allegedly superseding the work ethic. None of these propositions is true. It is important that, in the next two or three decades, they should be.

Ortega y Gasset thought he had observed the emergence of a fun morality in the early nineteen-twenties;[49] John Cohen thought he saw one (of a somewhat debased kind) in the 'spivery' which flourished in the time of scarcity following World War II. He thought that twentieth-century Britain had seen 'an enormous change in the comparative valuation of work and play, a shift of emphasis from production to consumption . . . This changed emphasis has been accompanied by a diminution in the seriousness of work.'[50] Martha Wolfenstein thought she had discovered the emergence of a fun morality in child-care literature.

She analysed themes in child-care literature since 1914: in the earlier years the infant was seen as a stern responsibility; by the nineteen-forties the infant was fun. Parents were now subject to a new imperative: they should enjoy their child. And more generally, 'Not having fun is not merely an occasion for regret, but involves a loss of esteem. I asked myself: What is wrong with me that I am not having fun?' Martha Wolfenstein thought that fun and play had assumed a new, obligatory aspect.[51] Nelson N. Foote thought that sex had become obligatory play. It was true that this play was conducted according to strict rules of reciprocity, but play usually had elaborate rules. Sex as play was appropriate to a leisure-based society: 'In an America which is coming to honour leisure and play, however, not only is our interest in sex capable of infinite elaboration through all the arts, but intercourse itself is likely to gain recognition as an art.'[52]

Anthony Crosland did his best, in the mid-nineteen-fifties, to speed a new fun ethic on its way; but he recognized the heavy weight of the tradition of the Webbs who, in their time, 'were no doubt right to stress the solid virtues of hard work, self-discipline, efficiency, research and abstinence . . .' But Crosland saw correctly the needs of a new age of affluence:

> Posthumously, the Webbs have won their battle, and converted a generation to their standards. Now the time has come for a re- action: for a greater emphasis on private life, on freedom and dissent, on culture, beauty, leisure and even frivolity. Total abstinence and a good filing system are not now the right sign- posts to the Socialist Utopia: or at least, if they are, some of us will fall by the wayside.'[53]

The discussion of contemporary work and leisure is bedevilled by the problem of definition, which is scarcely solved by talking of work and non-work. The non-work sphere of life may be subject to constraints and obligations, especially in the family, and wholly discretionary time may be spent with the seriousness of purpose that usually characterizes work. A sharp distinction between work and leisure is difficult to uphold; but 'discretionary time' is prob- ably a good working definition of the latter. (The line is by no means hard and fast: some senior executives and higher professionals may enjoy a good deal of discretionary time within the normal hours of work, but take home work which constrains their leisure. Routine workers make up for lack of autonomy in work through complete autonomy in leisure.[54]) But the general trend in a plural- istic, segmented society is for work and leisure to move further apart. Their final divorce is the hope for the future.

The process of segmentation can be seen in the privatized leisure of both factory workers and managers. Rapoport argues: 'Family and work are no longer subject to a single overarching set of role prescriptions in an integrated cultural whole, nor are family func- tions as residual as they were . . .'[55] Roberts argues similarly and

approvingly that the life of contemporary man is highly compart-
mentalized, and maintains that the nature of one segment is not
dependent on, and cannot be inferred from, another. Away from
work a man discovers a new self and adopts pursuits 'which bear
little relationship to the roles that his other self plays at work.
The splitting up of the individual's life into discrete parts is one
of the most distinctive qualities of life in modern industrial
society.'[56] But Roberts goes further: leisure has not only
'autonomy', it has primacy: 'the self-consciousness of modern
man is based mainly upon the interests and activities which he
pursues during his leisure . . .' It is not his work, but his leisure,
which shapes his notion of who he is: 'The individual's self-
concept is based upon and reinforced by, the activities he under-
takes during his leisure.'[57] In this sense, says Roberts, we are a
leisure-based society.

He is wrong. But hopefully, he is prophetic. The self-concepts of
people at work which are reported in Chapter seven, show how
work dominates the self-image. This is notably true of the actors; it
is also the case with the skilled factory workers. The most hedon-
istic, leisure-based self-concept of a factory worker was that of a
22-year-old single man. But even here there is an undertone of
concern with work:

> I am very egotistical and a very expert car driver. I am a drinker,
> and unfortunately this heads my list of hobbies. I'm a part-time
> intellectual (learning French) who works in a factory but tries to
> keep his brain active. I hate factory authorities, especially the
> types who try to put over their superiority. I'm a fisherman. I
> don't go regularly, but when I do, I find it a great relief of tensions.
> I hate petty dictators and people who 'create' over trivial things.
> I'm the exact opposite of a ladies' man: I can't find anything to
> say to females I don't know. That is probably why drinking
> heads my list of hobbies. I waste money and have no sense of
> value; I'm an easy-going type, with no sense of urgency.

In the late 'sixties the author investigated the aspirations[58] and
anticipated life-styles[59] of first-year undergraduates in a technological university. They were asked the following question: 'Imagine
you have reached the age of seventy and are looking back over
your life. What are the highlights and achievements you hope to
look back on? List these highlights and achievements with the age
at which you hope they would occur.'

The students who responded were all the first-year males in departments of science and engineering (261) and in the department of social sciences. The life-styles they envisaged were saturated with occupational concerns. This was especially the case with the students of science and engineering. Overall, 68 per cent of all the highlights mentioned were connected with career. Marriage and children constitute the only other sizeable categories, accounting for 18 per cent of all the references. The balance of 14 per cent relate to overseas travel unconnected with career (6 per cent), sports and hobbies (2 per cent), voluntary public work (0·5 per cent) and a miscellaneous 5·5 per cent.

*Table 7* Anticipated highlights in various spheres of life

|  | Career | Marriage | Children | Hobbies, Travel etc. |
|---|---|---|---|---|
| Students of science and engineering N.261 | 69·8% | 10·5% | 6·6% | 13·1% |
| (references 1372) | 957 | 144 | 91 | 180 |
| Social science N.33 | 59·2% | 10·6% | 11·9% | 18·3% |
| (references 235) | 139 | 25 | 28 | 43 |

In the responses of these students there was commonly a lock-step progression of career advancement and family building. But career was the 'independent variable' – family highlights (like having another child) followed on career achievements, except in the case of one social science student quoted below, for whom marriage and family seemed to be a possible substitute or perhaps recompense for achievement in a career.

The life-styles envisaged are illustrated by quoting the highlight lists of four randomly selected students of mechanical engineering, and four students of the social sciences. These are the lists of the engineers. The first: obtain degree; become a good designer; work in various overseas countries age 26–28; become a section leader; become a chief draughtsman (30); become a Member of the Institute of Mechanical Engineers (30); thirties a period of transition from chief draughtsman to technical director; become a Member of the Institute of Production Engineers (35); become technical director

(40). This particular student does not look beyond the age of 40, and he refers to nothing whatsoever apart from his career.

The second mechanical engineer hopes to get his degree and be established in a good job by the age of 25. At 27 he is promoted to a higher position; at 30 he is married and living in a fashionable house; at 35 he is the head of a development team; by 36 he has two children; by 54 both his children are happily married; at 55 he has a commanding position in the firm; at 65 he retires on a good pension.

The third engineer will obtain his degree; by 25 he will be travelling in several countries on business; at 26 he will marry; at 36 he is promoted assistant departmental head; at 37 he makes a successful contribution to engineering technology; at 38 he purchases a modern spacious house; at 42 he is promoted to a management position; at 50 he takes a world cruise; at 60 he retires after a rewarding career.

The fourth engineer obtains his degree; marries at 26; at 28 becomes the father of a boy and is promoted in his job; at 30 he becomes the father of a girl and is promoted again; at 40 he joins the board of directors; at 46 his son enters a university; when he is 51 his daughter marries; at 51 he celebrates his silver wedding; at 55 he becomes a grandfather; at 60 he is buying a detached bungalow by the sea.

The first social science student obtains his degree at 22 and 'an attractive management post in an industrial empire'; at 25 he gets his first managerial position which gives him scope to work on his own initiative and to travel, but also involves danger, hardship and a good salary; at 27 he marries and starts a family; at 32 he is elected to the board of directors and has sufficient security for more expensive holidays; at 45 he is made managing director with power to institute various necessary reforms; at 50 he becomes a grandfather; at 55 he retires and is now able to enjoy cultural and aesthetic things at his leisure.

The second social scientist obtains his degree and a job with a progressive firm. At 26 he says that 'mixed with this material success one can only hope for personal happiness in the form of marriage'. At 29 he is able to judge whether he is really succeeding with his firm; and, if he is not, he changes his job; at 29 he starts a family; from 35 his financial security is assured; by 45 he has progressed in the firm to the position of director. He enjoys 'success from this vital age onwards until by 70 he can retire knowing that his children and grandchildren are financially safe'.

The third social scientist will get a first, a doctorate, a chair in a big university at 35, and will research and write books and articles connected with his field of studies.

The fourth social scientist will get a good degree at 22, a good teaching job at 23 and marry at 24. At 29 he will be made head of department; at 30 his first child will be born, and at 32 his second. At 35 he will become deputy head and his third child will be born. At 42 he becomes headmaster of a secondary school. When he is 48 his first child enters a university. At 50 he is made head of a large comprehensive school and his second child enters a university. His third child enters a university two years' later. At 55 he is promoted to a post in a college; at 60 he retires; and at 62 he can see his children doing well in their jobs.

The forties (at least as seen twenty years in advance) appear to be the career-dominated decade as indicated by the frequency of career statements. By this age references to family have fallen to 10 per cent (from the overall 18), and references to career have risen to 76 per cent (from the overall 68).

Table 8 Proportion of references to career and marriage and children in each decade of life
(294 students)

| Decade | Career | Marriage and children |
|---|---|---|
| 20s | 65·0% | 22·3% |
| 30s | 69·0% | 18·4% |
| 40s | 75·8% | 10·0% |
| 50s | 66·9% | 15·7% |
| Average | 68·2% | 17·9% |

The preoccupation with careers among tomorrow's technocrats is not, perhaps, surprising. The career-lines they project into the future are orderly, progressive, linear. Only the second social science student is tentative, exploratory, envisaging the possibility of changing his career after an experimental start. Their problem will arise if organization-man careers decline sharply in numbers – as Wilensky, for example, predicts.[60] What will these endlessly working and lonely technocrats do – poised rather uneasily between family and career – when there is no work left?

## Discussion

In pre-industrial times, a man spent a great deal of his non-work time burying his relatives. By the time he was fifty he had buried nine of his immediate family, excluding uncles and cousins, and his grandparents who would have died before he was born. Himself one of five children, of whom three would have died by the time he was fifteen, he married at twenty-seven and in turn had five children. Two or three would die before he did. 'A l'époque traditionelle, le mort était au centre de la vie, comme le cimetière au centre du village.'[61] As death has receded, work and careers have assumed a position of centrality.

The very recession of death has made commitment to one calling for life ever less necessary or sensible.[62] The median duration of a marriage has almost trebled since the seventeenth century, from 15 to 41 years. There is now time for two or three careers (or perhaps one career and two or three uncareers). We have not yet come to terms with longevity or rephased the life-cycle to exploit its possibilities and promise of variety. A linear career makes good sense when life is short; a more episodic life-style is appropriate and possible when life is long.

Work within the structure, constraints and imperatives of an orderly career is acceptable to those who score low on the scale of counter-cultural attitudes (see Chapter five), but far less acceptable to those who score high. One of the scale items referred to seeking promotion and climbing the ladder of success: two-thirds of the (low-scoring) 'olders' agreed that this was natural and good, less than a quarter of the (high-scoring) students of art and drama.

Table 9 'To seek promotion and climb the ladder of success is natural and good'.

|  | Strongly agree or agree | Uncertain | Strongly disagree or disagree |
|---|---|---|---|
| Olders (N.63) | 41 (65·1%) | 15 (23·8%) | 7 (11·1%) |
| Students of fine art and drama (N.63) | 14 (22·2%) | 11 (17·5%) | 38 (60·3%) |

Chi-square 35·2   df 2   P< 0·01

The possibility of self-fulfilment through work, on the other hand, is accepted by a far higher proportion of the students of fine art and drama, but by a still higher proportion of olders.

*Table 10* 'Self-fulfilment can be found by working hard to be a success in our jobs'.

|  | Strongly agree or agree | Uncertain | Strongly disagree or disagree |
|---|---|---|---|
| Olders (N.63) | 44 (69·9%) | 8 (12·7%) | 11 (17·4%) |
| Students of fine art and drama (N.63) | 27 (42·9%) | 17 (27·0%) | 19 (30·1%) |

Chi-square 9·4  df 2  P< 0·01

The importance of work as a central life interest and a source of personal meaning still has strong champions, especially, perhaps, among educators. Thus Entwistle would have education reaffirm the centrality of work, for 'to take the earning out of living would be to impoverish life itself.'[63] Clive Bell was quite clear that work was not compatible with a civilized life. Work and success even in the higher professions brings more than touch of barbarism:

How many thousands of barristers, civil servants, and men of business, who left Oxford and Cambridge equipped to relish the best, have become, after thirty years of steady success, incapable of enjoying anything better than a little tipsy lust or sentimental friendship, cheap novels, cheaper pictures, vulgar music, the movies, golf, smoking-room stories, and laying down the law.[64]

Herbert Marcuse has kept consistently to the view that work dehumanizes and degrades, although he has changed his mind about the possibility of avoiding it. In his recent writings he has envisaged the possibility of work largely disappearing with the advent of automation; but there will be an extension of purposeful activity, based on the aesthetic principle rather than the performance principle. In *Eros and Civilization* he states his position most unambiguously:

No matter how justly and rationally the material production may be organized, it can never be a realm of freedom and gratification, but it can release time and energy for the free play of human faculties outside the realm of alienated labour. The more complete the alienation of labour, the greater the potential of freedom: total automation would be the optimum.

Like Marcuse, David Riesman has often changed his mind about the possibility of men being able to renounce the work ethic and turn to leisure for a more satisfying life. In his recent writings he departs from the hope he saw in leisure when he wrote *The Lonely Crowd*, and wants work to be refashioned 'so that man can live humanly on as well as off the job'.[65] He sees a fusion of work and leisure, rather than a separation (corresponding, as he thinks, to more general 'homogenizing' processes at work in society). But he knows that the middle range of 'organization men' are foolish to expect from their work the sense of significance that it formerly afforded: '. . . junior executives may realize that they are not indispensable and that, in an increasingly complex and bureaucratic society, they may be fools to drive themselves only in order to achieve a moderately greater income and vastly greater responsibilities.'[66]

There are signs in survey research on American university campuses that less work-dominated and more 'privatized' forms of life are finding favour with students. Hadden calls them 'The Private Generation'.[67] He found in a national sample of 2,000 college seniors that 82 per cent agreed with the statement: 'My private life will not be sacrificed even if it means making less money.' They wish to escape from bureaucratic constraints in work, and 85 per cent agree that: 'Whether I work for Government or business, I would like a job where I will be more or less my own boss.'

These surveys were carried out in the late 'sixties. In the early 'sixties Riesman had already discerned in the incipient counter-culture on the college campuses the promise of new values, de-emphasized work, and a new civilization:

> In the best of our college students we see a use of leisure that is often admirable . . . serious concern with current issues, with reading and companionship, and often a strong interest in music, drama, literature and nature. We need only compare these students, products of affluence, intelligence and civility, with many of their parents to see that the future of leisure is not merely a dangerous abyss.[68]

It is principally within the counter culture that an unequivocal and unapologetic 'fun morality' is to be found: work is not only de-emphasized and displaced from the centre of life, but the obligation to engage in 'productive' work is not recognized. The justification for activity is personal enrichment and extension of awareness, social service, or frankly enjoyment.

Ambition and striving for success are discreditable; in Charles

Reich's terminology: 'Consciousness III rejects the whole concept of excellence and comparative merit that is central to Consciousness II.'[69] Careers are as discreditable as the ambition they encourage: 'In terms of their own lives, Consciousness III people simply do not imagine a career along the old vertical, escalator lines.'[70] Work in general, and a career in particular, makes us less than human; and support from public funds through the Department of Social Security is no more reprehensible than a salary obtained from a university for research in Sanskrit, and far less than a salary obtained for work in advertising or munitions. 'The great villains of history were busy men, since great crimes and slaughters require great industry and dedication.'[71] Work, no less than power, corrupts. Neither has a wholly human face.

# 10

## A cautious optimism

We have argued that counter cultures arise in rich societies. But they are not simple and direct reactions to unprecedented wealth and new means of production: they are neither ascetic withdrawal out of surfeit and revulsion, nor joyous abandon at the prospect of still greater abundance. Counter cultures arise with steep population growth and intensive migration associated with great economic transformations. In these circumstances traditional social bonds are disrupted and old statuses brought into question. The counter culture is hungry for rootedness and community but lives a life of improvization in loose, shifting social networks. The counter culture is not alienated, but anomic.

There is no deep and irreconcilable split between the political and the aesthetic in counter-cultural actions and beliefs. The counter culture as a group of ideas or as groups of people is apparently splintered, contradictory, divided. But we have argued an underlying unity and demonstrated a high correlation among apparently divergent attitudes. The counter culture has shifted profoundly in emphasis in its short history over less than a decade. It is less innocent and naïve, more pragmatic and instrumental yet probably more interested in madness and meditation, in exploration of the disordered regions of society and the mind. The last boundary to be denied is between madness and sanity.

We have argued that the counter culture is marginal, and that in marginality lies ecstasy – sharpened perceptions and re-ordered perspectives which come from a position outside the taken-for-granted, the socially programmed and the culturally prescribed. It is perhaps only in margins that true learning and self-awareness are possible (as great educators through the ages, with their deep contempt for relevance, have intuitively known): in the margins we are robbed of familiar systems of classification which order, pre-process and filter the bombardment of impression and experience; the world is experienced with a terrifying immediacy and directness. Ecstasy has a ragged edge of melancholy. We have argued for due recognition and reinstatement of marginal men.

We have argued that the counter culture rises with weak rather than strong groups and 'grids' but aspires to the final dissolution of social roles and perceptual–experiential boundaries. And yet it seeks humanness in new categories, holiness in reclassification. It finds unreal and degrading the ancient boundary between men and animals: the counter culture is vegetarian and its imagination is haunted not by metamorphosed animals, but by metamorphosed machines. The confusion of men and machines is the new unclean-liness, the final abomination. We shall see science and scientists, technology and technologists, increasingly segregated and kept firmly in their subordinate, non-human place. In the new classification and definition of holiness the scientist is obscene. The consumption of unprocessed products is ritual purification which keeps man in his proper category and proclaims his holiness.

We have argued that the counter culture very deeply affects a minority of the 'new generation': it is rooted in the generational consciousness of those who were born around 1938–9, were in their 'teens in the late 'fifties, and today are rising forty. The new generational consciousness is the outcome not of repression and deprivation, but of a new affluence and openness; it is non-defer-ential, questioning the legitimacy of all power and authority (and led occasionally into tolerance by questioning the sanctity of the social contract itself. It dares even to question the authority and the legitimacy of majorities).

The counter culture is about human dignity and personal mean-ing: it finds the exercise of power no less degrading than sub-mission. And this is one of its central dilemmas: the innocent anarchism of its first efflorescence has been succeeded by a more realistic exploration not of impractical zero power, but of minimum power. It is involved, like Marcuse, in the difficult definition of 'surplus repression' and acceptance of some inescapable residual. The commune is its principal laboratory for experiments in minimum power. Even sharing needs some organization. There is a tendency for the milk bottles never to be put out.

The counter culture probably 'peaks' in the 'twenties. It is not an exclusively or perhaps characteristically adolescent phenomenon. There may be a second 'peaking' in the late forties, in the form of executive dropout. But this may be no more than early retirement, when 45-year-old accountants decide to live (modestly) on their savings and take up painting and weaving. We have no systematic – or even exploratory – study of executive dropout, which seems to be occurring more widely in America and perhaps gathering momentum here. But we now have no Empire to drop out into; and the Royal Geographical Society is less prone to finance drop-out explorers who disappear up the Niger or set up desert harems. They are to be met with their sleeping bags in colder climes: on the ferry to Iona, or writing fairy tales, painting, and making somewhat inept excavations on Islay and Mull. The Hebridean world is a magical (even mystical) marginal world with a potentially great counter-cultural future ahead.

We have argued that the counter culture is distinguished by its rejection of careers and even of work as conventionally defined; and we suggested at the outset that it had something of the appearance of genteel poverty. This is not the poverty made necessary by overall scarcity; on the contrary, it is voluntary poverty in the context of plenty. (It may take the form of choosing to work in an undemanding and fairly poorly paid job well below one's capacities and qualifications.) But neither is it renunciation and self-mortification. It has, indeed, the mark of an untamed aristocracy rather than a pinched gentility. Its essentially aristocratic posture is notable in its attitude to time, in its contempt for and aloofness from the organization and processes of material production; its disdain for plumbing; and its involvement not in cautious, incremental progressions, but in exploits – discontinuous, unpredictable, without an obvious past or certain future. The counter culture has rediscovered the exploit as a means of expression and education. Life is not decently, modestly, and unobtrusively cumulative: it is periodically explosive, a constellation of exploits rather than a finely graded array of achievements.

There is a sense in which the counter culture is a new leisure class. It is true that the counter culture rejects current conceptions of leisure, which it sees as dehumanized as work – routinized, commercialized, 'not the antithesis of the world of work but, with its pressures (it) identifies itself completely with that world.'[1] And the counter culture is no leisure class as Veblen conceived it: marked, above all, by 'conspicuous consumption'. The counter culture resembles Veblen's leisure class only in the 'irrelevance' of its preoccupations and contempt for industrial production. But Veblen's leisure class, for all its archaic traits of character and 'disserviceable anachronisms', was certainly not 'marginal': it was extremely busy, for it included the occupations of 'government, war, sports and devout observances'. It was deeply rooted in society, even through its leisure activities (in clubs, at race-meetings and country house parties) which added social prestige to power and so turned it into authority. It was rooted, too, through property and its management – and through public honours which tie otherwise very private men to society. The counter culture as leisure class has no such material or symbolic social ties: its marginality is more like the pauper's than the clubman's.

Curiously, the counter culture is often like the social world for which Veblen hankered, and with which he contrasted the new leisure class: peaceful, cooperative, small-scale rural communities which de-emphasized both property and proficiency:

'They are small groups of a simple (archaic) structure; they are economically peaceable and sedentary; they are poor; and individual ownership is not a dominant feature of their economic system . . . Indeed, the most notable trait common to members of such communities is a certain amiable inefficiency when confronted with force or fraud.'[2]

Veblen, at the turn of the century, was pointing the way to the greening of America.

## The significance of automation

We have argued that the counter culture in some sense anticipates a world of great wealth based on a highly automated production system. It does so in the sense that it recognizes the wisdom of living well within the level of consumption that automation makes theoretically possible. The full economic potential is a safety-net that may never be used.

Those who are 'into automation' have an unbounded faith in its revolutionary possibilities. Studies carried out in the nineteen-fifties are replete with examples of greatly increased productivity with a dramatically reduced labour force.[3] Norbert Wiener made confident predictions: it is perfectly clear, he maintained, that automation will produce unemployment 'compared with which the depression of the 'thirties will seem a pleasant joke.'[4] Marcuse saw in such developments unprecedented hope for humanity: 'Utopian possibilities are inherent in the technical and technological forces of advanced capitalism and socialism: the rational utilization of these forces on a global scale could terminate poverty and scarcity within the foreseeable future.'[5]

In England Bagrit argued in the mid-nineteen-sixties that 'We have now reached a point where we could be moving into a golden age for most human beings . . .'[6] He predicted (in his Reith Lectures in 1964) that the concept of charity would be obsolete within twenty-five years since the majority of people would be supported without being productive.[7] Gabor's vision is not dissimilar.[8] Even the middle ranks of 'organization men', it is argued, will be made superfluous by the new information technology.[9]

One of the most recent pronouncements by computer men in America chides the layman for his disbelief: 'The majority of persons outside computer circles totally underestimate (automation's) potential and the speed at which the changes are coming upon us.'[10] They foresee unprecedented changes in the next fifteen years: 'The potential wealth that the good use of computers opens up to us is staggering.' Their most cautious estimate is that within two decades the average American will work a four-day week and take three months' vacation a year.[11]

But it never seems quite to happen. On the contrary, labour shortages seem to become more acute and advanced economies survive only by importing cheap labour on a very large scale. (Thus in 1963 foreign workers constituted no less than 12 per cent of Switzerland's total population; a more modest 2·2 per cent in France and 1·5 per cent in Germany.[12]) 'Abnormal' circumstances always seem to intervene and upset predictions. Thus Pollock, in the nineteen-fifties, foresaw a large 'surplus population' and argued that only America's war economy in times of peace had prevented a reduction of the labour force by 15 per cent.[13]

Bagrit foresees a version of the counter culture as a direct outcome of automation, great wealth and a largely redundant population. The counter culture anticipates the future in a more subtle
and appropriate way. For the counter culture confronts the paradox
that an over-rich society cannot consume all that it can produce.
Rich postindustrial societies choke on their wealth. The counter
culture appropriately anticipates the future by cultivating a simple
life. The point at which the postindustrial society is most effective
is significantly below its level of maximum production. Thus, as
Illich points out (in *Tools for Conviviality* and elsewhere), we reach
a point in our consumption of motor cars where we lose more time
than we gain by using them: they create more distances than they
help to bridge. Our consumption of schooling, health services and
other commodities reaches a similar watershed. There will probably
be no need to wait hopefully for all men to renounce greed so that
consumption may fall to a level below which this inversion occurs;
transport systems and formal, qualified-teacher-run schools will
simply become inoperative: most adults would have to become
teachers and we should reach most urban destinations faster by
bike.

It is a further paradox of the highly developed postindustrial
society that many goods and services become more expensive as
they become less valuable to the consumer. Costs rise as utility
declines. (Motor cars are again a good example, and so is formal
education.) This is, perhaps, some consolation for the dispossessed.
But in over-rich societies many services previously available to most
people at low cost are accessible only to the very rich. This is partly
because we insist on professionalizing (and paying correspondingly
professional salaries for) quite humble services which require modest
talents (a partial solution to the overproduction of highly educated
men and women who expect high returns from their long years of
schooling). The deprofessionalization of subprofessional services (in
the less skilled sectors of education, medicine, social work, commerce and engineering) would be painful and perhaps politically
suicidal – but finally inevitable when we face up to the absurdity
that in societies of unprecedented wealth most citizens cannot
afford services readily available (albeit on an unprofessional basis)
in simple societies of abject poverty. The promised superabundance
of postindustrialism is credit that must never be cashed in full, a
promissory note that cannot be honoured. It is for life within limits
below the theoretical full potential of a postindustrial economy that

the counter culture is frugally vegetarian and without appetite for haute cuisine.

## The dialectical process

The counter culture is transforming itself, and there are signs that it is modified by, and in turn deeply modifies, the dominant society. This is the nature of the dialectical process. Modifications are not 'compromises'. The counter culture will not be 'absorbed', but its marginality is likely to be less stark, and its influence more widely pervasive – especially with reference to work, authority, levels of consumption and attitudes to pollution.

Americans who have come to equate the counter culture with separatist communes, social islands with only tenuous connections with the mainstream society, seem pessimistic about its future. ('In spite of the fervor of the initial bearers of the counter-cultural idea, its survival is quite an open question. Robert Owen's utopia in New Harmony, Indiana, is today only a memory. Noyes' Perfectionists at Oneida have been reduced to a trademark for silverware . . .'[14]) In an attempt to answer the question: Will the counter culture survive? they have engaged in ingenious historical-comparative studies.

Kanter examined the histories of ninety-one utopian communities founded in America between 1780 and 1860.[15] Thirty were sufficiently well documented regarding their beliefs, practices and internal structures to make comparative studies possible. Nine were regarded as successful because they survived for more than twenty-five years, twenty-one as unsuccessful because they survived for less. (The cut-off at twenty-five years was taken since this is 'a sociological definition of a generation' and a longer life-span implies that the founders were succeeded by at least one generation.) Among the successful were the Shakers (180 years) and Zoar (eighty-one years); among the unsuccessful Bishop Hill (fourteen years) and Wisconsin Phalanx (six years).

The successful were distinguished from the unsuccessful chiefly by the efficiency of their 'mortification mechanisms'. They effectively reduced the individual's sense of autonomous identity through confession, self-criticism and public denunciation; they were remarkable for abstinence and austerity and often for geographical isolation. 'A special term for the outside world, a negative attitude toward the outsider, the failure to read outside newspapers or celebrate national patriotic holidays, a distinctive language and distinctive style of dress also promote insulation.' Loyalty came from sacrifice, from renunciation or 'investment'.[16]

Celibacy is a potent mechanism of sacrifice and renunciation and appears to be a good predictor of utopian survival. But free love, though experientially opposite is 'functionally alternative': both celibacy and free love undermine the family and forbid individualistic ties. Both weaken the bond with the wider society. This appears to be the one ray of hope for the counter culture today.

But it is false to equate the contemporary counter culture with monasticism and its variants. (It is also inadequate to explain the survival of groups in exclusively social-psychological terms without reference to their place in the social structure.)

And in fact the most recent (1973) accounts that we have of American communes do not match the monastic model with regard to their culture, structure or relationship to the wider society. It is true that communes are changing, becoming more organized, and are engaged in more purposeful activity than formerly. One urban commune in Michigan continues after nine years with the same membership of twenty-two persons. But it changed around 1970 and its members see the earlier years as rather senseless and even hysterical. Today it provides a wide range of social services from a food co-operative to an artists' workshop and community gardening.[17]

Communications among communes is good: 'In the San Francisco Bay area a private commune newsletter circulates among over three hundred communes. Each issue is hand-lettered, hand-bound, tied with thread, and illustrated. Each copy is a work of art, hand-delivered to communes in its circulation list . . .'[18]

And even in New England communes have established good relationships with the local society: they interact with it, influence it, and are increasingly supported by it:

Before 1968 there were many stories in the papers of harrassment of communes, but these have largely disappeared. Good relations with neighbours are a high priority for communards who are more dedicated than desperate in their efforts to change society; 'They think we're crazy but they love us', is a typical comment from a rural commune in New England. Neighbours learn to respect the capacity of the rural communards for hard work, their interest in traditional wisdom and skills, and their willingness to help others. On the other hand, the neighbours have learned to tolerate (and in some cases to enjoy) a certain amount of nude farming, pot smoking, and blurring of sex roles as women show up to help on the hay waggon, leaving men to tend the babies.[19]

Culture and counter culture do not stand as polar opposites; the main culture provides more support for the counter culture which now has 'a new patience and historical sense, perhaps derived from Mao and Oriental philosophy'.

While work becomes more restrictive, the straight culture becomes more unbounded, expansive, as it is coloured by the counter culture with which it interacts. Daniel Bell has described the recent expansion of straight middle class culture:

> Everything is now available, and Hindu mantra and Tantric mandalas, Japanese prints and African sculptures, Eskimo music and Indian ragas all jostle one another in 'real time' within Western homes. Not since the age of Constantine has the world seen so many strange gods mingling in the meditative consciousness of the middle class mind.[20]

Even the English public schoolboy appears to have veered in the direction of the counter culture. It is true that English public schools still provide a disproportionate number of our Apollonian élites; but their product turns increasingly, apparently, to a more Dionysian style of life.

Public schoolboys, we are told on high authority, no longer wish to manage and to lead. In *The Director* (September 1973) Miss Joan Hills, Appointments Registrar at the Independent Schools Careers Organisation since 1948, claims that today's public schoolboy has an accent which is mid-Atlantic, disc-jockey, or carefully cultivated working-class; and an appearance which is cosmopolitan-dropout. 'The old idea of leading people has given way to a wish to help them or at least to communicate with them on the same level.' But these attitudes are not merely negative: they reflect the public schoolboy's 'positive desire for a new kind of society.' Public schoolboys who decide against higher education tend nowadays to end up not with firms in the City, which are still anxious for their services, but on the fringes of the art world, as antique dealers, art auctioneers, or on the staff of art galleries and museums. But the majority go on to universities and then seek professional qualifications for a career 'which they believe they will enjoy and preferably has some bearing on the quality of our life and surroundings'. Power is not coveted: 'Social goals . . . have become paramount, taking the form of a growing interest in the environment in all its aspects.' 'The art schools are all overflowing – art, after all, has a direct effect on the environment.' These apparent changes in the outlook of English public schoolboys are unlikely to have arisen from radical changes in the teaching, curriculum or ethos of the schools. The counter culture appears to have had an impact on one of the key institutions of the English Establishment.

When he studied utopian movements, Karl Mannheim tied their development closely to the social structure. More than forty years ago he foresaw something of modern counter-cultural utopias; and he feared for their survival because he believed they would no longer be rooted in social class. The new utopia would be a movement of intellectuals widely conceived: they would not merely be those who bore the outward insignia of education, but those who were 'interested in something else than success in the competitive scheme that displaces the present one.'[21] He feared their dissociation from society and the failure of the dialectical process.

The new utopia would be simply retreatist. Socially unattached intellectuals would be recruited from all strata of society and would have no social-class base; they would probably 'consciously renounce direct participation in the historical process. They become ecstatic like the Chiliasts, but with the difference that they no longer concern themselves with radical political movements.' The new ecstasy would be socially disembodied: 'This a-historical ecstasy which had inspired both the mystic and the Chiliast, although in different ways, is now placed in all its nakedness in the very centre of experience.' Existentialism, thought Mannheim, was the main reason for this: '. . . many non-academic thinkers like Kierkegaard, in the quest of faith, discard all the concrete historical elements in religion, and are ultimately driven to a bare ecstatic "existence as such".' By thus removing the chiliastic movement from the midst of culture and politics, the purity of ecstasy might be preserved, 'but it would leave the world without meaning and life'.

Ten years ago the author concluded *Youth and the Social Order* in despair. Youth, it seemed, would be contained, absorbed, after a protracted period of quarantine. This book ends on a note of qualified hope. It seems likely that more people will have opportunities for ecstasy, and more people will refuse to be things. Mannheim knew the deadness that was inevitable if the ecstatic counter culture failed:

> But the complete elimination of reality-transcending elements from our world would lead us to a 'matter-of-factness' which ultimately would mean the decay of the human will . . . The disappearance of utopia brings about a static state of affairs in which man himself becomes no more than a thing.

Our contemporary utopia is in fact caught up in political and social action; we cannot disentangle mystics and militants. There are fewer 'things' around than ten years ago. The counter culture changes, and straight society with it. But the future does not appear to be without meaning or life. Advanced, complex and rapidly changing plural societies are likely to raise unending problems of holiness and provide possibilities for ecstasy. Mannheim's dictum seems apposite: 'The meaning of history and life is contained in their becoming and in their flux.'

# Notes to chapters

CHAPTER 1

1  F. Musgrove, *Youth and Social Order* (1964, 1966, Routledge and Kegan Paul; 1965, Indiana University Press).
2  Margaret Mead, Social Change and Cultural Surrogates' in C. Kluckhohn and H. Murray, *Personality in Nature, Society and Culture* (1948, Alfred A. Knopf: New York).
3  David Riesman, *The Lonely Crowd* (1950, Yale University Press).
4  See J. Pitts, 'The Family and Peer Group' in N. W. Bell and E. F. Vogel, *An Introduction to the Family* (1960, Free Press: Glencoe, Ill.) and A. Berge, 'Young People in the Occident and Orient', *International Journal of Adult and Youth Education* (1964).
5  P. Abrams and A. Little, 'The Young Voter in British Politics', *British Journal of Sociology* (1965).
6  F. Musgrove, 'Inter-generation Attitudes', *British Journal of Social and Clinical Psychology* (1963). Cf. J. F. Morris, 'Adolescent Value-judgements', *British Journal of Educational Psychology*, 1958, and F. S. Niles, *The Influence of Parents and Peers on Adolescent Girls* (1968, unpublished M.Ed. thesis, University of Manchester).
7  N. W. Riley and M. E. Moore, 'Adolescent Values and the Riesman Typology: an Empirical Analysis' in S. M. Lipset and L. Lowenthal, *Culture and Social Character* (1961, Free Press: New York). See also B. M. Berger, 'Adolescence and Beyond', *Social Problems* (1963).

8 J. A. Kahl, 'Educational and Occupational Aspirations of "Common Man" Boys', *Harvard Educational Review* (1953).

9 W. A. Westley and F. Elkin, 'The Protective Environment and Adolescent Socialization', *Social Forces* (1957).

10 P. E. Jacob, *Changing Values in College* (1957, Harper: New York).

11 M. A. Davidson and C. Hutt, 'A Study of 500 Psychiatric Patients', *British Journal of Social and Clinical Psychology* (1964).

12 F. Zweig, *The Student in the Age of Anxiety* (1963, Heinemann: London), pp. xiii–xv.

13 See F. Musgrove, 'Childhood and Adolescence', *The Educational Implications of Social and Economic Change* (1967, Schools Council Working Paper No. 12: H.M.S.O.).

14 See F. Musgrove, 'The Problem of Youth and the Structure of Society in England', *Youth and Society* (1969).

15 Only some 14 per cent of males in the age-group 20–24, who left school at fifteen or under, were in middle-class occupations, compared with almost twice that proportion (27 per cent) of males over forty-five who left school at the same age. The disparity was less marked for those who left school at seventeen or above: 82 per cent of the men in the younger age-range were in middle-class occupations, 87 per cent of those over forty-five. The corresponding percentages for those who left school at sixteen were 55 and 72. See D. J. Lee, 'Class Differentials in Educational Opportunity and Promotion from the Ranks', *Sociology* (1968), Table VIII, p. 307.

16 See *Youth and the Social Order*, Chapter Three, 'The Invention of the Adolescent'.

17 Ibid., pp. 155–6.

18 H. Bourges, *The Student Revolt: The Activists Speak* (1968, Jonathan Cape, London), pp. 85 and 88.

19 Richard Startup, 'Why Students Wish to Reform University Government', *Research in Education* (1964).

20.

| | Occupationally frustrated students of music (N.13) | Occupationally frustrated students of painting and sculpture (N.33) |
| --- | --- | --- |
| Counter-cultural scale score: | 145·4 | 168·0 |
| | $t = 3·36$ df 44 $P < 0·01$ | |
| Activist (scale B) score: | 39·3 | 49·5 |
| | $t = 3·38$ df 44 $p < 0·01$ | |

21 *The Hornsey Affair* (1969, Penguin Books: Harmondsworth).

22 Ibid., p. 68.

23 Ibid., p. 187.

24 Ibid., p. 66.

25 Stephen Hatch, 'Students Protesters: Supporters and Opponents', *Research in Education* (1972).
26 See C. M. Arensberg and S. T. Kimball, *Family and Community in Ireland* (1940).
27 Kenneth Westhues, *Society's Shadow, Studies in the Sociology of Counter Cultures* (1972, McGraw-Hill Ryerson: Toronto), pp. 9–10.
28 Westhues, op. cit. p. 45.
29 Karl Mannheim, *Ideology and Utopia* (1960, Routledge: London), p. 190.
30 E.g. R. S. Kanter, 'Commitment and Social Organization. A Study of Commitment Mechanisms in Utopian Communities', *American Sociological Review* (1968).
31 E.g. Westhues, op. cit.
32 Mannheim, op. cit., p. 24.
33 Westhues, op. cit., p. 11.
34 Ibid., p. 18.
35 Ibid., p. 22.
36 Ibid., p. 15.
37 See Ross V. Speck, *The New Families* (1972, Tavistock: London).
38 Mannheim, op. cit., p. 179.

## CHAPTER 2

1 Lewis S. Feuer, *The Conflict of Generations* (1969. Heinemann: London), pp. 436–491.
2 L. Yablonsky, *The Hippie Trip* (1968, Pegasus: New York).
3 Education at Berkeley. *Report of the Select Committee on Education* (1966, Berkeley).
4 See D. Cohn-Bendit's interpretation of events in Hervé Bourges, *The Student Revolt. The Activists Speak* (1968, Panther Books), p. 107.
5 Charles A. Reich, *The Greening of America* (1971, Allen Lane, The Penguin Press), p. 164.
6 Herbert Marcuse, *An Essay on Liberation* (1969, Allen Lane, The Penguin Press), p. 22.
7 Jack Levin and James L. Spates, 'Hippie Values', *Youth and Society* (1970).
8 For an examination of the ethos of social-work and management training – which has many obvious echoes in the ethos of the counter culture – see Paul Halmos, 'The Personal Service Society', *British Journal of Sociology* (1967).
9 John Hoyland, 'The Long March Through the Bingo Halls', *Oz* (January/February 1973).
10 Ibid.
11 Reich, op. cit., p. 164.
12 See Ted Goertzel, 'Generational Conflict and Social Change', *Youth and Society* (1972).
13 Reich, op. cit., p. 2.

14 See Paul Levy, *The Really Interesting Question and Other Papers* by Lytton Strachey (1973, Weidenfeld and Nicolson).
15 See E. M. Forster, 'The New Economy with the Old Morality' in Anthony Arblaster and Steven Lukes (eds.), *The Good Society* (1971, Methuen).
16 See T. Blackstone and R. Hadley, 'Student Protest in a British University: Some Comparisons with American Research', *Comparative Education Review* (1971).
17 Richard Mills, *Young Outsiders* (1973, Routledge and Kegan Paul), p. 29.
18 J. Milton Yinger, 'Contraculture and Subculture', *American Sociological Review* (1960).
19 Robert-Gussner, 'Youth: Deauthorization and the New Individualism', *Youth and Society* (1972). For Roszak the counter culture is counter less to bourgeois economic organization than to positivist science: it is '. . . a cultural constellation that radically diverges from values and assumptions that have been in the mainstream of our society at least since the Scientific Revolution of the seventeenth century' (Roszak, op. cit., p. xii).
20 Mills, op. cit., pp. 75–6.
21 D. Matza, *Becoming Deviant* (1969, Prentice-Hall: Englewood Cliffs), p. 68.
22 Mills, op. cit., p. 60.
23 Mary Douglas, *Natural Symbols* (1970, Barrie and Rockcliff), p. 153.
24 For a study of this new counter-cultural pragmatism see William C. Crain, 'Young Activists, Conception of an Ideal Society', *Youth and Society* (1972).
25 Hoyland, op. cit.
26 Keniston, op. cit.
27 Jack Levin and James L. Spates, 'Hippie Values. An Analysis of the Underground Press', *Youth and Society* (1970).
28 Mills, op. cit., p. 133. 'Essentially a pop festival was a sacred drama – the collective re-enactment of the archetypal event in the career of the hip outsider' (p. 165).
29 See Jeremy Seabrook, 'Brief Sojourn', *New Society* (3 May, 1973).
30 Peter L. Berger and Brigette Berger. 'The Bluing of America', *The New Republic* (3 April, 1971). Cf. Roszak, op. cit.: 'At this point, the counter culture I speak of embraces only a strict minority of the young and a handful of their adult mentors' (p. xii).
31 Adam Curle, *Mystics and Militants* (1972, Tavistock), p. 72.
32 Ralph H. Turner, 'The Theme of Contemporary Social Movements', *British Journal of Sociology* (1969).
33 Kenneth Keniston, *The Uncommitted* (1960, Harcourt, Brace and World: New York), p. 197.
34 L. Kohlberg, *Stages in the Development of Moral Thought and Action* (1969, Holt, Rinehart and Winston: New York).
35 Bennett M. Berger, 'On the Youthfulness of Youth Cultures', *Social Research* (1963).

36 See Rosalind Morris, 'Squatters' Community', *The Observer* (4 March, 1973).
37 See Linda Blandford, 'Towards a New Jerusalem', *The Observer* (11 February, 1973).
38 Mills, op. cit., p. 113.
39 Curle, op. cit., p. 67.
40 *Directory of Communes* (1972, Bluebell Printing Company, King Street, Cambridge).
41 Kenneth Westhues, 'Hippiedom 1970: Some Tentative Hypotheses', *The Sociological Quarterly* (1972).
42 Edmund R. Leach, *A Runaway World?* (1968, O.U.P.), p. 44.
43 Bennett Berger et al., 'Child Rearing Practices in the Communal Family' in A. S. Skolnik and J. H. Skolnik, *Family in Transition* (1971, Little, Brown & Co.: Boston).
44 Ross V. Speck, *The New Families* (1972, Tavistock), p. 49.
45 Ibid., p. 179.
46 Westhues, op. cit.
47 Neal Ascherson and Colin Smith, 'The Mind of the Angry Brigade', *The Observer* (10 December, 1972).
48 David Matza, *Delinquency and Drift* (1964, John Wiley: New York), p. 69.
49 Howard S. Becker, *Outsiders* (1963, Free Press: New York), p. 42.
50 Ibid., p. 42.
51 E.g. Edwin M. Lemert, *Human Deviance, Social Problems, and Social Control* (1967, Prentice-Hall: Englewood Cliffs, N.J.).
52 Mills, op. cit., p. 74.
53 Ibid., p. 74.
54 Ibid., p. 98.
55 J. A. Jackson, *Migration* (1969, Cambridge University Press), p. 3.
56 S. M. Lipset, 'Student Politics in Comparative Perspective', *Daedalus* (Winter 1968).
57 K. E. Gales, 'A Campus Revolution', *British Journal of Sociology* (1966).
58 See A. H. Richmond, 'Sociology of Migration in Industrial and Post-Industrial Societies' in Jackson, op. cit.
59 S. N. Eisenstadt, *The Absorption of Immigrants* (1954, Routledge and Kegan Paul).
60 Donald A. Schon, *Beyond the Stable State* (1971, Temple Smith), pp. 23 and 28.
61 Edmund R. Leach, 'The Study of Man in Relation to Science and Technology', *Journal of the Royal Society of Arts* (June 1973).
62 Ibid.
63 Robert K. Merton, 'Bureaucratic Structure and Personality', in *Social Theory and Social Structure* (1957 revised edition, Collier-Macmillan: London).
64 See Peter M. Blau, *The Dynamics of Bureaucracy* (1963, University of Chicago Press).

65 See Harry Cohen, 'Bureaucratic Flexibility: Some Comments on Robert Merton's "Bureaucratic Structure and Personality"', *British Journal of Sociology* (1970).
66 M. Crozier, *The Bureaucratic Phenomenon* (1964, Tavistock), p. 184.
67 Schon, op. cit., pp. 111–115.
68 Mary Douglas, *Natural Symbols* (1973, Penguin), p. 81.
69 Ibid., p. 169.
70 Ibid: 'Whether it be rules of monetary exchange, debit and credit, or rules of etiquette and hospitality, the system constitutes an oppressive grid. Londoners too know what this can mean. As a system of control industrial society is impersonal. Some more than others feel their lives controlled not by persons but by things' (p. 90).
71 Ibid., p. 113.
72 Ibid., p. 114.

CHAPTER 3

1 H. J. Eysenck, 'Personality Patterns in Various Groups of Businessmen' in *Occupational Psychology* (1967).
2 Edmund Leach, *A Runaway World?* (1968, Oxford University Press).
3 Herbert Marcuse, *An Essay on Liberation* (1969, Allen Lane, the Penguin Press), p. 37.
4 Jacques Ellul, *The Technological Society* (1965, Jonathan Cape: London, trans. John Wilkinson), p. 404.
5 Ibid., p. 142.
6 Ibid., p. 425.
7 Ibid., p. 426.
8 Oswald Spengler, *The Decline of the West* (1926, Allen and Unwin: London, trans. Charles F. Atkinson), p. 505.
9 R. K. Merton, *Social Theory and Social Structure* (1957, Collier-Macmillan: London, ch. XVIII, 'Puritanism, Pietism and Science'.
10 Spengler, op. cit., p. 40.
11 T. Roszak, *The Making of a Counter Culture* (1970, Faber and Faber: London), p. 142.
12 A. Toffler, *Future Shock* (1970, Bodley Head: London), p. 320.
13 C. Hampden-Turner, *Radical Man* (1971, Duckworth: London), p. 367.
14 P. E. Slater, *The Pursuit of Loneliness* (1970, Beacon Press: Boston), p. 132.
15 Charles A. Reich, *The Greening of America* (1971, Allen Lane, the Penguin Press), p. 51.
16 See Norman O. Brown, *Life Against Death* (1959, Routledge and Kegan Paul), especially chap. XII, 'Apollo and Dionysus'.
17 Friedrich Nietzsche, *The Birth of Tragedy* (1909, Foulis: Edinburgh and London, trans. W. A. Haussmann), p. 22.
18 Ibid., p. 41.
19 Ibid., p. 26.

20 Ibid., p. 30.
21 Ibid., p. 26.
22 Spengler, op. cit., p. 183.
23 Ibid., p. 503.
24 Ruth Benedict, *Patterns of Culture* (1961, Routledge and Kegan Paul: London), p. 178.
25 Cf. Lauren Langman, 'Dionysus – Child of Tomorrow', in *Youth and Society* (1971).
26 Gordon Childe, *What Happened in History* (1943, Penguin), pp. 16–17.
27 I. C. Jarvie and Joseph Agassi, 'The Problem of Rationality and Magic', *British Journal of Sociology* (1967).
28 J. G. Frazer, *The Golden Bough* (1927, Macmillan: London), vol. 2, p. 510.
29 Ibid., p. 511.
30 Alvin W. Gouldner and Richard A. Peterson, *Notes on Technology and the Moral Order* (1962, Bobbs Merrill: New York), p. 61.
31 Ibid., p. 36.
32 Max Webber, *The Protestant Ethic and the Spirit of Capitalism* (1930, Allen & Unwin: London, trans. Talcott Parsons), pp. 181–2.
33 R. S. Lopez, 'The Trade of Medieval Europe: The South' in M. Postan and E. E. Rich, *The Cambridge Economic History of Europe* (1952, Cambridge University Press), p. 289.
34 E. M. Carus-Wilson, 'An Industrial Revolution in the Thirteenth Century', *Economic History Review* (1941).
35 M. Postan, 'The Trade of Medieval Europe: The North' in M. Postan and E. Rich, *The Cambridge Economic History of Europe* (1952, Cambridge University Press), p. 161.
36 Lopez, op. cit., p. 297.
37 Ibid., p. 298.
38 J. U. Nef, 'The Progress of Technology and the Growth of Large-scale Industry in Great Britain 1540–1640', in *Economic History Review* (1934).
39 R. H. Tawney, *Religion and the Rise of Capitalism* (1938, Penguin: Harmondsworth), p. 211.
40 H. M. Robertson, *Aspects of the Rise of Economic Individualism* (1935, Cambridge University Press), p. 8.
41 Ibid., p. 256.
42 Tawney, op. cit., p. 94.
43 H. Luthy, 'Once Again: Calvinism and Capitalism' in S. N. Eisenstadt, *The Protestant Ethic and Modernization* (1968, New York: Basic Books).
44 Tawney, op. cit., p. 218.
45 Weber, op. cit., p. 180.
46 Robertson, op. cit., p. 56.
47 Ibid., p. 56.
48 Merton, op. cit., 'The exaltation of the faculty of reason in the Puritan ethos – based partly on the conception of rationality as a curbing device for the passions – inevitably led to a

sympathetic attitude towards those activities which demand the constant application of rigorous reasoning . . . the combination of rationalism and empiricism which is so pronounced in the Puritan ethic forms the essence of modern science' (p. 579).

49 Weber, op. cit., p. 117.
50 Alan Macfarlane, 'Witchcraft in Tudor and Stuart Essex' in Mary Douglas, *Witchcraft Confessions and Accusations* (1970, Tavistock: London), and *Witchcraft in Tudor and Stuart England* (1970, Routledge and Kegan Paul: London).
51 Keith Thomas, *Religion and the Decline of Magic* (1971, Charles Scribner's Sons: New York), p. 498.
52 Michael Walzer, 'Puritanism as a Revolutionary Ideology' in S. N. Eisenstadt, op. cit.
53 Ibid.
54 Richard G. Wilkinson, *Poverty and Progress* (1973, Methuen), p. 81.
55 Gordon Childe, op. cit., p. 59.
56 Postan, op. cit., p. 160.
57 Lopez, op. cit., p. 293.
58 Norman Cohn, *The Pursuit of the Millennium* (1957, Secker and Warburg: London), p. 313.
59 S. T. Bindoff, *Tudor England* (1950, Penguin), p. 13.
60 Thelma McCormak, 'The Protestant Ethic and the Spirit of Socialism', *British Journal of Sociology* (1969).
61 Thomas, op. cit., p. 664.
62 Jacob Burckhardt, *The Civilization of the Renaissance* (1945, Phaidon Press: London), p. 273.
63 Ibid., p. 217.
64 Ibid., p. 52.
65 John Ruskin, *The Stones of Venice* (1881, George Allen: London), vol. 2, p. 9.
66 Ibid., p. 6.
67 Ibid., p. 46.
68 R. S. Lopez, *The Three Ages of the Italian Renaissance* (1970, University of Virginia Press), p. 16.
69 Alfred von Martin, 'Sociology of the Renaissance' in K. H. Dannenfeldt, *The Renaissance* (1959, Heath & Co.: Boston).
70 Lopez, op. cit., p. 15.
71 R. S. Lopez, 'Hard Times and Investment in Culture' in K. H. Dannenfeldt, *The Renaissance* (1959, Heath & Co.: Boston).
72 Peter Burke, *Culture and Society in Renaissance Italy 1420–1540* (1972, Batsford: London), p. 245.
73 R. S. Lopez, op. cit.
74 R. S. Lopez, *The Three Ages of the Italian Renaissance* (1970, University of Virginia Press), p. 14.
75 Burke, op. cit., p. 194.
76 Quoted Burke, op. cit., p. 200.
77 See John Larner, *Culture and Society in Italy 1290–1420* (1971, Batsford: London). 'The books produced by those who worked

in the Florentine chancery were written for pleasure, but also as exercises which demonstrated the suitability of their authors for the positions they held. This explains the large amount of "chancery writing" in Italy and the intimate connection, from the very beginning of humanism, between literature and government circles' (p. 207).

78 Burke, op. cit., p. 252.
79 Lopez, op. cit., p. 11.
80 Lopez, op. cit., p. 16.
81 R. S. Lopez, 'Hard Times and Investment in Culture' in K. H. Dannenfeldt, op. cit.
82 See Alan Macfarlane, op. cit.
83 Emile Durkheim, Suicide (1970, Routledge and Kegan Paul: London), trans. J. A. Spaulding and George Simpson, p. 257.

## CHAPTER 4

1 See Wordsworth's Preface to 'Lyrical Ballads'.
2 Théophile Gautier, Mademoiselle De Maupin (1835, Libraire Garnier: Frères, Paris), Preface, p. 28.
3 Thomas Love Peacock, 'The Four Ages of Poetry' in H. F. B. Brett-Smith, Peacock's Four Ages of Poetry (1921, Basil Blackwell: Oxford), p. 16.
4 T. H. Malthus, Population. The First Essay (1959, University of Michigan Press), p. 62.
5 R. Price-Williams, 'On the Increase of Population in England and Wales' in Journal of the Royal Statistical Society (1880).
6 See A Defence of Poetry.
7 William Godwin, Enquiry Concerning Political Justice, third edition, 1798, ed. K. Codell Carter (1971, Clarendon Press: Oxford), p. 301.
8 Ibid., p. 315.
9 Ibid., p. 276.
10 Ibid., p. 292.
11 Ibid., p. 303.
12 See Althea Hayter, Opium and the Romantic Imagination (1968, Faber: London), p. 334.
13 William Gaunt, The Aesthetic Adventure (1945, Cape: London), p. 16.
14 Hayter, op. cit., p. 157.
15 Ruth Benedict, Patterns of Culture (1961, Routledge and Kegan Paul: London), pp. 155, 79–80.
16 See S. Kelly (ed.), The Life of Mrs Sherwood (1854).
17 Joan Calvin Metcalf, De Quincey. A Portrait (1940, Harvard University Press), p. 62.
18 Cf. Benedict, op. cit., p. 80.
19 J. E. Morpurgo, The Last Days of Shelley and Byron. Being the Complete Text of Trelawney's Recollections (1952, The Folio Society: London), p. 90.

20 Quoted ibid., p. 91.
21 Graham Hough, *The Last Romantics* (1949, Duckworth: London), p. 37.
22 Mary Douglas, *Purity and Danger* (1970, Penguin), p. 72.
23 John Ruskin, *The Stones of Venice* (1908 edition George Allen and Sons), vol. 2 'The Nature of Gothic', p. 161.
24 Eric Gill, *Art* (1934, The Bodley Head: London), p. 111.
25 'The Nature of Gothic', p. 159.
26 Ibid., p. 172.
27 Robert Southey, *Sir Thomas More: or, Colloquies on the Progress and Prospects of Society* (1829).
28 Edgell Rickword, 'The Social Setting 1780–1830' in Boris Ford (ed.), *From Blake to Byron* (1970, Penguin), p. 22.
29 Harold Nicolson, *Swinburne* (1926, Macmillian: London), p. 14.
30 Ibid., p. 16.
31 Quoted Alfred Ainger, *Charles Lamb* (1888, Macmillan: London), pp. 153–4.
32 See Carl Van Doren, *The Life of Thomas Love Peacock* (1966, Russell and Russell: New York).
33 See Nicholson, op. cit.
34 See John Walsh, *Strange Harp, Strange Harmony* (1968, Allen and Unwin: London), p. 18.
35 Quoted in H. Mills, *Peacock, his Circle and his Age* (1969, Cambridge University Press), p. 73.
36 See Mark Roskill (ed.), *The Letters of Van Gogh* (1963, Fontana/Collins), p. 320.
37 Nicholson, op. cit., pp. 91–2.
38 Ibid., p. 163.
39 Ibid., p. 133.

## CHAPTER 5

1 See José Ortega y Gasset, *The Modern Theme* (1931, The C. W. Daniel Company: London), trans. by J. Cleugh.
2 Richard Flacks, 'The Liberated Generation: An Exploration of the Roots of Student Protest', *Journal of Social Issues* (1967).
3 See Raymond Cochrane, 'The Measurement of Value Systems in Deviant Groups', paper presented at the British Psychological Society Annual Conference, April 1972.
4 Jack Levin and James L. Spates, 'Hippie Values: An Analysis of the Underground Press' in *Youth and Society* (1970).
5 Factor: *'For uninhibited relationships, against the work ethic and organizational restraints'* (factor loadings in brackets)

It should be clear in any organization who is superior, and superiors should be respected (*reverse scoring*)　　(0·378)

In college and at work everyone should have some say in how things are run　　(0·393)

Pop art and pop poetry are a huge confidence trick
(*reverse scoring*) (0·353)

Everyone should be able to do just as he likes provided
he doesn't hurt anyone (0·457)

There is no particular virtue in persevering with the
same job or career throughout life (0·300)

Uninhibited relationships are manifestations of a
healthy curiosity and lack of guilt in a new generation (0·450)

The Beatles have made a distinctive and valuable contribution to our culture (0·464)

Work should only be done when it's fun (0·418)

Our educational system is on the whole fair
(*reverse scoring*) (0·586)

We must have respect for authority (*reverse scoring*) (0·543)

Legal marriage must be preserved (*reverse scoring*) (0·472)

6 Factor: '*Against boundaries and for a simple life*'.

The earth's natural resources are being unnecessarily
depleted to satisfy artificially created cravings (0·360)

Exams are wrong in principle: we should not try to
grade people (0·587)

National boundaries are unnatural and evil (0·659)

We should try to develop simpler forms of life (0·380)

Our society still makes too sharp a distinction between
men and women (0·588)

We must oppose the Establishment, not with an isolated
political programme, but with an alternative way of
life (0·308)

We are still maintaining too many artificial barriers
between academic subjects (0·413)

7 Factor: '*The commune scale: for handicraft, pop, mysticism,
against authority, the family and boundaries*'.

The present family structure is outmoded (0·319)

Exams are wrong in principle: we should not try to grade people (0·320)

In college and at work everyone should have some say in how things are run (0·505)

Pop art and pop poetry are a huge confidence trick (*reverse scoring*) (0·329)

Pop is for idiots (*reverse scoring*) (0·383)

We have a great deal to learn in this country from the Eastern mystics (0·358)

Pop has greater vitality than established culture (0·369)

We must oppose the Establishment, not with an isolated political programme, but with an alternative way of life (0·434)

We are still maintaining too many artificial barriers between academic subjects ((0·460)

Too much of our life today is ordered by faceless bureaucrats (0·385)

We ought to make far more things with our own hands instead of relying on mass production (0·396)

Communal living, in which children belong to all, is a highly desirable form of social organization (0·345)

8 The middle of the 48-item 5-point scale was removed by taking out one-fifth of the scores, i.e. 38. Thus low scores ranged from 48 to 125, the middle 38 ranged from 126 to 162 (inclusive), and the high scores from 163 to 240

9 High and low ranges on these 16-item 5-point scales were again obtained by removing the middle 20 per cent of the scale, thus low scores ranged from 16 to 41, the middle ranged from 42 to 54 (inclusive), and the high scores from 55 to 80

10 Apart from the factor-analysis, simple correlations with an activist 'marker' item ('Protests and sit-ins are desirable means of exposing injustice and corruption') gave a profile of the activist as: opposed to the existing family structure, supporting communes, believing that large gatherings can be self-regulating, opposed to barriers to communication, hostile to the police, and

sympathetic to drug use. The marker-item correlated very highly (at the 1 per cent level) only with the following seven statements in the attitude scale:

1 The present family structure is outmoded (r=208)

2 Large gatherings can regulate themselves perfectly well without direction from on high (r=256)

3 We all need vivid, exciting and exotic experiences which expand our minds (r=232)

4 The danger in outlawing 'pot' is that you make criminals of the most intelligent and sensitive people in the country (r=289)

5 Police violence and brutality in handling protest marches and sit-ins is generally overstated (*reverse scoring*) (r=312)

6 We should be less afraid of using touch in communicating with people (r=229)

7 Communal living, in which children belong to all, is a highly desirable form of social organization (r=252).
(P 0·01=208)

By contrast, when we take an anti-technology marker-item ('The good effects of technology are outweighed by its disadvantages'), we get, not a Godwin-Shelley profile, but a remarkably accurate 'Ruskin profile' – retreatist and environmentalist, concerned with the human character of work and simpler forms of life. Only seven attitude-scale statements correlated at the one per cent level with this anti-technology item.

1 The earth's natural resources are being unnecessarily depleted to satisfy artificially created cravings (r=351)

2 Work should only be done when it's fun (r=271)

3 We should try to develop simpler forms of life (r=210)

4 We have a great deal to learn in this country from the Eastern mystics (r=256)

5 We are in danger of letting technology run away with us (r=378)

6 We must oppose the Establishment, not with an isolated political programme, but with an alternative way of life (r=208)

7 We ought to make far more things with our hands instead of relying on mass production (r=255)

11 Mean scores of females on Scale A: Youngers (16–25): 49·65; Middles (26–35): 49·60; Olders (36–65): 49·80. Mean scores of males: Youngers (16–25): 53·1; Middles (26–35): 53·5; Olders

(36–65): 50·8. The difference between male Middles and Olders is not significant (t=1·07 NS).

12 Mean scores of females on scale B: Youngers (16–25): 40·3; Middles (26–35): 39·8; Olders (36–65): 33·0. (Difference between Middles and Olders=6·8, t=3·6, P < 0·001.) Mean scores of males: Youngers: 43·6; Middles: 43·5; Olders: 39·1. (Difference between Middles and Olders=4·4, t=2·02, P < 0·05.)

13 S. M. Lipset, 'Youth and Politics' in R. K. Merton and R. Nisbet *Contemporary Social Problems* (1971, Harcourt Brace Jovanovich).

14 Stephen Hatch, 'Student Protest Supporters and Opponents', *Research in Education* (1972).

15 Lipset, op. cit.

16 Peter Kelvin, 'What Sort of People Now? The New Society Survey', *New Society* (30 November 1972).

17 'Family structure outmoded.'

| | Strongly Agree or Agree | Uncertain | Strongly Disagree or Disagree |
|---|---|---|---|
| Fine art and drama (N.63) | 18 | 3 | 32 |
| Olders (N.63) | 7 | 13 | 43 |

Chi-square = 6·5 df2 P< 0·05

Even the fine art and drama students support the present family structure to a greater extent than 'chance expectancy':

| | Strongly Agree | Agree | Uncertain | Disagree | Strongly Disagree |
|---|---|---|---|---|---|
| fo | 11 | 7 | 13 | 22 | 10 |
| fe | 12·6 | 12·6 | 12·6 | 12·6 | 12·6 |

Chi-square = 10·5 df 4 P< 0·05

18 'Communal living highly desirable.'

| | Strongly Agree or Agree | Uncertain | Strongly Disagree or Disagree |
|---|---|---|---|
| Fine art and drama (N.63) | 11 | 15 | 37 |
| Olders (N.63) | 6 | 6 | 51 |

Chi-square = 7·6 df 2 P< 0·05

The fine art and drama students are opposed to communal living and child care to a greater extent than 'chance expectancy':

| | Strongly Agree | Agree | Uncertain | Disagree | Strongly Disagree |
|---|---|---|---|---|---|
| fo | 5 | 6 | 15 | 24 | 13 |
| fe | 12·6 | 12·6 | 12·6 | 12·6 | 12·6 |

Chi-square = 18·8 df 4 P< 0·01

CHAPTER 6

1 Kenneth Keniston, *Young Radicals* (1968, Harcourt, Brace and World: New York), p. 259.
2 Kenneth Keniston, *The Uncommitted* (1960, Harcourt, Brace and World: New York), p. 56.
3 *Young Radicals*, p. 340.
4 *The Uncommitted*, p. 181.
5 David Matza, *Delinquency and Drift* (1964, John Wiley: Chichester), p. 69.
6 R. K. Merton, *Social Theory and Social Structure* (1957, Collier-Macmillan: London), p. 162.
7 Joseph Priestly, *Observations on Education* (1788), p. 93.
8 Richard Flacks, 'The Liberated Generation', loc. cit.
9 See also Ted Goertzel, 'Generational Conflict and Social Change', loc. cit.
10 *Young Radicals*, p. 341.
11 Adam Curle, *Mystics and Militants* (1972, Tavistock: London), p. 23.
12 'Normlessness' and 'social isolation' are especially close to Durkheim's concept of anomie, but both are used as components in Dean's measure of alienation: see Dwight G. Dean, 'Alienation: Its Meaning and Measurement', *American Sociological Review* (1961).
13 A sense of powerlessness (e.g. in one's work organization) has been taken as an indicator of alienation; it has been shown, not surprisingly, to correlate with dissatisfaction: see John P. Clark, 'Measuring Alienation Within a Social System', *American Sociological Review* (1959).
14 R. Aron, *Progress and Disillusion* (1972, Penguin), p. 177.
15 Leo Srole, 'Social Integration and Certain Corollaries: An Exploratory Study', *American Sociological Review* (1966).
16 Herbert McGlosky and John H. Schaar, 'Psychological Dimensions of Anomy', *American Sociological Review* (1965).
17 Curle, op. cit., p. 27.
18 Donald A. Schon, *Beyond the Stable State* (1971, Temple Smith: London), p. 20.
19 J. F. T. Bugental and S. L. Zelen, 'Investigations Into the Self Concept I. The W-A-Y Technique' in *Journal of Personality* (1950).
20 M. H. Kuhn and T. S. McPortland, 'An Empirical Investigation of Self Attitudes', *American Sociological Review* (1954).
21 Students' self concepts

| | Students' self concepts Consensual | Subconsensual |
|---|---|---|
| High scorers | | |
| N. (Statements) | 55 (10·4%) | 249 (89·6%) |
| Rest | | |
| N. (Statements) | 168 (43·3%) | 220 (56·7%) |
| Chi-square = 12·34  P< 0·001 | | |

Adults' self concepts

| | Consensual | Subconsensual |
|---|---|---|
| High scorers | | |
| N. (Statements) | 58 (40·0%) | 87 (60·0%) |
| Rest | | |
| N. (Statements) | 313 (52·3%) | 286 (47·7%) |

Chi-square = 6·96  P< 0·01

22 Mary Douglas, *Natural Symbols* (1970, Barrie and Rockcliff: London), p. 57.
23 Ibid., p. 103.
24 T. Blackstone and R. Hadley, 'Student Protest in a British University: Some Comparisons with American Research' in *Comparative Education Review* (1971).
25 Kenneth Keniston, *The Uncommitted* (1960, Harcourt, Brace and World: New York), pp. 99–100.
26 Ibid., p. 73.
27 Theodore Roszak, *The Making of a Counter Culture* (1970, Faber: London), p. 47.
28 Jeff Nuttall, *Bomb Culture* (1970, Paladin), p. 160.
29 In a recent inquiry into religious beliefs and human relationships among nearly three thousand sixth-formers in thirty-nine comprehensive and public schools, Richardson and Chapman asked them to write an answer to the following question: 'As you consider your own future in modern society, what are your main hopes and fears?' The answers were largely in terms of pollution, overpopulation, the 'rat-race', anonymity and the loss of individuality: see Robin Richardson and John Chapman, *Images of Life* (1973, S.C.M. Press). One sixth-form boy replied in terms which clearly illustrate the connection between anomie and 'openness' which is argued in this chapter (and, indeed, throughout this book):

'Bored I am, and bored I shall remain, because there are too many people about for them to be treated as individuals. I am convinced that the population explosion is the root of all unhappiness. In the foreseeable future life will be sufficiently automated for there to be no need for masses of men to waste their lives doing exactly the same routine tasks as their fellows. Then we could happily reduce the population 100 times (in theory), live where we liked, do what we liked, and never have to gaze on the ugly faces of our own species unless we wanted to. We could become personalities again. Life to someone else's specifications inevitably seems future, and when that life is buried so deep in the midst of innumerable others that it would not be missed if it were not there, it begins to become utterly pointless. The only reason I have not yet shuffled off this mortal coil of my own accord is that in my family I still have a certain amount of significance. I am surprised that the suicide rate is not climbing faster as there seems but a small step nowadays between the nonentities that we are in life and the nonentities that we are in death' (p. 129).

## CHAPTER 7

1 The interviews were conducted by Mr Roger Middleton, Research Associate, Department of Education, University of Manchester.
2 Ivan D. Illich, *Celebration of Awareness* (1973, Penguin Education), p. 18.
3 Ibid., p. 19.
4 Peter L. Berger, *A Rumour of Angels* (1971, Penguin), p. 96.

## CHAPTER 8

Cf. Jean Fourastié, *Machinisme et Bien-Etre* (1962, Les Editions de Minuit: Paris), p. 236.
2 Peter Laslett, *The World We Have Lost* (1965, Methuen: London), p. 105.
3 F. Parkin, 'Working-class Conservatives: A Theory of Political Deviance' in *British Journal of Sociology* (1967).
4 Laslett, op. cit., p. 174.
5 For an attempt to relate involvement in pop culture to inferior home background and low commitment to school see B. Sugarman, 'Involvement in Youth Culture, Academic Achievement and Conformity in School' in *British Journal of Sociology* (1967). For a more perceptive understanding of pop music see W. Mellers, 'Pop, Ritual and Commitment', *Journal of the Royal Society of Arts* (1974).
6 See G. P. D. Phelps, *Differential Commitment to School and Patterns of Peer Group Culture* (1973, unpublished Ph.D. thesis, University of Leicester).
7 Bryan Wilson, 'Youth Culture, the Universities and Student Unrest' in C. B. Cox and A. E. Dyson, *Fight for Education. A Black Paper* (1969), Critical Quarterly Society.
8 See D. Child and F. Musgrove, 'Career Orientations of Some University Freshmen', *Educational Review* (1969); F. Musgrove, 'Self Concepts and Occupational Identities', *Universities Quarterly* (1969). It is remarkable how seldom students take other students as their reference group: see F. Musgrove, 'University Freshmen and their Parents' Attitudes', *Educational Research* (1967); D. Child, 'Some Reference Groups of University Students: a Follow-up Study', *Educational Research* (1970).
9 S. N. Eisenstadt, 'African Age Groups. A Comparative Study', *Africa* (1954).
10 S. N. Eisenstadt, *From Generation to Generation* (1956, Routledge and Kegan Paul: London), p. 239.
11 Richard Flacks, op. cit.

12 Ted Goertzel, 'Generational Conflict and Social Change', *Youth and Society* (1972).
13 Karl Mannheim, 'The Problem of Generations' in K. Mannheim, *Essays on the Sociology of Knowledge* (1952, Routledge and Kegan Paul: London), ed. Paul Kecskemeti, p. 291.
14 Bennett M. Berger, 'How Long Is a Generation?', *British Journal of Sociology* (1960).
15 Peter Burke, *Culture and Society in Renaissance Italy 1420–1540* (1972, Batsford: London), pp. 266–8.
16 Alex Simirenko, 'Mannheim's Generational Analysis and Acculturation', *British Journal of Sociology* (1966).
17 R. Serge Denisoff and Mark H. Levine, 'Generations and Counter-Culture', *Youth and Society* (1970).
18 Lewis S. Feuer, *The Conflict of Generations* (1969, Heinemann: London), p. 33.
19 Ortega y Gasset, op. cit., p. 15.
20 Mannheim, op. cit., pp. 295–6.
21 For an interpretation in these terms of the coercion of hippies, street-people and students in the People's Park confrontation at Berkeley in 1968, see Sheldon Wolin and John Schaar, 'Berkeley: The Battle of People's Park' in C. E. Kruytbosch and S. L. Messinger, *The State of the University* (1970, Sage: California). 'The life-styles and values of the Park people were forever escaping the categories and procedures of those who administer the academic plant' and university bureaucracy 'is experiencing increasing difficulty, because human life is manifesting itself in forms which are unrecognizible to the mentality of the technological age.'
22 Ralph H. Turner, 'The Theme of Contemporary Social Movements', *British Journal of Sociology* (1967).
23 Walter Bagehot, *The English Constitution* (1879), especially chapter IX. Bagehot pointed to the resistance to 'the introduction of effectual policemen' and the allegedly inquisitorial Census of 1851. 'The natural impulse of the English people is to resist authority.'
24 W. G. Runciman, *Relative Deprivation and Social Justice* (1966, Routledge and Kegan Paul: London).
25 Gabriel Almond and Sydney Verba, *The Civic Culture* (1963, Princeton). For a useful discussion of the deference debate see Dennis Kavanagh, 'The Deferential English: A Comparative Critique' in *Government and Opposition* (1971).
26 David Butler and Donald Stokes, *Political Change in Britain* (1971, Pelican: Harmondsworth).
27 Robert McKenzie and Allan Silver, *Angels in Marble* (1968, Heinemann: London).
28 Ibid., p. 189.
29 F. Parkin, 'Working-class Conservatives: A Theory of Political Deviance' in *British Journal of Sociology* (1967).

30 P. R. Abramson, 'Middle Class Traitors' in *New Society* (3 May, 1973).

31 E. R. Tapper, *Secondary School Adolescents: A Study of the Formation of their Role Aspirations and Attitudinal Patterns* (unpublished Ph.D. thesis, University of Manchester, 1968).

32 T. Allen Lambert, 'Generations and Change' in *Youth and Society* (1972).

33 Most of these interviews were conducted by Mrs Patricia Hawes, Research Assistant, Department of Education, University of Manchester.

34 Brian Salter, 'Attention Must Be Paid' in *Education Guardian* (21 November, 1972).

35 R. G. Gregory, *The Grove: R. G. Gregory's First Hand Account of a Dispute in a Provincial Comprehensive School* (1971), duplicated by Wrekin Libertarians.

36 For extensive survey data on schoolboys' acceptance or rejection of the authority systems of their schools, see Robin Richardson and John Chapman, *Images of Life* (1973, S.C.M. Press). Sixth-form boys in day public schools are more critical of the authority system than sixth-form boys in comprehensive schools: 41 per cent agree that 'There is too much concern with power and privilege throughout the school'; 31 per cent of the comprehensive school boys agree with this statement (p. 179). This majority support for the status quo is in line with our data on a sixth-form grammar school sample reported in Chapter 5. But among the minority of critics, criticism may be very bitter indeed: 'I feel critical in school about the authority of head-masters who are bloody hypocrites. At our school for example the headmaster has a committee which he says runs the school. In fact they do not . . . I would like to see student control of a school meeting and deciding important matters', 'I feel most critical of small-minded, vicious, out-dated, bigoted, self-centred, mean, two-faced, deceitful, ignorant, self-flattering deputy head-masters who wield too much power and restrict freedom and the arts beyond a state of durance. The man is a real danger' (pp. 201–2).

CHAPTER 9

1 H. J. Wilensky, 'Orderly Careers and Social Participation: The Impact of Work on Social Participation', *American Sociological Review* (1961).

2 For a concrete illustration of the way in which dancing was intimately bound up with work, leisure and religion see Eileen Power's account of the daily life of Bodo, a medieval peasant (*Medieval People*, 10th edition 1963, Methuen).

3 See Gareth Williams, 'The Economics of the Graduate Labour Market' in H. Greenaway and G. Williams, *Patterns of Change*

*in Graduate Employment* (1973, Society for Research into Higher Education).

4 See Ivar Berg, *Education and Jobs. The Great Training Robbery* (1970, Praeger Publishers: New York). Berg investigated the nature of 4,000 jobs and the educational qualifications of their incumbents over an eight-year period (1957–65). 'The data do not support the blanket inference that employers always reward educational achievement more than performance, but they afford presumptive evidence that this is the case' (p. 48).

5 See E. G. Whybrew, 'Trends in the Labour Market for Highly Qualified Manpower' in Greenaway and Williams, op. cit.

6 P. R. G. Layard, J. D. Sargan, M. E. Ager and D. J. Jones, *Qualified Manpower and Economic Performance* (1971, Allen Lane, The Penguin Press).

7 Ibid., p. 121.

8 Dael Wolfle, *The Uses of Talent* (1971, Princeton University Press: New Jersey). This estimate is based on the assumption that men are actually 'worth' to the economy what they are actually paid.

9 Karl Mannheim, 'The Nature of Economic Ambition and Its Significance for the Social Education of Man' in K. Mannheim, *Essays in the Sociology of Knowledge* (1952, Routledge and Kegan Paul), p. 247.

10 *Directory of Alternative Work*, 3rd edition (October 1972), Pershore Road, Birmingham.

11 Harold J. Wilensky, 'Work as a Social Problem' in Howard S. Becker (ed.), *Social Problems: A Modern Approach* (1966, John Wiley), p. 164.

12 Georges Friedmann, 'Leisure and Technological Civilization', *International Social Science Journal* (1960).

13 Joffre Dumazedier, *Toward a Society of Leisure* (1967, Free Press: New York), p. 73.

14 Ellul, op. cit., pp. 401–2.

15 Aron, op. cit., p. 141.

16 Ibid., p. 159.

17 Fourastié, op. cit., p. 242.

18 W. H. Whyte, *The Organization Man* (1960, Penguin Books), p. 11.

19 Ralf Dahrendorf, *Class and Class Conflict in Industrial Society* (1959, Routledge and Kegan Paul), p. 68.

20 Weber, op. cit., p. 181.

21 Robert Blauner, 'Work Satisfaction and Industrial Trends in Modern Society' in R. Bendix and S. M. Lipset, *Class, Status and Power* (1967, Routledge and Kegan Paul).

22 Robert Dubin, 'Industrial Workers' Worlds: A Study of the "Central Life Interests" of Industrial Workers', *Social Problems* (1956).

23 E. Chinoy, *Automobile Workers and the American Dream* (1955, Doubleday and Co.: New York), p. 82.

24 Wilensky, op. cit.
25 Stanley Parker, *The Future of Work and Leisure* (1971, Mc-Gibbon and Kee: London), p. 81.
26 Wilensky, op. cit.
27 For the evidence on leisure-patterns revealed by the Detroit study see H. J. Wilensky, 'Mass Society and Mass Culture: Interdepence or Independence' in *American Sociological Review* (1964). Type of work, rather than social class level, influenced leisure pursuits: 'In general data both here and in other studies suggest that as predictors of life-style variables – especially cultural tastes and ideology – sex, age and social-economic stratum are far weaker than religion, type of education, work and career – variables that represent positions in established groups.'
28 Louis H. Orzack, 'Work as a "Central Life Interest" of Professionals', in *Social Problems* (1959).
29 C. Sofer, *Men in Mid-Career* (1970, Cambridge University Press), pp. 327–8.
30 Ibid., p. 9.
31 Kingsley Davis and Wilbert E. Moore, 'Some Principles of Social Stratifications' in R. Bendix and S. M. Lipset, *Class, Status and Power* (1967, Routledge and Kegan Paul: London); 'Social inequality is thus an unconsciously evolved device by which societies insure that the most important positions are conscientiously filled by the most qualified persons.'
32 Sofer, op. cit., p. 312.
33 Dahrendorf, op. cit., p. 56.
34 J. M. and R. E. Pahl, *Managers and their Wives* (1972, Penguin), p. 107.
35 Ibid., p. 258.
36 Ibid., p. 256.
37 Ibid., p. 266.
38 Ibid., p. 189.
39 Ibid., p. 258.
40 J. H. Goldthorpe, D. Lockwood, F. Bechhofer and Jennifer Platt, *The Affluent Worker: Industrial Attitudes* (1968, Cambridge University Press), Table 10, p. 26.
41 Ibid., p. 84.
42 H. J. Wilensky, 'Work as a Social Problem' in Becker, op. cit.
43 J. H. Goldthorpe, 'Attitudes and Behaviour of Car Assembly Workers' in *British Journal of Sociology* (1966).
44 John Cohen, 'The Ideas of Work and Play' in *British Journal of Sociology* (1953).
45 Ian Lewis, 'In the Courts of Power – The Advertising Man' in Peter L. Berger, *The Human Shape of Work* (Macmillan).
46 Raymond L. Gold, 'In the Basement – The Apartment-Building Janitor' in Peter L. Berger, op. cit.
47 Erich Fromm, *The Sane Society* (1963, Routledge and Kegan Paul: London), p. 179.

48 Peter L. Berger, 'Some General Observations on the Problem of Work' in Berger, op. cit.

49 Ortega y Gasset, *The Modern Theme* (1931, The C. W. Daniel Co.: London), trans. by J. Cleugh, p. 82. Ortega y Gasset saw a fun ethic in the treatment of art, 'the sense of life as a sport and a festivity'. This he saw as a revolutionary attitude: 'The face of the nineteenth century bears through its extent the grim signs of a day of toil. Our present youth seems disposed to give life the careless aspect of a day of merrymaking.'

50 John Cohen, 'The Ideas of Work and Play' in *British Journal of Sociology* (1953).

51 Martha Wolfenstein, 'The Emergence of Fun Morality' in *Journal of Social Issues* (1951).

52 Nelson N. Foote, 'Sex as Play' in *Social Problems* (1954).

53 Anthony Crosland, 'Open-Air Cafés' in Anthony Arblaster and Steven Lukes, *The Good Society* (1971, Methuen: London).

54 Cf. F. P. Noe, 'Autonomous Spheres of Leisure Activity for the Industrial Worker and Blue Collarite' in *Journal of Leisure Research* (1971): 'The integration of the blue collarite and executive into the industrial organization is partly achieved by their differential use of autonomy . . . the executive finds freedom and flexibility in leisure within the work role, (yet) he is conversely limited by the leisure alternatives available to him in the outside world. The blue collarite has limited leisure alternatives within the workplace, but he has the controlling edge over his leisure outside the workplace'.

55 R. Rapoport, 'Work and Family in Contemporary Society' in *American Sociological Review* (1965).

56 K. Roberts, *Leisure* (1970, Longman: London), p. 34.

57 Ibid., p. 93. Similarly: '. . . to regard the styles of life that people adopt in their free time as being simply derived from the nature of their jobs would be an injustice to the autonomous and central role that leisure plays in the lives of many of the members of modern society' (pp. 25–6).

58 F. Musgrove, 'Social Class and Levels of Aspiration in a Technological University' in *Sociological Review* (1967).

59 F. Musgrove, 'Self Concepts and Occupational Identities' in *Universities Quarterly* (1969).

60 See H. J. Wilensky, 'Work, Careers and Social Integration' in *International Social Science Journal* (1960).

61 Fourastié, op. cit., p. 235. The sense of death was all-pervasive: 'Cet homme, s'il vivait jusqu' à 50 ans, ce qui était assez rare – une chance sur cinq . . . avait vécu deux ou trois famines . . . il avait, en plus des morts, vécu les maladies de ses frères, de ses enfants, de ses femmes, et de ses parents et les siennes propres, il avait connu deux ou trois épidémies de maladies infectieuses, sans parler des épidémies quasi-permanentes de coqueluche, scarlatine, diphtérie . . .' (p. 234).

62 Cf. H. R. Stub, 'Education, the Professions, and Long Life' in *British Journal of Sociology* (1969).

63 Harold Entwistle, *Education, Work and Leisure* (1970, Routledge and Kegan Paul: London), p. 26.

64 Clive Bell, op. cit., pp. 128–9.

65 David Riesman, *Abundance for What?* (1964, Chatto and Windus: London), p. 170.

66 Ibid., p. 188.

67 J. K. Hadden, 'The Private Generation' in *Psychology Today* (October 1969).

68 Riesman, op. cit., pp. 190–1.

69 Charles A. Reich, *The Greening of America* (1971, Allen Lane, The Penguin Press), p. 167.

70 Ibid., p. 177.

71 Philip E. Slater, *The Pursuit of Loneliness* (1970, Beacon Press: Boston), p. 139. Slater takes a characteristically counter-cultural stance when he reverses the Puritan attitude to sloth: 'One thing must be said for idleness: it keeps people from doing the Devil's work' (p. 139).

## CHAPTER 10

1 Mills, op. cit., p. 14.

2 Thornstein Veblen, *The Theory of the Leisure Class* (first published 1899), (1970, Unwin Books), p. 24.

3 See for example W. S. Buckingham, 'Automation, Employment and Economic Stability', and William A. Faunce, 'Automation and Leisure' in H. B. Jacobson and J. S. Roucek, *Automation and Society* (1959, Philosophical Library: New York).

4 Norbert Wiener, *The Human Use of Human Beings* (2nd edition 1954, Doubleday Anchor Books: New York).

5 Herbert Marcuse, *An Essay on Liberation* (1969, Allen Lane, The Penguin Press), p. 4.

6 Leon Bagrit, *The Age of Automation* (1966, Penguin Books), p. 65.

7 Ibid., p. 83.

8 Dennis Gabor, *The Mature Society* (1972, Secker and Warburg).

9 See Michael Rose, *Computers, Managers and Society* (1969, Penguin Books), and H. J. Wilensky, 'Work, Careers and Social Integration', *International Social Science Journal* (1960).

10 James Martin and A. R. D. Norman, *The Computerized Society* (1970, Prentice-Hall: Englewood Cliffs: N.J.), p. vi.

11 Ibid., p. 419.

12 See N. Peppard, 'Migration: Some British and European Comparisons', *Race* (1964).

13 Frederick Pollock, *The Economic and Social Consequences of Automation* (1957, Basil Blackwell: Oxford), p. 58.

14 K. Westhues, *Society's Shadow* (1972, McGraw-Hill Ryerson: Toronto), p. 40.

15 See R. M. Kanter, 'Commitment and Social Organization: A Study of Commitment Mechanisms', *American Sociological Review* (1968).

16 Cf. E. Aranson and J. Mills, 'The Effect of Severity of Initiation on Liking for a Group', *Journal of Abnormal and Social Psychology* (1959).

17 Judson Jerome, 'The New Plenitude', *The American Scholar* (Summer 1973).

18 Ibid.

19 Ibid.

20 Daniel Bell, 'Technology, Nature and Society', *The American Scholar* (Summer 1973). 'Straight' culture may be modified by more deliberate counter-cultural infiltration. One American observer, Michael E. Brown, recognizes and illustrates that the politically militant and culturally defiant are joining forces, and maintains that 'many hippies have gone underground – in an older sense of the word. They have shaved their beards, cut their hair, and taken straight jobs, like the secret Jews of Spain; but unlike those Jews they are consciously an underground a resistance.' The counter culture is expanding but less visible: 'the hippie culture is growing as it recedes from the eye of the media'. See 'The Condemnation and Persecution of Hippies' in Brigitte Berger (ed.), *Readings in Sociology* (1974, Basic Books: NewYork).

21 See *Ideology and Utopia*, p. 232.

# Index

# Index